AROUND THE WORLD
WITH
CITIZEN TRAIN

THE SENSATIONAL ADVENTURES
OF THE REAL PHILEAS FOGG

AROUND THE
WORLD
WITH
CITIZEN TRAIN

THE SENSATIONAL ADVENTURES
OF THE REAL PHILEAS FOGG

ALLEN FOSTER

MERLIN
PUBLISHING

Published in 2002 by

Merlin Publishing
16 Upper Pembroke Street
Dublin 2
Ireland

www.merlin-publishing.com

Text Copyright © 2002 Allen Foster
Arrangement and design Copyright © 2002 Merlin Publishing
except
Photographs courtesy of the individuals and institutions noted between pages 64–65
and pages 224–225.

The author and publisher have made every reasonable effort to contact copyright
holders of text quoted and photographs reproduced in this book. If any involuntary
infringement of copyright has occured, the owner is requested to contact the publisher
so that omissions can be rectified in the next edition.

ISBN 1-903582-11-3

A CIP record for this book is available from the British Library.

Typeset by Pierce Design, Dublin
Printed by Mackays of Chatham
Jacket design by Slick Fish Design

To my Mother and Father

The world is a book and every step turns a
new page.

— **Lamartine**

Acknowledgments

This book would not exist without three people to whom my gratitude is inexpressible: Selga Medenieks, Chenile Keogh and Elizabeth Senior. Many thanks to them for their continued faith and belief in *Around the World with Citizen Train* – and especially for their much-tested patience!

There are numerous other individuals and organisations worldwide whose help and assistance were crucial to the book's evolution. In particular, I would like to express my appreciation to the National Library of Ireland, Dr Edmund B. Sullivan, Dr Dennis B. Downey, the *Rail Splitter* archivists, and the many photo libraries whose researchers spent many hours digging out forgotten prints.

Special thanks to John O'Sullivan, Techstore, Kevin Carr photography and, last but not least, to Margaret Nicholas. I first came across George Francis Train in her wonderful book *World's Greatest Cranks and Crackpots* (Hamlyn, London, 1995), pp. 71–77.

Contents

Preface

Around the World in Eighty Days is one of the world's most popular adventure novels. Few people realise that Jules Verne's classic tale of a race around the world against time was inspired in part by the incredible life of an eccentric American businessman.

Amongst other things, George Francis Train was the real Phileas Fogg. He was also, at different times, a capitalist, communist, royalist, revolutionary, genius, lunatic, visionary prophet, fool, pacifist, warmonger, presidential aspirant, candidate for Dictator of the U.S.A., transportation pioneer, globe-trotting traveller, writer and, ultimately, an eccentric.

Train enjoyed great success in all his varied careers. He was a contradictory and impulsive character – an extraordinary figure who led an incredibly jam-packed life. The one thing that can be said with certainty about him was that at heart he was all-American.

One fine July morning in 1870, the aptly named Train, a wealthy Boston businessman, set out on one of the most famous journeys ever made. He travelled around the world in eighty days, excluding some time spent in a French prison. Two years after his return he found himself immortalised in Jules Verne's celebrated novel. Verne's protagonist was named Phileas Fogg, but the source was obvious. Train was sickened to see his crowning achievement appropriated by another.

"He stole my thunder," he protested. "*I'm* Phileas Fogg."[1] Train, who managed to cram several lifetimes into one by doing everything at incredible speed, was never one to be modest about his own achievements. He was always an inspired self-publicist.

Verne's Phileas Fogg was a clipped, precise Englishman, a pillar of the Reform Club; Train, on the other hand, was an erratic, unconventional Bostonian and a dyed-in-the-wool Yankee. Fogg was a cool, unemotional man; Train was impulsive and explosive. Fogg made the journey for a bet in the best British sportsmanlike manner; Train did it for the sake of it and for the glory. While Fogg brought back a princess, Train probably only brought back dirty laundry. Train's Passepartout (Fogg's faithful servant-companion) was his long-suffering cousin and private secretary, George Pickering Bemis.

Train's birth was every bit as dramatic as his life. He was born in 1829 during a snowstorm in Boston. Soon after his birth the family moved to New Orleans to start a new life. Tragically, George found himself orphaned at the age of four when a yellow fever plague wiped out his family. He was raised by his strict Methodist grandparents in Boston; they hoped to make a clergyman out of him. In the event, he became an atheist.

Train had his own plans for the future. He joined his uncle's shipping firm and advanced rapidly by his own merit, becoming a partner by the time he was only 21. While still only a teenager, Train was instrumental in the building of some of the world's largest and fastest ships for the firm.

Three years later Train set up his own trading house in Melbourne, Australia. It was tremendously successful on both personal and commercial levels. As one of the most prominent Americans in Australia he helped promote better transport and commercial institutions. At one point he was offered the presidency of the abortive Five-Star Republic.

In Europe, Train rubbed shoulders with an assortment of royalty and communists, and took some time off to dash to Russia for a chat with the Czar's brother, the Grand Duke Constantine. Racing back to France, he persuaded the Queen of Spain to back the construction of a railway in the backwoods of Pennsylvania. This was the beginning of the Atlantic and Great Western railroad. He also promoted and built the first tramways in Britain in the face of strong opposition. It did not help matters that Train bravely supported the unstable and by no means secure Unionist cause in the face of fiercely hostile British opposition.

Train is often called America's first foreign correspondent because of the informative letters and articles he sent to American newspapers about the numerous countries he visited. On his triumphant return to America, Train's popularity and reputation soared. He immediately launched into political and commercial ventures. He promoted the great Union Pacific railway despite the advice of short-sighted industrialists, such as Vanderbilt, who told him it would never work. Train made a fortune from real estate when the great railway running from coast to coast opened up huge swathes of western America.

Train also found the time to run for the office of President of the United States of America. His campaign was not helped when he grew bored in the middle of it and decided to make a whirlwind trip around the world in eighty days. On his return journey he got caught up in revolution in France. He claimed to have helped set up the short-lived Marseilles Commune aiding the communist take-over of the city. He was attacked by soldiers and almost shot, imprisoned, and allegedly poisoned, but certainly treated badly. It was left to his omni-competent assistant Bemis to organise a rescue attempt. He enlisted the intervention of the French novelist Alexandre Dumas (a friend Train and Verne had in common), the U.S. President, and of the *New York Sun* and the *London Times* to free him. Eventually he was bailed out and expelled. Bemis wryly commented: "It is doubtful if any other man was ever so politely put out of a country as was George Francis Train."[2]

Having lost a precious thirteen days, the gentlemen hired a private train and raced across France to the Channel. Once in England, Train headed straight for Liverpool, caught a boat by the skin of his teeth and arrived in New York exactly eighty days after setting out, excluding his forced stop in the Lyons prison. Arriving back in America, he recounted his adventures for the benefit of newspaper reporters. Train was quite correct to believe that Jules Verne used him as a model for Phileas Fogg in his famous novel *Around the World in Eighty Days*. There are several "coincidences" between the real adventure and the fictional one undertaken by Fogg that suggest Verne plagiarised Train's life story. Overall, Train managed to lap the globe four times, beating records each time. On his final attempt he did it in sixty days.

Train was dismissed as a crank when he supported the then disputed cause of women's suffrage. Due to political wrangling he was imprisoned and declared a lunatic after he supported Victoria Woodhull in a libel case. Train took his cue from the verdict and set off on a new career as a professional crank.

He stood for the position of Dictator of the United States, charged admission fees to his campaign rallies and drew record crowds. He became a vegetarian and adopted various fads in succession. Instead of shaking hands with other people, he shook hands with himself, the manner of greeting he had seen in China. For a time he also refused to talk to anyone, except children, and wrote messages on a pad when he wanted to communicate. These were means, he explained, of storing up his psychic forces. He even invented a new calendar based on the date of his birth.

In his old age Train turned his attention to the children he met daily in New York's Central Park, who, he declared, were alone worth talking to. When he died, more than two thousand children trudged through a bitter January night to place their tributes of flowers on his bier. Beggars and industrialists were seen side by side paying their tributes to this remarkable man.

Few people have lived the kind of rip-roaring adventurous life as did George Francis Train. The world is a poorer place for it.

---

[1] Don C. Seitz, *Uncommon Americans* (The Bobbs-Merrill Company, Indianapolis, 1925), p. 178.

[2] Quoted in Willis Thornton, *The Nine Lives of Citizen Train* (Greenberg, New York, 1948), p. 210.

ONE

Escape from the "City of the Dead"

George Francis Train's birth was every bit as dramatic as his life. He came into the world during a snowstorm on March 24, 1829, at No. 21 High Street, Boston. While George was still an infant the family moved to New Orleans, where his father Oliver opened a store. In his later years Train claimed he could remember almost everything since he was four years of age, from the beautiful, sun-drenched household garden of his childhood, teeming with flowers, right down to exactly how the old clothesline used to look weighed down with linen – the resting place of long-bodied insects that he and the other children called "devil's darning needles", or mosquito hawks. They used to hit the line with poles to frighten the insects, which would scatter flying away on their filmy wings.

Another poignant memory he retained was of going down to his father's store, filling his pockets with dried currants, and then watching his father there at work. His idyllic childhood ended abruptly when a yellow fever epidemic swept over the vibrant city of New Orleans, leaving behind a city of dead. The Train family suffered with the rest of the citizens and the memory of it was burnt into his consciousness for the rest of his life. Doctors and undertakers went to the grave just the same as their clients. It was impossible to give so many a decent burial:

> "[T]he fear of the plague had so shaken the human soul that men stood afar off, aghast, and did only what they had to do in a coarse, brutal, swift burial of the dead.
>
> There were no coffins to be had, and no one could have got them if there had been enough of them. Corpses were buried, all alike, in coarse pine boxes, hastily put together in the homes – and often by the very hands – of the relatives of the dead."[1]

One of those coarse pine boxes was brought into the Train household. George did not know what it was or for what it was made. Then he saw the dead body of his little sister, Josephine, quickly put into it. He was too young then to understand what was happening, but he never forgot it. Even towards the end of his life the memory made him cry.

After the box was nailed up and marked "To the Train Vaults", the family sat and waited for the coming of the "dead wagon". This was the name given to the horse-drawn carts that the city authorities sent to collect the numerous dead, just as it sent out scavenger carts to take away household refuse. The "dead wagon's" approach was heralded by the cart driver's cry: "Bring out – Bring out your dead!" This sound filled the now-empty streets, getting louder as it drew nearer and nearer. New Orleans had every appearance of a city from the Middle Ages.

The driver, no doubt fearful for his own safety, never entered the stricken houses. He remained on his cart, shouting out his heartrending cry for the populace, now virtually imprisoned in their homes, to bring out their dead to him.

George heard the wagon stop under a window of their home. He watched as his father and others lifted up the coarse pine box containing the body of his dead little sister, carry it to the window and throw it into the "dead wagon". The wagon rattled away down the street, stopping under the window of each house in turn, while all over the doomed city echoed the cry: "Bring out – Bring out your dead!" A few days later another of George's little sisters, Louise, died. The same callous procedure followed and the pine box was hastily loaded onto a wagon already loaded with similar boxes.

George now began to feel the loss of his two sisters. Only one was left, Ellen, who was "as frail and as lovely a flower as ever bloomed". Tragically she, too, succumbed to the plague. George went with his parents to the cemetery where each of his sisters were laid to rest. One day the arrival of a much larger, rough-looking box made from unplaned boards puzzled him. His nurse had to tell him it was for his mother. He was astonished to see that they did not throw the box containing his dead mother into the wagon. It was too heavy to do so and four or five men had to come into the house to take it out. Like his sisters' caskets, it was marked "To the Train Vaults". Now there was just George and his father left.

One day a letter came from George's grandmother, instructing Oliver Train to "send on some one of the family, before they are all dead. Send George". Oliver Train acted on this advice and immediately made preparations to send George to Massachusetts. He wrote a card and pinned it onto George's coat, just like a label or tag on merchandise to be shipped. It read:

"This is my little son George Francis Train. Four years old. Consigned on board the ship Henry to John Clarke, Jr., Dock Square, Boston; to be sent to his Grandmother Pickering, at Waltham, ten miles from Boston. Take good care of the Little Fellow, as he is the only one left of eleven of us in the house, including the servants [slaves]. I will come on as soon as I can arrange my Business."

George and his father went down to the river to put George aboard his ship, the *Henry*. She lay out in the broad, muddy Mississippi. Seven other vessels were anchored between her and the shore. Planks were laid on the riverbank up to the side of the nearest ship. They climbed up these and continued over the other ships until they reached the *Henry*. As they passed over the last ship before the *Henry*, George's father kissed him and said a tearful goodbye. He tried to hide his tears by putting a handkerchief to his face. George did not cry. He was too captivated by all of the new sights around him, as well as being too small to realise what the parting meant. "The ship seemed a new world to me. I had no eyes for tears – only for wonderment."

Now George found himself on board the *Henry*, with no-one to look after him, as "part of the cargo". The ship floated down the Mississippi, slowly on and on towards the gulf, bringing him out into the great ocean into the great world, along the Gulf Stream towards Boston. Travelling alone did not bother him. Everyone made him welcome and, if the truth be told, probably spoiled him. There was just too much to do, see and feel to find time to be lonely.

There was only one other cabin passenger besides George. He would sit opposite George at meal times. For their first meal on board they ate flapjacks. George was very fond of them, preferring to eat them with syrup or molasses. After a while he noticed that his companion did not eat molasses with his flapjacks. George could not understand why anyone would want to eat flapjacks without molasses, so he reached over and tried to pour some on his friend's plate. Just at that moment a heavy sea struck the ship, throwing George with the entire contents of the molasses jug forward, covering the man's trousers. George later dryly noted that, of course, the man was furious and did not appreciate the boy's efforts to teach him that molasses was the proper accompaniment to flapjacks. Surprisingly, they afterwards became good friends.

The voyage lasted twenty-three days, but George had not been long aboard before he became friendly with everybody. He had the run of the ship and, with no-one to look after him, he led a wild sort of life, never washing or changing his clothes. Sometimes he also stayed in the cabin with his molasses-hating friend, but more usually would be found in the fo'c'sle at all hours. He lived with the sailors on deck or in the riggings, although he liked the fo'c'sle best and felt right at home there.

George was a keen observer of everything and soon cursed and swore as well as any of the sailors. One of the games the sailors used to play with George was to go up into the rigging and call down to him that there was a great plantation up there. They would throw lumps of sugar to the boy, pretending these were from monkeys in the plantation. Only four years of age, he believed it all.

As soon as the ship anchored at Boston, George's uncle and a little dog came out in a boat to fetch his nephew. When they reached the wharf his uncle took George to his tobacco store in Dock Square, where a chaise was waiting to take him to George's grandmother at Waltham. They drove through the Massachusetts countryside towards their destination. Finally, they stopped at a little gate leading to an old farmhouse that stood half a mile away. This was the home of his grandparents, the Pickerings, who were strict Methodists. Oliver Train had married their eldest daughter Maria.

George's grandmother and aunts were astonished to see the filthy state he was in. They were also shocked to hear George swear, but before they dealt with his spiritual cleanliness they insisted that he must change his clothes and have a good scrubbing. The first thing the ladies had done was to organise a sort of town meeting where George would narrate the story of his voyage, but first he was to be washed and given different clothes. George was indignant when they did not believe him about the sailors getting sugar from the plantation up in the riggings and the monkeys throwing it down to him. He gave them an ultimatum: "If you don't believe my story about the plantation in the rigging and about the monkeys and the sugar, you cannot wash me or change my clothes." For three days they laid siege to him, but he held firm. Finally, George relented when the exasperated ladies said that they believed him.

George never heard anything from his father again. No trace of him could be found in New Orleans. His very existence had been erased and forgotten. No-one could be found who had ever heard of Oliver Train, or knew anything of his store. The family took it for granted that he had died from the plague like George's mother and sisters.

As this occurred prior to the invention of the daguerrotype, there were no photographs of his father or any others of George's family. Likenesses made in those days were expensive miniatures on ivory. The only images of his family George had were the precious memories of a four-year-old. To his surprise, sixty years later George received a letter from one of his cousins, Louisa Train, from Michigan. She told him that her own parents had died, leaving the contents of their house to her. She continued:

"In moving an old bureau, it fell to pieces, and, to my surprise, two documents rolled upon the floor. These papers relate to you. One of them was a letter from your father to his mother, written from New Orleans shortly before you left that city. In it he says:

'You can imagine my loneliness in being in this great house, always so lively, with eleven persons in it, including my own family — now all alone. George is with his tutor. He is a very extraordinary boy, though only four years old. The other day he repeated some verses, of which I can remember these lines:
"I am monarch of all I survey;
My right there is none to dispute;
From the center all round to the sea,
I am lord of the fowl and the brute.""'

One of George's aunts would later discover another letter written by Oliver Train. It was heartrending, penned on the day George was put on the *Henry.*

"New Orleans, June 10th, 1833.

Dear Sisters Abigail and Alice:
'Tis just two years since I left this place for New York, and arrived in Boston the evening of the 3d of July. I hope MY DEAR BOY will arrive safe and pass the 4th of July with you. He is now on board the ship (and the steamboat alongside the ship) to the Balize. I have written several letters by the ship, and found I had a few moments to spare which I will improve by addressing you. I refer you to the letters to Mother Pickering for particulars — as I have not time to say much. I can only say, my dear girls, that I am very unhappy here for reasons you well know. I part with George as

though I was parting with my right eye — *but 'tis for his good and the happiness of all that he should go; take him to your own home, care, and protection;* he is no ordinary boy, but is destined for a great scholar.

I am left here without a friend except my God! in a city where the cholera is raging to a great extent — 100 are dying daily! and among them some of the most valuable citizens. A sweet little girl about the age of Ellen, and an intimate acquaintance of George's, who used to walk arm in arm with him, died this morning with the cholera, and a great number of others among our most intimate acquaintances have passed on. Mrs. Simons died in six hours! What is life worth to me? Oh, my dear sisters! could I leave this dreadful place I would, and die among my friends! The thoughts of my dear Maria and Ellen fill me with sorrow! I have mourned over their tombs in silence. I have been with them in my dreams, and frequently I meet them in my room and talk with them as though alive. All here is melancholy. When shall I see you, God only knows! I have relieved my heavy heart of a burden — a weight that was almost unsupportable.

In parting with my lovely boy *I have bequeathed him to Mother Pickering as a legacy — it being all that I possess! You will take a share of the care and I know will be all that mothers could be for your dear sister Maria's sake!*

Give my love to Grandpa Bemis, Father Pickering, and all the rest of the family. Say to them that my mind is constantly with them, *and will ever be so. I have written in great haste and very badly, as I am on board the ship and* all is confusion, *with the steamboat alongside. Farewell, my dear sisters! Do write me a line. If you knew how much I prize a letter from you, you would write often. Adieu, and believe me your affectionate brother,*

OLIVER TRAIN."

For the next six years George earned his keep on the farm. Otherwise, he was pretty much left to his own devices, except for receiving religious instruction. He ran errands; there was always something for him to do. He was ambitious and inquisitive, and was never afraid to ask questions about something he did not know or understand. Life on the farm was busy. George would do household chores, such as setting a table or preparing a meal. He learned to sow, reap, plant, plough, hoe, mow and harvest. He even had a little garden of his own where he grew onions, lettuce, cucumbers, parsnips and other vegetables. There were not a lot of books on the farm. The only ones his family had were Walter Scott's *Waverley* novels, Jane Porter's *Scottish Chiefs*, Watts's *Hymns*, and the Bible, as well as a weekly religious paper from Boston called *Zion's Herald*. George was a voracious reader and soon got through this meagre library.

When George was ten years of age, he began going to the old Quincy market ten miles away in Boston. He soon got used to travelling there alone and selling the farm produce and vegetables. On these mornings George had to get up at four o'clock in order to prepare and harness "Old Tom", the Pickerings' faithful and trustworthy horse. He would arrive at the market before dawn, back up the wagon against the Market House and wait for light. Then he would feed Old Tom. Now and then, if the weather was particularly bad, he would put the horse in a stable for a few hours, at a cost of fifty cents, and give him a feed of oats. After the market business was done, George would go to Cambridgeport to purchase groceries and other supplies for the farm. He would buy a meal before driving home and giving his grandmother an itemised account of his sales and purchases. He followed this routine for the next few years.

George had no difficulty amusing himself. He roamed the countryside at will, setting box-traps for rabbits and snares for partridges. He had a small gun and a little dog for companionship, with which he would hunt rabbits or squirrels. This little dog, a type of mongrel fox terrier, was the only real friend he ever had. They were constant companions, seldom parted. In the winter, when the old house was cold, very cold, George used him to keep warm in bed. Through his farming and hunting activities, George earned his own keep and even was able to save some pocket money.

Of course, he went to school. The schoolhouse was two and a half miles away. To reach it George had to follow a path that ran across half a dozen farms, then a mile through a forest. He quickly learned the elementary skills of reading, writing and mathematics. One of George's earliest ambitions was realised when he was chosen as leader of the school.

In his old age, around the time that Train was dictating his autobiography, he happened to read an account of the collision between the *Priscilla* and the *Powhatan* in the Sound off Newport. The lives of five hundred passengers were threatened. It brought to mind a catastrophe that had occurred over sixty-two years before. Over and over again George relived the horrors of that day in his mind. It was a stormy, bitter day in January 1840. George was in the little schoolhouse at Pond End. It had snowed for most of the day and everything was covered. As the day advanced, the snow fell incessantly, piling up heavily around the schoolhouse, covering the surrounding landscape.

As the day went on, everyone grew anxious. Every now and then someone's parents arrived on a sleigh to take their child home. George began to think with dread about how he would get home through the blinding snow. Suddenly there was a tap on the door. The teacher answered it, then called: "George, your uncle Emery Bemis has just arrived from Boston in his sleigh, and wants to take you home with him."

When George got into the sleigh it was immediately clear to him that his uncle was very sad. Emery Bemis sat quietly for some time, while he collected his thoughts, then turned and spoke:

> "George, I have some terrible news for your grandmother. She is at the farmhouse now, waiting to see her youngest daughter, your Aunt Alice. Your grandmother expects me to bring her. She was coming from New York on the steamer Lexington, with the dead body of her husband [and his brother and father], which she wanted to bury in the family graveyard. There were three hundred passengers on the ship. The Lexington was wrecked and burned in the Sound, and three hundred persons were lost — burned or drowned. Your aunt was lost. Only five passengers were saved."

It's not surprising that this incident was fixed permanently in George's memory. Another peculiar thing about the destruction of the Lexington struck him. When the ship was smashed to pieces, part of the pilot-house, containing the ship's bell, remained intact and floated away before getting lodged on some rocks near the shore. The bell rang out mournfully, "clanging dolorously in every wind". To George it seemed to be "tolling perpetually for the dead of the Lexington".

Many years later Train made use of this incident in a speech for one of his political campaigns. He said that "the Democratic Party of the day was adrift from its ancient moorings, and was always calling up something of the remote past. It was like the bell of the Lexington, caught upon the rocks that had wrecked the ship and tolling forever for the dead".

Lectures were often held in Waltham's Rumford Hall. Lecture

night was always highly anticipated in the community. One day the committee that organised these lectures received a remarkable letter:

> "To the Library Committee, Waltham:
>
> *I will come to lecture for $5 for myself, but ask you for four quarts of oats for my horse.*
>
> RALPH WALDO EMERSON."

Ralph Waldo Emerson went on to become one of America's most influential authors, philosophers and thinkers. Then virtually an unknown, he gave Waltham the same philosophical lecture that would make him famous. In his speech, called "Nature", he eloquently expressed transcendentalism's main principle of the "mystical unity of nature".[2] Train was highly impressed and would remain a devoted disciple of Emerson's for the rest of his days. In his autobiography he acknowledged how lucky he had been to hear Emerson first-hand:

> "*He delivered it many times afterward, when his name was on every lip in the civilized world, and he received $150 to $500 for each delivery. He was just as great then, in that hour in the little old town of Waltham; it was the same lecture, with the same exquisite thought and marvelous wisdom; but it took years for the world to recognize the greatness and the beauty and the wisdom of him, and to value them at their higher worth. The world paid for the name, not for the lecture or the truth and beauty.*"

Train's grandparents wanted to make a clergyman out of him. He had others ideas about his future and commented: "that sort of thing was not in me." Although he had grown up in a strict religious atmosphere, Train turned out to be an atheist. Later on in life he paid tribute to his upbringing:

> "*[T]he scheme of morality proved a good thing for me, and served to guide me aright in all my wanderings about the world and up and down in it. I think it very good testimony to the soundness and virtue of my moral training that I have wandered around the world four times, have lived in every manner known to man, have been thrown with the most dissolute and the most reckless of mankind, and have passed through almost every vicissitude of fortune, and have never tasted a drop of intoxicating liquor, and have never*

smoked. I have kept all of the commandments — those of Sinai and those of the Methodists.

In my period of wealth and prosperity, I have entertained thousands of men, have seen thousands drinking and drunken at my table — and under it; but I never touched a drop of my own wine or of the wine of others. I have paid a great deal of money for the purchase of all sorts of tobacco, and for all sorts of pipes — narghiles, hookas, chibouks — as presents for others; but never touched tobacco myself in any way. I have been in every rat-hole of the world — but I never touched the rats. It is for these reasons that I am seventy-three years young, and am hale and strong to-day, and living my life over again like a youth once more."

He was sent ten miles away to Mr Leonard Frost, at Framingham, for further education. He stayed there for three months. This constituted his college education. One day he happened to overhear his aunts talking about his future. They had wisely come to the conclusion that a clergyman's life was not right for George. They debated the idea of sending him out to learn a trade, since it was clear that he would not be a clergyman, a doctor, or a lawyer; they reasoned that he must become a blacksmith, or a carpenter, or a mason. George did not want to be any of these things.

As soon as he got an opportunity, he told his aunts of his intention to go down to Boston and find a position somewhere. "They were astounded," he later recalled:

"They could not believe their ears. But I went.

The city seemed bigger than ever, now that I had to face it and conquer it, or have it conquer me. But I was not beaten before the fight. I began walking through the streets with as bold a heart as I could summon, and kept searching the windows and doors for any sign of 'Boy wanted'. I had seen such notices pasted up in windows when I came into the town on marketing trips."

Finally, George saw such a sign on a drugstore in Washington Street and walked in to apply. The owner offered George his board and lodging in exchange for looking after the place. George happily started work, wearing his Sunday suit. The first night he slept above the store. About one o'clock in the morning the bell rang. Someone wanted the doctor at once:

"I said I wasn't a doctor, and that the doctor was not there. The messenger ran off. This was bad enough, to be routed up in the middle of the night that way. The next day the druggist went away from the store on some business. I sampled everything edible in the place. I tried the different kinds of candy, and sirups, and then went out and bought some lemonade and a dozen raw oysters. The result may be imagined."

After a few minutes of discomforting illness George quickly decided that he had had enough of the drug business. He told the druggist so, shut the door, and left the store "a disappointed and lonely little fellow". He contemplated returning home, but decided to persevere in the city. He was determined to get another job, but not in a drugstore. Then he was inspired. He decided to try a grocer named Joseph A. Holmes, at the corner of Main Street and Brighton Road. Holmes's reply was music to his ears: "You have come just in time. We want a boy." He asked what wages Train wanted.

"Just enough to live on."

"You can live with us," Holmes said, "and I will give you one dollar a week." That meant fifty dollars a year. It was an enormous sum to the eager fourteen-year-old and he began to work at once, very hard.

"My work was to drive the grocery wagon up to Old Cambridgeport, take orders, and fill them. I had to get up at four o'clock in the morning to look after the horse, just as I had done on the farm, and to get everything ready for the trip. I had the orders of the day before to fill and to deliver at the college. Besides, I had to work in the store after I came back from Old Cambridgeport. In the evening I had to look after the lamps, sweep out, put up the shutters, and do numberless other little things about the store. The store was closed at ten o'clock at night. Then I would put out the lights, which were old-fashioned oil lamps.

It was a long day for a boy – or for a man. I worked eighteen hours every day… This life continued for about two years. In that time I had learned to do almost everything that was to be done about a grocery store. I had really learned this in the first six months.

One of my many little duties was to make paper bags. I had to cut the paper and paste it together. Another task was to take a hogshead of hams, put each ham in bagging, and sew it up. Then I

had to whitewash each particular ham. That was a nice business!
It went against my nature more than any other part of my mani-
fold labors in the store."

Mr Holmes was a deeply religious man. In fact, he was a Baptist dea-
con. That did not bother Train, as he had grown up amongst such people, but he did despise Holmes's habit of chewing tobacco, and his constant urging that Train join the Bible class in his Sunday school.

Train was restless, but something was about to occur that would
affect the course of the rest of his life and start him on the road to
adventure.

---

[1] Unless otherwise indicated, quotations are sourced from George Francis Train, *My
Life in Many States and in Foreign Lands* (D. Appleton and Company, New York, 1902).

[2] "Ralph Waldo Emerson" in *Encyclopedia Britannica* (15th edition, Chicago, 1994),
Vol. 4, pp. 473–474.

TWO

Learning the Ropes

One day a gentleman in an elegant, horse-drawn carriage drove up to the store and asked if there was a boy there named Train. Mr Holmes called George and introduced him to the visitor. He told George that the stranger, Colonel Enoch Train, wanted to speak with him.

The first thing Colonel Train said was: "I am surprised to see you, George. I thought all your family were dead in New Orleans. Your father was a very dear friend of mine – and your mother, too... He was my cousin. But we had heard that you were all dead. Where have you been?"

George told Colonel Train that he had been living with his grandmother at Waltham for the last ten years. After George had responded to all his queries, Colonel Train drove back to Boston. As George watched the departing carriage, "brave and disturbing" thoughts came to him. Colonel Train's surprise appearance was timely, as George had learned everything he could about the grocery store business and was longing for a change.

The next day George acted on an impulse and went to Boston. Although he had no definite plan of action when he set out, by the time he reached his destination he knew what he was going to do. He went directly to his uncle's shipping house at No. 37 Lewis Wharf. The huge granite building of Train & Co. seemed enormous to George then, "as if it contained the whole world of business and enterprise". He would return years later and think it very plain and ordinary.

George walked in purposefully and asked to see Colonel Train. The Colonel shook hands cordially and said he was very glad to see his nephew. George boldly asked: "Where do I come in?"

"Come in?" gasped his uncle at this effrontery. "Why, people don't come into a big shipping house like this in that way. You are too young."

"I am growing older every day," replied George. "That is the reason I am here. I want to make my way in the world."

"Well," responded the Colonel, regaining his composure and smiling at his nephew, "you come in to see me when you are seventeen years old."

"That will be next year," replied George. "I am sixteen now. I might just as well begin this year – right away." The Colonel tried to put him off in different ways but George persisted. He meant to stay.

"I will come in to-morrow," concluded George before leaving, content with how events had gone and certain that he would be successful. The Colonel must have been relieved to see him go, expecting that it would be the last he would see of the impetuous youth.

Early next morning George went to the shipping office, took a seat at one of the desks and waited. After a short while Colonel Train came in and was astonished to see George sitting there, ready for work.

"You here?" he stammered. "Have you left the grocery store?"

"Yes, sir… I have learned everything there is to learn there and in fact had done so before I had been there six months. I want a bigger field to work in."

"You don't mean to say you have come here without being invited?"

"As I was not invited, that was about the only way for me to come. As I am here, I might as well stay," he said, settling himself in his seat at the desk.

Colonel Train threw a puzzled look at the company bookkeeper, Mr Nazro, but George saw that the Colonel admired his persistence and bravado. He had won the first trial of arms. "Well," his uncle said after a while, once again turning to the bookkeeper, "we shall see if we can find something for you to do."

"I will find something to do."

He smiled cordially at George and said, "I will make a man of you."

"I will make a man of myself," the boy countered.

The Colonel asked Mr Nazro to try to find something for George to do.

A ship called the *Anglo-Saxon* had just arrived from Liverpool under the command of Captain Joseph R. Gordon, with goods for a hundred and fifty consignees. Nazro handed George the portage bill, showing the amount to be collected from each of the consignees, and asked him to convert it from English currency to American money. George thought Nazro had given him this task to get rid of him, but George had previously converted currencies while working at the store. He coolly asked Nazro what the current rate of exchange was.

"$4.80 to the pound," replied the clerk.

"That is just 24 cents to the shilling, two cents to the penny," George replied and went right to work. He started at noon. By six o'clock that evening he was finished and handed back the list, much to

Nazro's astonishment that the task had already been completed.

"You can see for yourself," George said. "There it is, all made out properly and correctly."

"How do you know it is right?" Nazro said uncertainly.

"Because I have proved it."

This task decided his fate. Nazro, satisfied with George's work, told him that the office hours were from eight until six.

The next morning, when George arrived promptly at the office, Nazro handed him the bundle of bills that he had worked on the day before, gave him a collector's wallet to put them into, and instructed him to go out and collect the amounts due. This must have seemed an overwhelming task to George, as he was not familiar with Boston. Although he had lived on the edge of it for years, he had not ever had the opportunity to become familiar with any part of it except the old Quincy market, where he had sold the farm's produce. Nevertheless, George set out undaunted by the task, intent on succeeding.

Working his way through the city, street after street, he collected as he went. He kept up a steady pace, never stopping. By the afternoon he had worked his way to the end of the list and had collected nearly every bill due. When he returned to the office and handed the wallet and money in, Nazro was once again astonished. Nearly all of the bills had been collected and all the money was correct to a cent, despite the fact that George did not carry a list. He preferred to rely on his memory.

George's next job was to see that each of the hundred and fifty persons received his goods. This gave him an opportunity to meet a large number of important people. He even met the unassuming Nathaniel Hawthorne, author of *The Scarlet Letter*, in the Custom House on a visit from Salem.

One day in 1847 a gentleman who looked like a farmer came into the office and asked to see Mr Train. George replied that he was Train. "I mean the old gentleman," said the caller. George told him that although Colonel Train was out of the office at that time, he would be able to help the gentleman, adding that he was in a hurry as the *Washington Irving* was sailing in an hour.

"That is just what I am here for," replied the stranger. "I want to sail on that ship; I want passage for England." There was one stateroom free, so George offered him both berths for the price of one: $75. The man quickly agreed, taking out from his pocket an old packet that had twine wrapped around it, and counted out seventy-five dollars. Train threw the money into the drawer without bothering to count it and started to fill in a passenger slip. "What is your name?" he asked the stranger.

"Ralph Waldo Emerson," was the reply. It must have been one of the few moments in Train's life when it was his turn to be astonished. He remembered Emerson from his lecture many years before in Waltham. This was Emerson's second journey to England. He was on his way to resume his acquaintance with Thomas Carlyle, the essayist and historian, and would write *Representative Men* and *English Traits*. Train's chance meeting with him was one of great significance: "I began to take great interest in him, read him carefully, and have continued to read him throughout my life. He has had more influence upon me than any other man in the world."

One day in 1848 George was standing on the pier waiting the arrival of the *Ocean Monarch* amongst a crowd of several thousand people. Although telegraph had been established four years earlier, it had not yet been brought from Nova Scotia to Boston, so the only means of communication was the semaphore, which was a brass trumpet. When a ship entered the harbour, the captain would take it and, standing on the bridge, shout out the latest news. As it happened, the *Persia* under Captain Judkins came in ahead of the *Ocean Monarch*. George was standing at the end of the pier and saw Captain Judkins place the trumpet to his lips and shout hoarsely: "The Ocean Monarch was burned off Orm's Head. Four hundred passengers burned or drowned. Captain Murdoch taken off of a spar by Tom Littledale's yacht. A steamer going to Ireland passed by, and refused to offer assistance. Complete wreck, and complete loss."

Everyone was stunned. The scene was indescribable. After the deadly silence with which the dreadful news was received, it took a while for it to sink in, but soon chaos broke out. George took advantage of the lull and rushed towards the street end of the pier. He leaped on his waiting horse and galloped off. After crossing the ferry he raced madly through Commercial Street and up State Street to the Merchants Exchange. There, standing on a chair amid a solemn hush, he announced the tragedy word for word, speaking with almost the same intonation that the captain had used.

That was not the only time George was quick off the mark after a shipwreck. Enoch Train once chartered the *Franklin* to take a cargo of tar, pitch and turpentine from Wilmington, N.C., to Baring Brothers, London, and return with a cargo of freight. She was due from England thirty-five days after the scheduled departure date. George, who was by now in charge of all the shipping, was on the lookout for the *Franklin* and listened in horror to news coming to him over a semaphore that a large ship had been wrecked just off the Boston harbour light house. The captain did not know for certain what ship it was, but asked if a Train & Co. vessel was due. Instantly the thought struck George that it might have been the *Franklin* making a faster than expected passage.

He was at the pier the following day when some wreckage floated into the harbour bearing the name *Franklin*. To the astonishment of all Boston, the valise of one of the *Franklin's* officers washed ashore the following day at Nantucket. In amongst the many letters was one giving instructions telling how "to sink the vessel off the light house, as she was fully insured".

Train saw at once that this circumspect "evidence" cast a suspicious shadow over the ship's sinking. If it was proven to be true, which of course it was not, since all aboard the ship drowned, then the ship's insurers would probably be successful with a claim that the ship's captain had sunk her deliberately for the insurance money. On the face of it, it was an open-and-shut case of barratry, or fraudulent breach of duty, by the master of the ship.

Losing no time, Train went straight to the office of Rufus Choate, then the most famous lawyer in New England. He hurriedly explained the matter and his urgent need for legal assistance. "Will you accept a retainer of $500?"

Without even waiting for a receipt, Train dashed out of Choate's offices, across the street to the office of another lawyer, Daniel Webster. A political heavyweight, Webster was a former Secretary of State and current Senator for Massachusetts. Combining his careers as a statesman, lawyer and orator, he was his era's foremost advocate of American nationalism. "Come in," roared a great, deep voice in response to George's knocking. Inside, Webster sat imposingly at a large desk. George wasted no time on shallow pleasantries and offered him a cheque for a thousand dollars. "Mr Webster, we want your services in a very important case. Will you accept this as a retainer?" Needless to say, Webster quickly consented. Thanks to George's initiative in hiring these lawyers with their "matchless array of legal ability", Train & Co. won the case against the insurers.

Seeing the kind of profits made by merchants, it was inevitable that Train started to engage in business ventures on his own account. His first speculation involved the shipment of onions to Liverpool. Although the onions were of a high standard and carefully packed under his personal supervision before they were shipped, Train's confident expectation of a good profit was dashed when he received an unhappy message from England: "Onions arrived; not in good order. Debit, £3 17s 6d." Of course, George was very disappointed by the failure of his first venture, but he learned from his mistake and never made it again. When he was later promoting his shipping business between America and Australia, he would quote this experience as a cautionary lesson of what might be expected by people who shipped perishable and fragile goods around the world.

He was not put off by the bitter taste of failure and quickly engaged in a second venture, involving the shipment of fish on ice to New Orleans. This enterprise proved more successful; encouraged by its profitability, Train kept his eyes open for other opportunities. The foundations for Train's shipping career came from an unexpected source:

> "I am ashamed to confess how I began this career, which made me a shipper of cargoes to the other end of the earth. But as I was too ignorant at the time to know much better, or, indeed, to give any thought at all to the matter, I shall, in the interest of truth, make a full confession. I became a smuggler of opium into China!
>
> It happened in this way. One of our captains, who was about to start with a cargo for the Orient, asked me if I did not want to send over something for sale, as he thought a good profit might be made on a shipment of something in demand there. 'What would be a good thing to send?' I asked. 'Opium,' said he laconically.
>
> Opium meant nothing to me then. I had never thought of it in any way other than as a marketable product and an object in cargoes. So I went to Henshaw's, in Boston, and got three tins of opium, the best he had. This I placed in charge of the captain, and he smuggled it into China, and got a good price for it, to the profit of himself and me.
>
> But the smuggling did not end there. I had instructed him to lay in a supply of curios, silks, and other oriental things, and bring them to Boston ...
>
> I had not, at that time, the slightest idea that I was doing wrong. I felt entirely innocent of defrauding two governments, and did not realize that I was a smuggler. The wrong of the transaction I fully understood afterward."

Colonel Enoch Train's older ships, like the *Cairo*, the *St Patrick* and the

Dorchester, had originally been built for traversing the South American trade routes, but these slow ships were hopelessly outclassed when Enoch decided to compete for trade on the transatlantic route to Liverpool. When he started to sail this route, he found that eastbound cargoes were scarce, so his ships had to make the triangular run from Boston to New Orleans. There they would pick up cargo, such as cotton, and then sail on to Liverpool before making the return journey to Boston.

The Colonel soon realised that this bulk freight enterprise had little appeal compared to the lucrative transatlantic passenger opportunities that the new Cunard steamers or even direct sailings to Liverpool by fast ship from Boston had all but sewn up. Faced with the realisation that with his existing small ships he had no chance of breaking into this potentially enormously profitable market, he decided to commission larger, faster ships.

In 1844 the Colonel set his plan in motion, commissioning Donald McKay to build a 400-ton clipper. This was named the *Joshua Bates*, in honour of the American partner of the British banking company Baring Brothers, who was his original London representative when he first entered the north-Atlantic trade routes. McKay, who would later become one of the most famous shipbuilders of his time, was persuaded by Enoch Train to move from Newbury port and set up a new shipyard at the foot of Broder Street, east Boston. From his new base McKay built a series of ships that put Train & Co. in the running on the trans-Atlantic routes, and made him famous as the premier American shipbuilder.

McKay was extremely successful in building bigger and faster ships for Train & Co., so much so that in a few years the average size of clippers doubled to 800 ton. The success of these new ships rippled though the shipbuilding world, leading to a new renaissance, making American clippers famous the world over. A further spur to the development of clipper ships came when gold was discovered in California in 1848. Prospectors dashed to the gold fields by every means and at any cost. Thousands of people were eager to get to California and make a fortune, and were quite happy to pay high prices if it meant getting there by the fastest clipper ship. The more practical men were quick to realise that the real money to be made was in supplying goods to these same desperate prospectors. The ships that got these goods to California first made excellent returns for their owners. Fortunes were made and lost on these speculations.

Traffic heading for California exploded along the three routes: the long, tiring and dangerous trek overland filled with many hazards; across the isthmus of Panama; or the long voyage around South America braving the ferocious seas at Cape Horn. In January 1849 alone, ninety ships sailed for California, carrying 8,000 people.[1] Determined not to miss out on this lucrative trade, George convinced his uncle that they once again needed larger, faster ships to compete. All he had to do was convince McKay. As it turned out, this was not difficult.

"I want a big ship," George demanded, "one that will be bigger than the Ocean Monarch."

"Two hundred tons bigger?"

"No... I want a ship of 2,000 tons."

If Mackay so much as raised an eyebrow at this request to build what would be the world's largest clipper, it is not recorded. To put George's demand in context, it is worth remembering that the Ocean Monarch was an 800-ton vessel and was considered enormous. Yet here was George Train wanting to build a ship over twice its size – a ship that would herald a historic revolution in shipbuilding. Fortunately, McKay was someone who just got on with it.

Soon not only shipbuilders but the whole world, it also seemed, were talking about this new ship. As the Flying Cloud, as it came to be known, took shape in the shipyard, crowds came to watch the proceedings. When she was launched in May 1851, thousands of people crowded onto the docks, some even on nearby rooftops to cheer her on. The ship bore great expectations from the very beginning.[2]

Duncan McLean, in the Boston Daily Atlas on April 25, 1851, wrote a thorough description of the ship and predicted a bright future: "If great length, sharpness of ends, with proportionate breadth and depth, conduce to speed, the Flying Cloud must be uncommonly swift, for in all these she is great." With a similar sentiment, a Boston editor went so far as to write: "If the Flying Cloud does not prove true to her name for speed and excellent sea qualities, then we are no judge of maritime matters."[3] Luckily for his reputation, he was proved right. The Flying Cloud's first voyage from New York to San Francisco was made in eighty-nine days and twenty-one hours, under the command of Captain Josiah Perkins Cressey, with a full cargo of freight and passengers. She paid for herself in that single voyage there and back. The previous record had been one hundred and twenty days. On one day she made 374 miles in twenty-four hours.

Though Train & Co. built the Flying Cloud, she never sailed under the company's unique flag: a bright, red square with a white diamond in the centre.[4] By the time the ship was completed, other shipowners were clamouring to buy her. When a carrot of $90,000 was dangled before the Trains by the House of Grimmel, Minturn & Co. of the Swallow-Tail Line of Liverpool, the temptation of making a quick, hundred-per-cent profit was too much for them to resist. It was one of the proudest moments of George's life when he received the $90,000 cheque, but Enoch later said that parting with this magnificent ship was one of his life's major regrets.

The Trains lost no time in commissioning an even bigger ship from McKay. This enormous clipper, named *Monarch of the Seas,* was a 2,200-ton ship – two hundred tons larger than the *Flying Cloud.* News that this even bigger vessel was being built rapidly circulated around the world, resulting in almost daily enquiries from other shipping lines eager to buy her. It was another proud moment in George's life when, at the age of nineteen, the largest ship in the world was entered in his name. Once again, the temptation to make a quick profit made the Trains sell her, this time to a German buyer for $110,000. The Trains were immensely proud to be associated with these magnificent ships.

The California trade was highly profitable and Train & Co. became one of the leading shippers with their fleet of fast clippers. One of their biggest ships was purpose built for the Boston to San Francisco run. This was the *Staffordshire*, a sister ship of the *Flying Cloud* of the same size and tonnage. She was sent to California on her first trip under Captain Richardson, full of freight and passengers. Three hundred passengers paid $300 each for the trip around the Horn. This single voyage made the Trains $90,000 and paid the entire cost of building and equipping the ship before she had even sailed.

When the Californian gold rush had first exploded into a public mania, George had intended going there himself and setting up his own house, as he foresaw "a great development in trade and permanent business there". But circumstance kept him on the sidelines in Boston, watching as others made fortunes doing this.

Realising that the ships returning from Liverpool often returned with few passengers, George instantly seized on this as an opportunity to increase business by encouraging immigration to America. After all, he reasoned, America needed more people to populate its wide expanses; if by providing these he happened to increase Train & Co.'s profits, then that was no crime. In particular, George focused on the Irish, who were in dire straits at home after a disastrous famine that had devastated the country.

The first step he took was to hire as many Irish longshoremen and stevedores as possible. He persuaded them to pass on information about America and how to immigrate to their families and friends throughout the country. Then he set to work arranging a cheap and convenient means of passage for them. George claims to have invented a new form of prepaid passenger certificate, along with the small one pound sterling bill of exchange. The bill of exchange enabled immigrants to send money back home to their relations in Europe. He then advertised in the Boston *Pilot*, the Catholic newspaper of the day, with a letter of endorsement from the Archbishop of Boston:

> *"The Boston and Liverpool Packet Line of Enoch Train & Co. have arranged to issue prepaid passenger certificates and small bills of exchange for one pound and upward. This firm is highly respectable, and has established agencies throughout Ireland for the benefit of Irish immigrants.*
>
> ✠ FITZPATRICK, Archbishop of Boston."

Train claimed that this advertisement and the Archbishop's approval were the catalyst for the increase of Irish immigrants into America.[5]

---

[1] Stephen E. Ambrose, *Nothing Like It in the World* (Simon & Schuster, New York, 2000), p. 48.

[2] According to *Western Ocean Packets*, a history written by Basil Lubbock in the nineteenth century: "McKay's ships were celebrated for their strength; they were designed to carry a tremendous press of sail in heavy weather without straining. In light winds they were not fast, but then packet ships did not sail in the latitudes of light winds." This passage was cited in Edward Laxton, *The Famine Ships* (Bloomsbury, London, 1996), p. 144.

[3] Quoted in Willis Thornton, *The Nine Lives of Citizen Train* (Greenberg, New York, 1948), p. 18.

[4] Edward Laxton, above, n. 2.

[5] Among the most famous immigrants that travelled on the Trains' ships were U.S. President John F. Kennedy's ancestors. They travelled to America from Ireland aboard the *Washington Irving* in 1844: Edward Laxton, above, n. 2, p. 148.

THREE

A Beautiful Stranger

Four years after the young grocery clerk joined his uncle's firm it was decided that George should go to England to manage the Liverpool office of Train & Co. Enoch agreed to his nephew's request for a holiday before he was to take up his new position and told George to take two months and see as much of America as he could. George had earned it. In those four short years he had worked hard and gained the respect of many people, not least that of his uncle who had placed more responsibilities on George as his confidence in him had grown.

After a brief stay in NewYork, George hurried on to Washington via Cape May, making the trip by boat, train and stagecoach. As soon as he reached Washington he called in on Daniel Webster, whom he had once retained to act on Train & Co.'s behalf. Webster, now re-elected Secretary of State, welcomed Train and arranged for him to meet President Zachary Taylor.[1] Webster also gave George a handwritten letter of introduction to give the President, which would later prove useful.

At the White House Train soon gained an audience with the President, who sat at his desk with his feet resting on another chair. Urging the President to stay seated, George presented him with the letter of introduction from the Secretary of State. At the President's request, George took a seat opposite him. From this vantage point the two men sized each other up. Train observed:

> *"He wore a shirt that was formerly white, but which then looked like the map of Mexico after the battle of BuenaVista. It was spotted and spattered with tobacco juice.*
>
> *Directly behind me, as I was soon made aware, was a cuspidor, toward which the President turned the flow of tobacco juice. I was in mortal terror, but I soon saw there was no danger. With as unerring an aim as the famous spitter on the boat in Dickens's American Notes, he never missed the cuspidor once, or put my person in jeopardy."*

It is not recorded what the President thought of his encounter with Train. He was courteous to his guest, though, and interested enough in him to question him for half an hour about New England, the shipping business, and the purpose of George's voyage to Liverpool. In particular, he was interested in the shipping business and the prospects for developing trade with England.

At Train's request, the President autographed Webster's letter, taking up a quill and writing "Z. Taylor" across it. With his highly prized letter in hand, George dashed from the White House to the National Hotel. Henry Clay, one of the best-known politicians of his day, received him. Train was disappointed to see that Clay's shirt was as stained and smeared with tobacco juice as the President's. Clay also agreed to autograph Webster's letter, dryly referring to Webster's recurring financial difficulties by observing that at least two signatures were usually necessary on Webster's paper.

George made a flying visit to Mount Vernon, Georgetown, and West Point military academy before going on to Saratoga Springs, the Mecca of high society. Train booked into the fashionable United States Hotel and had an enjoyable stay. This was his first exposure to high society and he was entranced by what he saw around him. The whirl of spirited activity made for a memorable stay, after which Train headed westwards.

At Syracuse train station an event occured that was to change his life. There was a group of about half a dozen students saying their goodbyes to a beautiful girl. Something about her struck George.

"Look at that girl with the curls," he urged his travelling companions.

"Do you know her?" they asked.

"I never saw her before… but she shall be my wife."

Without too much further thought, he quickly picked up his luggage and rushed over to the train she was on. He lost no time in finding a seat opposite her in the same car, determined to strike up a conversation at the first opportunity that occurred or that he could create. An elderly gentleman, whom he presumed was her father, accompanied her.

A chance to ingratiate himself into their company arrived sooner than he expected. When the elderly gentleman was unable to budge a carriage window, George quickly sprang across the aisle offering help with an eager: "Permit me to assist you." After a brief struggle, the young man succeeded in raising the window. In no time at all a conversation was struck up. Soon George had found out that the young lady was the daughter of Colonel George T.M. Davis of Louisville, Kentucky, who was an aide to General Scott in the Mexican war and later chief clerk of the War Department in Washington. The gentleman accompanying Miss Davis was not her father, but a family friend who was escorting the lady to her home in the west, a Dr Wallace.

When George learned that they were going to Oswego, he immediately declared that he was also going in that direction. Though this was far from the truth, it was in keeping with his character: "In such matters – for love is like war – quickness of decision is everything." He would have followed her to the end of the world. At Niagara Dr Wallace was happy to allow George to escort Miss Davis around the sights. Train was smitten with her:

> *"I was foolish enough to do several risky things, in a sort of half-conscious desire to appear brave – the last infirmity of the mind of a lover. I went under the Falls and clambered about in all sorts of dangerous places, in an intoxication of love."*

Fortunately, George's Southern belle felt the same way. "[O]ur love was mutually discovered and confessed amid the roaring accompaniment of the great cataract," confessed Train. In typical Train style, the couple were engaged to be married within forty-eight hours. Sadly, they had to part at Niagara, as she had to continue the journey homeward. Never disconsolate, George made the most of the rest of his holiday, dashing to Canada before returning to Boston to sail on the *Parliament* on July 25, 1850.

Eight weeks of travelling had almost worn Train out. His health also took a battering on the way to Liverpool and he was ill for most of the voyage. By the time he reached his destination, George had lost thirty pounds and had to be taken off the steamer and carried to the house of Mr Thayer, the Liverpool partner of Colonel Train. It was another two months more before he had completely recovered.

As soon as he was able to, George went down to Train & Co.'s office and took charge. This allowed Mr Thayer to return to America, leaving George in complete control. He immediately set about reorganising the Liverpool operation with a view to developing the business. One of its weaknesses, he found, was the irregularity of sailings between Liverpool and Boston. To remedy this, George quickly put two ships a month on a regular schedule on this route. He also arranged sailings for Philadelphia and New York.

Liverpool port was very conservative. The operators were content to conduct business as it had always been carried out in the past and never tried to improve efficiency or introduce better work practices. George was astonished to find that the port was only open from six in the morning until six at night. This meant that twelve hours were lost a day, with tremendous consequences in a business that required every minute of time available. If there was to be any profit in the shipping business, vessels had to be sent on their way without delay. They could not afford to be waiting for ports to open at daylight. The speed with which they were unloaded and reloaded, ready to set sail again, affected their profitability in a competitive marketplace. In short, Train and others like him could not afford these twelve unproductive hours. Train had supposed that the leading maritime nation understood this, but he was wrong.

He immediately began to urge the working of ships at night to save turnabout time. It had never been done; the port authorities feared the danger of fire and the weight of tradition. Train was surprised, to say the least, when they turned his request down:

"It was feared that we should burn the structures and destroy the shipping and docks. These dignified gentlemen even laughed at me for suggesting such a foolhardy undertaking."

Train realised that there was only one way to get the authorities' attention. He organised all of the American shippers into a committee and threatened the port authorities that unless they were permitted to load and unload at night, they would all abandon Liverpool for some other port. Faced with this threat, the authorities yielded reluctantly, and fires and lamps glared for the first time on the Liverpool docks for night work. This made a tremendous difference to the shippers. Some fifty years later, the shipping magnate J.P. Morgan, who occasionally sought advice from Train, copied his colleague's tactics and forced further concessions from the Liverpool dock board by threatening to move to Southampton.

Business boomed for the Liverpool branch of Train & Co. Their principal exports were "crockery from the Staffordshire potteries, Manchester dry-goods, and iron and steel, and what were known as 'chow-chow', or miscellaneous articles". By this time, Train had a one-sixth interest in the Liverpool branch of Train & Co. His share of profits for the first year was ten thousand dollars, an enormous income by any standard in 1850.

George's first British holiday was spent in Scotland, where he stayed for a week. While he was at Balmoral, Queen Victoria happened to be there. Later Train went to Braemar, on the way to Aberdeen. While Train was talking to a group of students in a hotel there, he suddenly found himself in the midst of tremendous uproar and excitement, when a horse carriage drew up. The students informed him that it was the Prime Minister, Lord John Russell, returning from an audience with the Queen.

Train immediately saw the chance for some sport at the students' expense. Turning to them with a smile, he said: "I wonder how his lordship knew I had come to Braemar? I hope to have the pleasure of speaking with him."

The students laughed. One of them said: "Look heah, Mr. Train, that sort of thing won't do heah, you know. We don't do things as you do in America." Another suggested that Train's attempt to approach Lord Russell would be met with brute force by the Prime Minister's bodyguards.

In response, Train took out a card and wrote: "An American, in the Highlands of Scotland, is delighted to know that he is under the same roof with England's Premier, Lord John Russell, and, before he goes, would ask the pleasure of speaking with his lordship for a moment." He carefully folded this card in the letter that had been given to him by Mr Webster – the one signed by the President of the United States and Henry Clay – and sent it to Lord Russell.

In a few minutes the door opened and Lord Russell's secretary came in and asked for "Mr. Train". Train confirmed his identity to the secretary. The secretary replied, "Lord John Russell waits the pleasure of speaking with Mr. Train of Boston." Train proudly followed him out of the room, to the amazement of the group of students, who didn't do things that way in England. Train was rewarded with a pleasant half-hour's chat with the peer and Lady Russell.

In his book, *My Life in Many States and in Foreign Lands,* Train referred to this incident and to the courteous reception at Braemar. He recorded that he had later received a warm letter from Lady Russell. "It was so kind of you," it said, "to remember us at Braemar, and to send us your Young America Abroad, which his lordship and I have read with a great deal of pleasure. When you come to London, come to see us. – FANNIE RUSSELL."

While in England Train availed of every opportunity to see and study the country, with the idea of finding out what made it tick. He always tried to do this in every country he visited, remarking: "I have

gone through the world as an inquirer and observer of men and things."
On another holiday, this time in Wales, he was fortune enough to meet
one of Britain's richest people, the Duke of Devonshire. Train's for-
wardness once again paid dividends, for by the time he had said his
goodbyes to the Duke, he had managed to wrangle an invitation to
Chatsworth, the Duke's famous stately home. As soon as Train returned
to Liverpool, he organised a group of friends and arranged to visit. On
their arrival at Chatsworth's nearby railway station, Train was pleasantly surprised to be mistaken for the Prince of Hesse-Cassel by the Duke's
waiting retainers. Chatsworth impressed Train immensely and he
repeated the, perhaps apocryphal, story that George IV was offended
when invited there because his own residence was shabby in comparison.

Another stroke of luck resulted in Train making the acquaintance at
Chatsworth of Sir Joseph Paxton, who went on to design the Crystal
Palace for the following year's Great Exhibition in London. Train
received an invitation to the exhibition and claimed that he had suggested a solution to a particular dilemma that its builder, Frank Fuller,
faced:

> "[A] problem arose, in the construction, as to what to do with a cer-
> tain beautiful and aged elm that had been an object of reverence
> and stood in the way of the proposed building. It had finally been
> decided to cut it down, in order to get it out of the way.
>
> 'What!' said I, 'Cut it down – this exquisite tree?'... 'The palace
> is here for time... and this tree may be here for eternity. Spare the
> tree.' 'But how?' they asked. They were bewildered – did not have a
> thought of what to do, except to hew down the venerable tree. 'Build
> your palace around it,' I said. This simple device had not occurred
> to them, but it saved the elm."

Train says that Fuller was delighted by the suggestion and went on to
propose that Train undertake the building of an American-style hotel in
London. Years later Train said that he did make plans to do this, but they
came to nothing.

In 1851 Train was almost tempted from his position of abstinence
of alcohol by no less a person than a Bishop. At dinner one day with his
friend Lord Bishop Spencer of Jamaica, whom he had met in Saratoga
Springs, Train faced a dilemma:

> "It was the 'closest call', as we say in the West, that my temperance

Methodist principles ever had. I was asked, as a great mark of dis-
tinction, to taste the pet wine of the bishop. The bishop himself
acted as chief tempter of my old New England principles. He
handed me a glass, saying: 'Mr. Train, this is the wine we call the
"cockroach flavor". I want you to drink some of it with us,' and he
glanced around his table, at which were seated many titled
Englishmen and women.

What was I to do? Should I, caught in so dire an emergency,
drown my principles in the cup that cheers and inebriates? Was all
my Methodism and New England temperance to go down in ship-
wreck? The exigency nerved me for the task, and I found a courage
sufficient to carry me through. I had never tasted a drop of wine,
and I was not going to begin now. I glanced about the room, and
slowly raised the glass to my lips. I did not taste the wine, but the
other guests thought that I did. 'We all know,' I said, 'that the wine
at your lordship's table is the best.' This passed without challenge
and, in the ripple of applause, my omission to drink the wine was
not observed."

Later in the evening Train went in style in the carriage and company of
the Bishop to a grand reception given by the American ambassador
Abbott Lawrence. He was wondering why several ladies were paying
such close attention to an elderly gentleman, when another lady asked
Train if he had seen the duke. Since there were two or three dukes present, he asked which one. "Why, the Duke of Wellington!" she
exclaimed, looking at Train as if he was from another planet. Only now
did Train realise he had been looking at the hero of Waterloo, who had
vanquished the threat of Napoleon:

"I now took occasion to get a good look at the venerable old man.
It was the first time, and proved to be the only time, I ever saw him.
He would not have impressed me, I think, had it not been for the
light of history which seemed, after I once knew it was he, to illu-
minate his face and frame."

Train was a prince among American social climbers. Knowledgeable,
wealthy, reasonably handsome and always fashionably turned out, Train
was eminently presentable in society. He loved every minute of it.

In the summer of 1851 George returned to America to marry his
Southern belle and take her back to England with him. He arrived in

Boston shortly before the Bunker Hill Day celebration. As an up-and-coming citizen it was only natural that he was appointed an aide to the Grand Marshal. Naturally, he hired the best horse he could and proudly wore a red, white and blue sash, cutting a dash in the parade. In the midst of all the celebrations, a telegram arrived from a friend warning him that all was not well in Louisville, Kentucky. His friend urged him to set everything else aside and hurry to Louisville with all possible speed.

Despite not understanding this cryptic message, he had enough sense to act immediately and left the parade, hurrying to his hotel room to make preparations to go Kentucky. Before he left Boston and much to his alarm, he found out what his friend had been referring to. Apparently his approaching marriage to Miss Davis had stirred up latent North-South rivalry. Several patriotic southerners were trying to save Miss Davis from marrying a Yankee by marrying her themselves. Racing to Louisville, George took no chances and insisted on marrying her immediately, determined not to let her slip through his fingers.

Wilhelmina Wilkinson Davis and George Francis Train were married on October 5, 1851 in the Episcopal Church of Louisville. The bride was only seventeen years old; the groom was twenty-two. They set out on their honeymoon that same day, stopping at Cincinnati. The Burnett House was the most popular hotel in the city at the time, so the couple stayed there. It was also reputed to be the first hotel in the country – perhaps even in the world – to have a "bridal suite". It cost the princely sum of fifteen dollars a day, which was more than extravagant in comparison to the normal charge of two dollars for a hotel room. Nothing was too good for George's bride.

The newlyweds went directly to Boston, where they stayed at Winthrop House. No doubt George lost little time introducing his bride to his family. Now with a wife to think of, he managed to negotiate a better partnership in Train & Co. and it was decided that he would return to England in the spring.

They sailed on the *Daniel Webster* from Boston. Only five days into the voyage, the ship ran into heavy weather. This did not concern them too much, since the McKay-built ship was sturdy and well capable of handling such weather. George knew, though, that many less seaworthy ships would be vulnerable in such a storm, so they kept a constant look out for vessels in distress. At the height of the storm Train spent most of his time on the bridge scanning the forward horizon. Suddenly something rose and took shape: it was the outline of a vessel – a shipwreck!

When George pointed it out, Captain Howard was reluctant to go to the rescue, but George insisted that they change course and offer assistance.

"Mr. Train," Howard protested, "we sea captains are prevented from going to the rescue of vessels, or from leaving our course, by the insurance companies. We should forfeit our policy in the event of being lost or damaged."

"Let me decide that... We can not do otherwise than go to the assistance of these persons."

The *Daniel Webster* bore swiftly down on the struggling vessel, which was in a worse condition than they had imagined. Effortlessly thrown around by the waves, the ship seemed in danger of going down at any moment. Men and women were clinging to her rigging, hanging over her sides, and trying to get hold of spars and timbers that would keep them afloat when they entrusted themselves to the mercy of the sea. The doomed vessel was the *Unicorn*, bound from Ireland to St John's, Newfoundland, with passengers and railway iron.

It was this iron that had been the cause of the wreck. Loosened by the stormy weather, it had broken away from its fastenings. With nothing to stop it moving about freely, the iron had punched holes in the ship's hull and ended seriously overbalancing it on one side. Another ship had already rescued as many passengers as it could accommodate. The passengers that were left behind seemed to have little chance of survival unless the *Daniel Webster* could get to them. The seas were running so high that it was impossible to bring the *Webster* along side. To make matters worse, the *Unicorn*'s crew had found whiskey in the cargo and in their desperation were drunk and unmanageable. They were of no help in evacuating the ship's miserable passengers.

The *Webster*'s small boats were launched in a final effort to save as many passengers as possible. It was their only hope. Train commanded one launch and Captain Howard another and rowed to the *Unicorn*. They discovered many passengers had already perished. Dead bodies tossed in the sea about the ship. They tried in vain to get close enough to reach the survivors, but it was impossible.

"Throw the passengers into the sea," Train shouted to the *Unicorn*'s captain, "and we will pick them up. We can't get up to you." In this manner two hundred people were saved and brought aboard the *Daniel Webster*.

Now they realised that the *Daniel Webster* was not equipped to accommodate and feed these survivors. For a while it seemed that they might have escaped drowning only to starve to death. The question of finding somewhere to put the survivors was solved by rigging up some of the ship's extra sails and tarpaulin as protection for them on deck and in the hold. As a result they were all fairly comfortable, though there was no food. There was hardly enough for the crew and passengers already on board: the delay caused by the ship's deviation from its course had already made an extra demand on supplies. Luckily, George had a brainwave. Thinking quickly, he remembered there was a cargo of corn meal on board. He also recalled that during famine times the Irish had survived by eating this.

"Open the hatches!" George cried out with, as he reported, "the enthusiasm of the philosopher who cried 'Eureka'!" The food problem was soon solved. Two barrels were cut in half, making four large tubs. They made large spoons from the staves of other barrels. Adding boiling water to the corn meal, they made a hot and filling meal, which the half-starved men, women and children relished. They lived on this until the ship reached England. No doubt George was proud that they had been able to save all two hundred without losing a life on the remainder of the journey. Captain Howard received a handsome medal from the life-saving society of England and the incident greatly increased the shipping company's reputation.

Once in Liverpool, George and Wilhelmina went to live at the house of a Mrs Blodgett in Duke Street, an arrangement considered much more genteel in Victorian England than staying at a hotel. The house was a favourite meeting place of American sea captains and shippers, a sort of central rallying point for all the Americans in Liverpool. It must have been hard for Wilhelmina to adapt from her home in the American South to these new surroundings.

There was appalling poverty, but living conditions for all classes were improving. There were signs of progress everywhere. In short, people had every reason to believe that things were getting better and that they would continue to do so for the indefinite future. The year before, while George Francis had been in Liverpool alone, the public opinion of Queen Victoria's husband, Prince Albert, had rocketed when he had set up the Exhibition of All Nations in the Crystal Palace in Hyde Park, to showcase Britain's cutting-edge technological achievements. Although the exhibits were now gone, the Crystal Palace still stood as a testament to its success. Victorian England was the first urbanised, industrialised society on earth and it evolved with stunning rapidity. Great wealth existed side by side with appalling poverty.[2]

It was a busy time for both Train and his wife. He continued his efforts at Train & Co., occasionally arguing the best course of action with George Warren, Enoch's former representative in Liverpool, who continued to work there and with whom he did not always agree. Willie Train directed her efforts towards the well-developed expatriate social circuit; the constant functions were excellent ways of meeting the local dignitaries and business community.

Train's first efforts as an after-dinner speaker proved highly successful and he was soon in demand. He was in his element, as he loved the limelight and felt quite at home at these various banquets and showy gatherings. Although he did not drink or smoke, or indulge in any other accepted vice, he was no party pooper and became a popular figure.

He was also very prominent in business circles. Charles Mackay, a fellow American and partygoing poet, liked to introduce his friend as "Express" Train, and once wrote that George "walked up the Liverpool Exchange like a Baring or a Rothschild". Train was highly flattered by this kind comparison, as he thought very highly of both men. Years later, he acknowledged that the "best men of Liverpool had made me welcome everywhere, in all circles of business or of society".

Towards the end of 1852 the Trains returned to Boston. Willie Train was about to have their first child and George, not unnaturally, wanted to negotiate a better interest in the business. Willie Train gave birth to a daughter, Lily; tragically, she died five months later.

When they arrived back home, George had a meeting with Colonel Train about business conditions in England. George innocently proposed that he should have a partnership interest in the Boston house, as well as the branch in Liverpool. Train could see that Enoch's business style, involving total control by one individual, was outdated. To his surprise, his uncle was not only startled but also highly indignant.

"Would you ride over me roughshod?" he accused George. After some discussion, a compromise solution was arrived at. George was given a partnership interest equalling $15,000 a year. With their signed contract in his hands, George, still angry at his uncle's reluctant reaction to his request, made a dramatic gesture.

"Colonel, as you do not seem to care to take me into the firm, here is your contract!" He tore it into pieces, gave it back to his stunned uncle, and declared his intention of setting up his own business in Australia.

Enoch Train did not know what to do for a moment. He probably realised that he could not restrain George's impulsive nature for long.

At best he could only guide his nephew and, knowing he was never going to be able to stop him doing want he had made up his mind to do, he probably thought it better to come to some kind of an understanding.

They settled the dispute amicably, parting company on friendly terms. It was agreed that George should go to Melbourne to start his own house. Colonel Train suggested that he take one of the company's most experienced captains, Ebenezer Caldwell, with him, whose experience Enoch hoped would counteract George's youthful rashness. The good captain certainly had an impeccable background. From 1838 he had commanded the *Forum* for the "Packet Line" between Boston and New Orleans. His first command for Train & Co. was the ship *Washington Irving* in 1845. Since 1849 Caldwell had been in charge of the *Plymouth Rock*.[3]

Forsaking whatever interest he may have had in Train & Co., George agreed to a partnership with Caldwell, one of Boston's most respected and reliable sea captains, to form the new shipping house of Caldwell, Train & Co., with a nominal capital of $50,000.[4]

It would not be too far from the truth to say that few Americans even knew of Australia until the discovery of gold, first in New South Wales and then in Victoria, brought its existence to their attention in late 1851. News of the find spread like wildfire, just as in California. However, some were familiar with Australian waters, especially New Englanders. Ships from Boston, Salem, and other ports had called at Sydney from about the time of its settlement to trade or purchase supplies while on sealing and whaling expeditions. But half a century passed before the first American ship visited Melbourne. The year after the discovery of gold, seventeen American ships came. The greatest influx was in 1853.

Prior to the gold rushes, Victoria was a pastoral colony of around 97,000 British settlers, almost entirely dependent on wool exports and trade with Britain. In 1851 only £122 was spent on imports from the United States. The next year this rocketed to £60,363. With the rapid growth of American interests in Australia, the need for reliable information regarding conditions in the "new" continent became of paramount importance. The Boston *Post,* then the leading newspaper in New England, enthusiastically proposed that Train send regular reports concerning the social, economic and political conditions of the rapidly-changing colony. George promptly agreed and wrote a unique sequence of well-received letters, sharing with American readers his observations of the excitement, extravagance, and economic growth of the turbulent gold rush years of 1853, 1854 and 1855.[5]

As early as 1853 America's leading independent newspaper, the New York *Herald*, predicted Australia's development as a market for American goods, "industry, skill and enterprise" much larger than California. It also believed that with a "free and independent government", which it foresaw would soon come, Australia's "social, commercial, and political" importance would "advance with rapid strides, and the trade between that continent and ours... increase in an equal ratio". The editor noted later in the same year that the new partners, who belonged to the "solid men of Boston", would take their part in the "spreading of the Anglo-Yankee race throughout the world" – part of America's "manifest destiny".[6]

The business outlook for the company looked extremely favourable. Among other things, the firm was appointed as gold purchasing agents for the firm of Duncan, Sherman and Co. However, George was one of the few who realised that the real money to be made was by supplying goods and other items to the expanding population, not by risking everything in a potentially fruitless attempt to find gold.

Nothing was left to chance. Everything the new company would need in Australia was to be brought from Boston, from ledger books and business forms right down to the clerks that would use them. This "singularly audacious venture" reached a point of no return when Captain Caldwell sailed from Boston with some clerks on the *Plymouth Rock* bound for Melbourne in 1853, arriving in May, a few days before the Trains came as passengers on board the *Bavaria*.

It was a long and monotonous voyage, taking ninety-two days. To relieve the boredom, George tried to keep occupied. He fished for porpoise and shark, and even baited seagulls. Anything to pass the time.

---

[1]   "David Webster" in *Encyclopedia Britannica* (15th edition, Chicago, 1994), Vol. 12, pp. 549–550.

[2]   Michael Crichton, *The Great Train Robbery* (Arrow, London, 1975), pp. *xi–xvii*.

[3]   Carl C. Cutler, *Queens of the Western Ocean* (Annapolis, 1961), pp. 371–2, 447–8; Melbourne *Argus*, May 20, 1853.

[4]   Boston *Post*, January 25, 1853.

[5]   E. Daniel and Annette Potts, eds, *A Yankee Merchant in Goldrush Australia* (Heinemann, Melbourne, 1970), pp. *v–vi.*

[6]   New York *Herald*, February 15 and December 2, 1853.

FOUR

"One of the most promising men in Melbourne"

Nothing had prepared George for what he saw when the *Bavaria* finally rounded Point Nepean to anchor off Sandridge point, Melbourne's port. Nearly six hundred ships were anchored in the harbour. For the second time within a few years it seemed that the whole world had gone wild over the discovery of gold and were now flocking to Australia. It was plain to see that the future was promising for Caldwell, Train & Co. Renting space at 13 Elizabeth Street, the new arrivals sold everything imaginable, including clothing, guns, flour, building materials, patent medicines, mining tools, coaches and carts, and wagons and buggies. In addition, they acted as agents for about twenty New England insurance companies and represented the White Star shipping line of Liverpool. George went into Melbourne at once and secured buildings to house the cargo, then arranged to have lighters (flat-bottomed boats for unloading ships) ferry it up the Yarra-Yarra river.

Melbourne itself was a small but promising city. Its population had exploded from ten to forty thousand people within a few years and was expanding as fast as new properties could be built.

"It was, of course, a frontier town, crude and raw, with few of the advantages of civilisation. The people were too busy with their search for gold and profits to think much of the conveniences or luxuries of life." For instance, the "only good hotel" was the Squatters' Hotel, the popular name for the Prince of Wales Hotel at Port Phillip, and it lacked every sort of comfort.

Fed up with paying grossly inflated rent for unsuitable premises, Caldwell, Train & Co. had a more suitable one built to Train's specifications by Sinclair and Sons. In May 1854 the blue granite store and warehouse was erected in the heart of Melbourne's business district on the corner of Flinders and Elizabeth streets, opposite the biggest structure in the city, Flinders Street railway terminus. The building was described by a contemporary newspaper as "elegant and commodious... unrivalled in the city of Melbourne... if not in Australia".[1]

The premises was easily distinguished by its three large, arched doorways, which led to a storeroom and two offices finished in local cedar. Massive teak columns supported the first floor, where captains of the White Star Line had their offices, and an attic. The most admired part of the establishment was a graded yard and a 10,000-gallon water tank for draining the roof and flushing the sewer.[2] Train claimed that the building cost $60,000.

It was clear that the firm also needed to have its own storage facilities at Sandridge point, since the area suffered from a severe shortage of warehouses. As this was where ships were unloaded and where the railway from Melbourne terminated, Caldwell, Train & Co. put up a substantial two-and-a-half-storey timber warehouse. It was made in Boston and shipped out in sections. This is the building Train later remembered as being six storeys high and costing $25,000.[3]

Train claimed that he successfully convinced the local businessmen that a railway line built over the short, two-mile distance from Sandridge point to Melbourne would be a much more convenient way of transporting goods than by ferrying cargo ten miles up the Yarra-Yarra. In fact, as his letter of June 23, 1853 shows, the Hobson's Bay Railway Company, which was established the year before, already had the project well underway, even before Train had put a foot on Australian soil.[4] The line was opened on September 13, 1854.

With warehouses at each end of the railway line, what was by now Melbourne's leading American firm was able to have passengers and cargo landed at Sandridge and taken by train, instead of by the slower and more expensive lighters, to the city.[5] From their Elizabeth Street office, Caldwell and Train sent American and English shippers circulars on trading conditions and requirements in an attempt, often a fruitless one, to regulate the type and quality of goods consigned to them for sale on commission. Sometimes printed in full in American newspapers, they were free of the exaggerations of which Train accused others and revealed the difficulties of gauging demand for goods in a market which would not receive them before six months had passed.[6]

Amid the quickly erected buildings, Caldwell, Train & Co.'s imposing offices stood out. The firm's method of conducting business over marble-top counters and providing champagne luncheon hospitality for customers soon made the firm prominent in the Melbourne business community. The extent of the firm's success can be judged by the fact that its commissions for the first year's business amounted to over $95,000.

The rough, frontier city might have daunted others, but Train was extremely enthusiastic about his prospects: "Melbourne, though situated so far out of the way, cannot fail to be a great city. All we require is a little energy and a great deal of money to make the wheel turn rapidly."[7] The city did not have a proper Merchants Exchange or Chamber of Commerce where merchants could meet. This was something other major ports took for granted. Train wrote disgustedly: "I should never have thought of finding a commercial exchange in the rear of a slop-shop inn."[8] He and Caldwell lost no time organising merchants, shippers and other interested parties so that the business community could be kept informed of daily arrivals and market conditions.

They joined forces with the builder of a new hotel, the Criterion, ensuring that a suitable hall was available for merchants' use. Vital information, such as statistics and newspapers from all corners of the world, was made available to the members. These resources were far too rare and valuable to be monopolised by any one individual, but no-one showed a greater interest in them than Train himself. One of his associates recalled:

> "No keener eye ever scanned their columns... than the eyes of Mr. Train... Any excision or mutilation of their contents always aroused his displeasure, and in great distress he would direct my attention to it and say, 'keep a sharp eye on those papers, and try to find out who mars them'."[9]

Train had his own reasons for keeping a close eye on the newspapers. He had started to write articles for them. Few American newspapers employed professional foreign correspondents and were usually glad to accept letters or correspondence from any reasonably reliable source. His articles were full of highly vivid, shrewd and observant insight into world affairs. Train benefited from the additional attention both to his business and himself.

In due course Train and Caldwell became active members of the Chamber of Commerce, taking their turn on the governing committee. Train wrote several reports on matters considered by the Chamber and his resignation – caused eventually by his decision to return home – at the meeting of November 7, 1855 was received with unanimous regret by the other members. As well, the two partners were among a group of compatriots whose concern at the inadequate provisions to protect Melbourne from fire led to the formation of volunteer firefighting units along American lines.[10]

One of George's most successful sidelines was the importation of vehicles. Initially he had brought a chaise from Boston for his own use. It was so light in comparison to the heavy, lumbering Australian ones that people were amazed when it stood up well to the notoriously rough and muddy tracks that served as roads. Soon people were urging George to import similar vehicles from America. Every ship began to bring Concord wagons, chaises, and vehicles of all sorts. In particular, the carriages and chaises attracted a lot of attention, as these were the first vehicles of the kind that had ever been seen in Australia. George was happy to make a huge profit and improve Australian transport. He later claimed credit for backing the famous coaching firm of Cobb and Co.; he did extend generous credit to Freeman Cobb for the purchase of coaches, but so did other Americans.[11]

By now the Trains found life at the rough hotel "very dreary and very inconvenient". It certainly was not an acceptable accommodation to Willie, who was expecting a second baby. Their situation improved no end when George bought a two-storey house just outside the city. It was large enough to accommodate the firm's clerks and even, for a time, the U.S. consul and his wife. Having a steward and stewardess on hand from one of the firm's ships meant that life was a great deal more comfortable than it had been at the hotel.

Another important aspect of Train's Melbourne career was his connection with Pilkington and Wilson's White Star Line, one of the two regular passenger lines between Liverpool and Melbourne. Both the Black Ball and the White Star used clippers, and the friendly rivalry which ensued between them was of great benefit to the public, helping to improve the service considerably. The legendary *Marco Polo*, built in New Brunswick, was the first clipper entered in the Australian trade. Flying the Black Ball flag of James Baines and Company, she sailed in 1851 from Liverpool to Melbourne in an astonishing sixty-eight days.[12] This record was broken three years later by the *Red Jacket*, one of the most famous clippers to sail under the White Star flag, whose graceful lines earned her the reputation of being the handsomest of the large, American-built clippers.

Rumours of mutiny had drifted around Melbourne when the *Red Jacket's* captain pressed charges against five cabin passengers (three of whom had actually been put in irons during the voyage) for insubordination and riotous conduct. A counter-suit brought against Captain Reed challenged his right to impose on passengers his views regarding punctuality, behaviour and dress, as well as a curfew; decrees against card-playing which "led to gambling, inebriety, and conduct too disgraceful to repeat"[13] reflected the captain's puritanical background. The episode actually stemmed from his determination to break all previous sailing records on the route, regardless of passenger comfort or safety.

Train shared this determination. The previous White Star vessel, the *Golden Era*, had been unloaded and made ready for departure from Melbourne in thirty days. To reduce this time for the *Red Jacket*, Train persuaded the Customs to allow her cargo to be unloaded without delay and hired a steam tug to tow her outside Port Phillip Head, as winds were poor. In the extraordinarily short time of fifteen days she left for the Heads where she was to be joined by Reed, who was wanted by the police to answer the charges made against him by his irate former passengers.

Captain Caldwell was on board and temporarily in command. The flooded markets and fluctuating business conditions had decided him to sell out and return with his son to Boston. He tied up the Sheriff's officer and his assistant who had boarded the clipper to serve warrants on Reed, and he then ordered the crew to put them into the accompanying steam tug.[14]

Among the passengers on the *Red Jacket* was Willie Train. As their first child had died at five months of age – albeit in Boston – the couple were fearful of health conditions in Melbourne. In addition, they entertained hopes that she was carrying a future President of the United States and wanted the baby to meet the constitutional requirement of being born on American soil. It was not until some time later that George found out that a child automatically has its parents' nationality, no matter where it is born. The child was a girl and they named her Susan.

Meanwhile, Train was having difficulties in Melbourne. All bills of lading were customarily signed by the ship's captain. As Samuel Reed was being sought for arrest by the police, naturally enough he was not present to sign the bills: two sheriffs were waiting patiently for him to make an appearance. In Boston, Train had often signed bills of lading in the absence of any captain and did not hesitate to do the same now. Train would later say that when the Melbourne bankers saw that he had signed these papers for nearly 58,500 ounces of gold worth around $2,000,000, "they were scared nearly out of their boots". Evidently, they had never heard of such a procedure and thought their insurance cover was rendered void by his unorthodox action. Their fears mounted when they heard that Train's wife and his business partner were also on board the *Red Jacket*. It had not escaped their attention that the ship also happened to be the fastest clipper ever to visit Melbourne. Captain Reed's circumstances did not help to allay their fears, either. They were sure Train meant to steal the gold from under their noses and that it would never be seen again.

Train later recorded: "[I]t occurred to these bankers that I was going to run off with this gold, and become a Captain Kidd or a buccaneering Morgan." It must have seemed to the bankers that their worst nightmares had come true. They lost no time communicating their concerns to the government, who in turn dispatched two men-of-war after the clipper, though only a miracle could help them to catch the fugitive ship. Meanwhile, the *Red Jacket*, with her trim sails bellied with wind, was swiftly sweeping down Hobson's Bay. At Point Nepean Caldwell ordered that the steam tug take the two sheriffs back to Melbourne. Of course, the officials were furious at this outrageous expulsion, but could do nothing about it now that they had entered international waters. Immediately after they had left the ship, a little yacht, the *Flying Eagle*, quickly came alongside and put the elusive Captain Reed aboard.

The hopelessly outclassed men-of-war soon abandoned their useless pursuit. Train optimistically predicted that the return passage to Liverpool would take only sixty-five days; his estimate was off by only eight days. He later claimed that the *Red Jacket* made the run to Liverpool in sixty-four days. For these two months the bankers and authorities waited anxiously for news, while Train calmly went about his everyday business. When the word finally came from Liverpool that all of the gold had arrived safely, these same people gave Train their hearty congratulations. But he could see they could never forgive him for taking matters into his own hands, defying convention and the authorities.

Australia was very much like the American Wild West. With its tough pioneer conditions it was a harsh place to live. Originally used as a convict settlement, it now attracted every kind of opportunist and adventurer. There were also many well-educated and respectable people though, as Train testified, Melbourne was a rough-and-ready frontier town. He was disgusted to see the body of a hanged criminal displayed in the front window of a drinking saloon, decorated with flowers and ribbons.

"We made some tremendous profits in Melbourne", Train recalled, "the sort that makes one's blood tingle and transforms cool men into wild speculators." He also found time to meet numerous famous people who happened to travel to Australia. He always made it a point throughout his life to collect the autographs of any celebrities he encountered. It was quite common for stars of the stage to include Australia while making a world tour. Train met many actors. He was astonished to meet Edwin Booth and Laura Keene stranded in Melbourne. Their visit to Australia had only met with a brief success in Sydney; elsewhere it had no appeal to the unpolished audiences of gold prospectors. They were glad to accept Train's offer of a free passage on one of his ships.

The greatest sensation during Train's time in Australia was made by the arrival of Lola Montez. She "danced and pirouetted on the necks and hearts of men". On her arrival she lost no time in calling on Train to make a complaint against the Captain of one of the ships for which Train was an agent. Train pacified her and did everything he could to ensure her visit was a success. One night he called at the green room of a theatre where she performed and danced every night to packed house. He was relaxing on a sofa while waiting for her to finish her performance when "[s]uddenly the door flew open, and in rushed something that looked like a great ball of feathers. This ball flew towards me and I was enveloped in a cloud of lace! The bold little dancer had thrown her foot over my head!"

During his Australian stay Train explored the outskirts of Melbourne – Geelong and the goldfields around Ballarat – visited Sydney on the American steamer the *Golden Age*, and spent a few days travelling in Tasmania. The latter trip was made partly on behalf of the Chamber of Commerce, to help promote the use of the White Star Line for a regular bimonthly mail service.

The trip to Sydney came about as a result of an invitation extended to the Trains by the captain of the *Golden Age*, who was a relative of George's. After "a short but delightful visit" to the fast-growing city, the *Golden Age* headed back to Melbourne. Shortly after leaving port she ran into one of the "most terrific storms" that Train ever encountered. As the storm mercilessly attacked the ship, few aboard believed that she could withstand such force. In the midst of the storm Train saw one of the most prominent and richest of the Sydney merchants coming across the deck, "thrown hither and thither by the tossings of the ship", carrying a very heavy package.

"For the love of goodness, what have you there?" Train asked in amazement.

The man came up close up to him and replied: "Mr. Train, I know you have some influence here on the ship. I have brought with me one thousand sovereigns. They are here" – and he tapped the bag he carried in his hands. "I want you to go with me to the captain and give him this amount for putting me off in a small boat."

"A small boat would not live a minute in this sea," Train responded.

"I am prepared to take my chances," the merchant replied, "as it would be better there than here, for the ship may go down any moment."

Train refused to go to the captain with such a foolish request and urged the man to be calm, reassuring him that the ship was well built and would weather the storm. It did no good, for the man was petrified with fear. Fortunately, the storm subsided as quickly as it had come. The rich merchant took his thousand sovereigns back to his room. Train, once again, had proved he could keep his head in a crisis.

As an agent for Boston insurance people, Train had a natural interest in the safety of all vessels in the vicinity. One morning the entire city of Melbourne was startled to hear that a great clipper had gone down or ashore on Flinders Island, off Point Nepean. At once Train made it his business to see what could be done to save the ship and crew. He hired a tug, organised a rescue party, then "steamed as fast as the tug's engines would carry her through the driving seas" down Hobson's Bay. As they neared it, they saw that the ship was a complete wreck and there were no signs of life aboard her. Train did not give up. He ordered the tug-boat's captain to make for the island:

"I had a vague hope that the crew had somehow managed to get ashore in the boats or on floating timbers. The captain did not relish this part of his work, and his fears were soon justified, for we very narrowly escaped shipwreck ourselves in the wild seas. We had, finally, to wait until the waves went down a little, before attempting to land on Flinders Island. We got up as near as we could, however, and then we saw signals flying from shore. We signaled in reply, and the wrecked crew understood that we were waiting for the sea to run less wildly before attempting to reach land.

The wind died down slowly, and it was hours before we could approach the coast. As soon as possible, I got out with a crew in a small boat and went to the island. We had a most difficult time in getting through the surf and avoiding the breakers, but we finally reached shore. There we found Captain Brown with his wife, the ship's officers and the crew, all alive and well. They had managed to live on shell-fish and wallaby – the small bush kangaroos. They

had not been able to take anything from the ship, and could not,
of course, reach her after she had been abandoned. We got them all
aboard the tug, and carried them safely to Melbourne. The
American consul afterward sent them all home by way of
Liverpool."

This was the second rescue of shipwrecked crew and passengers that
Train had made, and he was quite rightly proud of it.

By 1854 miners in the gold fields of Ballarat and Bendigo were
extremely disaffected with their treatment. In particular, the fact that
the government had once again raised the prospector's licence fee was
bitterly resented, since they had not even been granted a single representative in the provincial government. Organised resistance to the government began to gain popular support. Armed resistance was not far
away. While some were happy to argue for parliamentary reforms and a
reduction of licence fees, others wanted complete independence for the
Ballarat area and the creation of what they proposed to call "The Five-
Star Republic". They were quite prepared to fight for it.

Train kept a close eye on all these developments; how closely is
shown by his own dispatch of October 28, 1854 on the beginnings of
the disturbances:

"Last week the diggers rose en masse *against a judicial decision*
which liberated a notorious publican by the name of Bentley, who
was arrested for murder. That night mob law was supreme!"[15]

A huge crowd had gathered about Bentley's hotel and burned it to the
ground. Troops had to be called out. Train summed up the volatile situation: "Give the colonists their own way and they will remain loyal –
cross their path and they will have a flag of their own!"[16]

The miners also had their eyes on him. As they were aiming to create a new republic independent of Great Britain, they automatically
looked to the United States of America for their ideal model. Train was
probably the best-known American in Australia. He had introduced and
promoted the Fourth of July celebrations. Such an occasion was
recalled by one of the American diggers, Charles D. Ferguson:

"Fourth of July was coming, and arrangements had to be made for
the celebration, for the Americans had always observed the day and
the Canadians and British-Americans joined in the festivities of
the occasion, and seemed to take as much interest in it as those

from the United States... It was on the occasion of a public din-
ner that day that I met and heard the noted George Francis Train.
He was then connected with the American firm of Caldwell, Train
& Co. The toast he responded to was 'Young America', and never
before or since did I listen to a more eloquent speech. He was then
looked upon as one of the most promising men in Melbourne."[17]

All things considered, the American was a natural candidate for the
miners' revolutionary cause. They went as far as to offer Train the presidency of the proposed republic when it came about. In the meantime,
they offered him a position as their representative in the colonial legislature for the Maryborough district. However tempting their proposal
may have been, Train was smart enough to realise that their revolution
had no hope of success and he refused the position.

The rebellion was quelled when the government forces overran the
rebels' stockade called "The Eureka". Just before this, one of the
American leaders, James McGill, had been sent out to intercept some
government arms being sent out from Melbourne. At the height of the
panic McGill walked daringly about defying posters offering a reward
of one thousand pounds sterling for his capture, dead or alive. One
morning during this calamity, Train was sitting in his office when McGill
coolly walked in, as if he were only going about his everyday business,
not flitting from place to place in fear of his life.

"I hear," he said to Train, "that you have some $80,000 worth of
Colt's revolvers in stock, and I have been sent down here to get them."

Train glanced back at the man and studied him closely. In a flash the
identity of his visitor struck him. "Do you know," Train replied, "that
there is a reward offered for your head of one thousand pounds?"

"That does not mean anything," smiled McGill as if that were only
a joke. "They can not do anything," he added, as if this would allay any
fears Train might have.

"This will not do," Train angrily protested. "You have no right to
compromise me in this way."

"We have elected you president of our republic," McGill protested.

"Damn the republic!" was Train's less than eloquent reply.

"Do you mean to tell me that you refuse to be our chief?"

"I do... I am not here to lead or encourage revolutions, but to carry
on my business. I have nothing whatever to do with governments or
politics; and you must get out of here, if you do not want to be hanged
yourself, and ruin me."

Just then someone knocked at Train's door. Luckily, Train had wisely locked it as soon as he realised who his visitor was. He hurried to the door and asked who was there. His heart must have missed a beat when the Chief of Police, Captain McMahon, identified himself.

"Do you know that rascal McGill is in the city? His men are at Warren Heap, but he himself has actually come into Melbourne! I want a dozen of those Concord wagons of yours immediately." As soon as Train saw the way was clear, he took McGill out into the street and straight to the nearest barber. The fugitive's hair was cut and his moustache shaved off. Train made him put on a workman's suit of clothes. He bundled McGill into his private chaise and drove him down to the bay. He took McGill aboard one of the ships he knew was about to sail, telling the men he had brought them a new stevedore. McGill pitched in and worked alongside everyone else.

Meanwhile, other Americans appealed on McGill's behalf to the Australian government and were successful in convincing the authorities not to prosecute McGill on condition that he left the country. Three days later the ship sailed to America via England, taking Train's chance of the presidency of the "Five-Star Republic" with it.

As Willis Thornton observed: "It was his first sniff of the delicious odor of political power, which was later to become so sweet to his nostrils."[18]

---

[1]   *Argus*, May 12, 1854; *The Age*, January 29, 1855, quoted in E. Daniel and Annette Potts, eds, *A Yankee Merchant in Goldrush Australia* (Heinemann, Melbourne, 1970), p. xv.

[2]   E. Daniel and Annette Potts, eds, *ibid.*

[3]   *Argus*, June 2, 1854.

[4]   Boston *Post*, October 20, 1863, reproduced in E. Daniel and Annette Potts, eds, above, n. 1, pp. 22–26.

[5]   New York *Herald*, October 26, 1854.

[6]   e.g. New York *Herald*, March 12, 1854.

[7]   Quoted in Willis Thornton, *The Nine Lives of Citizen Train* (Greenberg, New York, 1948), p. 42.

[8]   *Ibid.*, p. 43.

[9]   *Ibid.*

10 E. Daniel and Annette Potts, eds, above, n. I, p. *xvi*.

11 *Ibid.*, p. *vi*.

12 Arthur H. Clark, *The Clipper Ship Era* (New York, 1910), pp. 266–272.

13 *Argus*, quoted in E. Daniel and Annette Potts, eds, above, n. I, p. *xviii*.

14 *Ibid.*

15 *Ibid.*, p. 155.

16 *Ibid.*, p. 156.

17 Charles D. Ferguson, *The Experiences of a Forty-Niner during Thirty-Four Years' Residence in California and Australia* (Cleveland, 1888), p. 328.

18 Willis Thornton, above, n. 7, p. 53.

When Commodore Perry signed the treaty of Kanagawa on March 31, 1854 the world looked on, believing that at last Japan was opening up to foreigners. Not wishing to waste any precious time, Train began planning to open a branch of Caldwell, Train & Co. in Yokohama. A man well ahead of his time, Train had a visionary plan for the future. He believed that the way ahead for both his and his uncle's interests was to expand by allowing new blood and capital to enter into the business. This would allow them to become a global shipping house, with branches in Boston, Liverpool, Melbourne and Yokohama.

It's ironic that he planned this just as the American merchant fleet of clippers was going into a sharp decline. The British, spurred into action by the American domination of global trade, had put all their energies into the development of new steam ships. Although the early side-wheelers were no match for the clippers, the new screw-driven steamers surpassed them. The British soon gained the upper hand with this innovation and exploited it to the fullest.

George's idea failed at the first hurdle, since he was unable to convince his uncle of the scheme's merits. Colonel Train's persistent demand that he must own all his ships put an end to the plan. He would not even consider allowing others to come in with new capital and perspectives while he retained a controlling interest. His stubborn and not unnatural, though short-sighted, desire to control everything completely not only put an end to George's proposal, but eventually to his own company. Gradually Enoch's business declined and in the panic of 1857 his firm was sunk.

After less than three years in Australia, Train left to sent up a new branch in Japan. He left behind a string of considerable achievements in Melbourne. Sixty years later the Rev. C. Stuart Ross, an Australian who had worked in the newly established Melbourne Commercial Exchange in his youth, described Train's contribution:

"But of all the foreign elements then attracted to our young Colony, there were none that took such hold, stamped it with a new quality of keenness, penetrated it with a new spirit of energy and enterprise, as the American element... One of those, George Francis Train, a splendid type of intelligence and smartness of his countrymen, and known in his day as 'Young America', pressed his way to the front rank as one of our most respected and popular merchants...

He was then a young man of indomitable energy, faultlessly dressed, always swinging an elegant cane in his hand; his jaunty air, breezy manner, and genial volubility, made him a general favourite. I was a boy of only thirteen years of age, but his dash and hopefulness, his bright and cheery spirit and charming personality strongly attracted me, and I used to regard him as the smartest man on the floor of the Exchange...

In many ways George Francis Train and his compatriots — shrewd, hard-headed business men, their souls kindled with the fire that glowed in the Great Republic and energized its sons to proud achievements — helped our State in its time of need."[1]

As well as being very successful financially, Train had gained a great deal of valuable experience in Australia and prized his time there. In a tribute to the country he wrote:

"Twelve months' experience in Melbourne during the memorable years of 1853 and '54 will prepare one to raise his shingle in Japan, open an ice-cream saloon in the African desert — form a co-partnership in Patagonia — or attempt any enterprise, however hazardous!"[2]

On November 3 the Melbourne *Herald* newspaper announced his impending departure, adding strange praise for a man whose activities allegedly led to an offer of the presidency of an Australian Republic: "In common with the whole of his countrymen, who are very numerous here, Mr TRAIN has practised a strict and honourable abstinence from all participation in our local and national politics".[3] The merchants arranged an impromptu farewell party at which Train made another eloquent, crowd-pleasing speech. A tribute to Train and an account of the evening was reported by the Melbourne *Age*[4] and reprinted by the New York *Herald*,[5] the paper with which Train would be most associated throughout his life. In glowing terms it paid tribute to Train's far-reaching influence on the commercial life of the city and indeed the country. The newspapers also reported the other toasts and speeches, including one by J.W. Tarleton, Esq., the American consul. Train's achievements and character were honoured so abundantly that the man of the moment was moved to respond to the toasts in kind. The *Age* paraphrased his finale thus:

> "Mr. Train concluded a speech, which was marked throughout with much elegance of words and style, by predicting that Victoria would shine as a star of the first magnitude under the auspices of the new constitution. He thanked them most heartily and sincerely for the honor they had done him in giving him so substantial a mark of their approbation, and assured them that it would be the pride of his life to refer to the hearty enthusiasm with which his friends in Victoria had greeted his departure from among them. Mr. Train resumed his seat amid great and long-continued cheering...". [6]

After Train's departure, the *Age* printed another tribute to Train's Australian career:

> "Notwithstanding the important interests on his hands, and his devotion to business, Mr. Train, by some miracle of industry, has found time for extensive reading and scholastic attainment, and perfected his pen in an easy and graceful style, and speaking as if elocution had been one of the chief objects of his study. To these qualities we may add the more endearing ones of strict integrity, great moral worth, and habits of life without a blemish. Throughout the colony, and amongst all classes, he is a universal favorite. He was urged by the mining interests to represent them in the Colonial Legislature, but his consent could not be obtained. The unanimity with which this nomination was tendered him, is the best evidence of the respect and confidence entertained for him by the great interest of the colony.
>
> On the occasion of his recent departure from Melbourne, the prominent merchants and citizens of that place gave him the testimonial of a public dinner, and the speeches then delivered exhibited their high appreciation of his qualities and bearing as a merchant and a man, and of his invaluable services in advancing the best interests of the Colony." [7]

The *Argus* summed up contemporary Melbourne opinion in its editorial, saying that Train's "energy, spirit, and restless activity have had an effect, not fully appreciated we believe, in stirring up a spirit of emulation amongst his brother merchants... it would be difficult to trace the full effect of his example in vitalising our whole commercial system."[8]

Train sailed on the *Dashing Wave* heading to Japan by way of Java, Singapore and China with high hopes for the future. He wrote entertaining and informative letters describing his various ports of call for the New York *Herald*. They were well received. The paper praised his reports, concluding:

> "We hope, when Mr. Train reaches this country, that, notwithstanding the success which has crowned his efforts abroad, he will conclude no longer to expatriate himself. Though proud of such men to represent us abroad, we cannot afford to lose their services at home." [9]

The natural beauty of Java captivated him. The colour of its trees, the rich shades of the flowers that flourished everywhere, and the sheer beauty of the place, fragrantly perfumed by flowers, aromatic herbs, and spices, overwhelmed him. It was here in Java surrounded by these abundantly beautiful flowers that he first came to admire their beauty. He always claimed that his daily custom of wearing a fresh spray of flowers in his lapel buttonhole began with his new-found infatuation with flowers on this island. After a brief stop in Singapore, which Train thought was a very dirty and busy port, he continued on to Hong Kong on a P. & O. steamer.

In Hong Kong Train met E.H. Green, the future husband of Hetty Green, who would become known as America's richest and meanest woman. They were bound for Macao and China on board a little steamer called *The Spark*. It was an eventful voyage as they encountered the usual hazards of travelling in Chinese waters: pirates and typhoons.

At the Boca Tigris, the mouth of the Canton (or Pearl) river, the steamer was overtaken by a typhoon. Seeking shelter from its wrath, the crew anchored near an island in the midst of a number of junks. Pretty soon it became apparent that these were pirate ships. The pirates drew closer to the defenceless steamer and prepared to attack. After they had anchored close to *The Spark* Train noticed that a "dozen of the ugliest ruffians" were staring in through the cabin windows.

On investigation he found Green sitting cool as anything, facing the windows, with his feet up on a table making faces at the pirates. This bizarre scene astonished Train:

"He was the coolest man, I think, that I ever saw. Nothing moved him out of his imperturbable calm. The Chinamen were scowling at him, but this did not at all disconcert him. If he was going to be killed by these devils, he seemed to be thinking, he might as well die in a cheerful humor."

It must have seemed an easy target was in the pirates' grasp. The little steamer's coal had been used up and there was no hope for any rescue. Luckily for Train and Green, they were rescued out of the lion's mouth by some quick thinking. Someone had the bright idea of using the vessel's woodwork to fuel the engines. With little time to waste, the passengers and crew attacked the ship's deck, getting enough fuel to fire up the engines. Suddenly, to the pirates' complete amazement, *The Spark* steamed out and away, out of the pirates' reach. The steam ship was too fast for a sailing junk and it was able to reach Macao safely.

At the time Macao was the headquarters of slave trading in the region. Train had heard of this horrible traffic in human flesh at Singapore, but could not believe it until he saw it with his own eyes. The unsuspecting Chinese victims were lured from the country's interior with tempting stories of other Chinese who had gone to America and had done well for themselves. Slave traders tricked these unfortunates into believing they would be transported to America. In reality they were shipped to the Guano islands of Chincha, off the coast of Peru.

Train climbed to the top of a hill for the purpose of observing the slave traders' barracoons, where the slaves were kept while awaiting transportation to their final destination. He wrote reports of this inhumane trade for the New York *Herald*, describing the slavery and giving the names of the boats that had recently sailed with full cargoes of slaves. Amid the subsequent widespread publicity it was discovered that Americans were involved. Train was in no doubt that his reports helped break up this savage trade.

Train and his new friend Green travelled on to Canton, arriving there during the Chinese New Year. The city astonished Train. "It was dirty and miserable beyond imagination, with narrow streets and indescribable filth." At a glance it was immediately apparent that it was an extremely busy commercial centre:

"The river was covered with junks and larger vessels at Whampoa, the lower port, floating the flags of every nation. Warehouses, the 'godowns' [signifying putting items down in a warehouse] of the

A poster featuring George Francis Train surrounded by scenes from his life's adventures.
The faint autograph at the bottom reads: "With kind regards of Geo. P. Bemis, Private Secty
to Geo. Francis Train, New York, New York, 1890."

Courtesy of the State Historical Society of Wisconsin [WHi (X3) 53024].

GEORGE FRANCIS TRAIN.
Entered according to Act of Congress, in the year 1862, by CURTIS GUILD, in the Clerk's Office of the Dist. Court of the Dist. of Mass,

ABOVE: A published collection of Train's speeches in England supporting the Union effort during the Civil War. He was America's first "foreign correspondent", covering the Lincoln Administration from Europe (April 1862).
Jonathan H. Mann Collection, The Rail Splitter Archives.

LEFT: An autographed picture of GFT in his early thirties, dated both 1862 and 1872, from a *carte de visite* by Silsbee, Case & Co. of Boston.
Miscellaneous Papers (George Francis Train), Manuscripts and Archives Division, The New York Public Library, Astor, Lenox and Tilden Foundations.

BELOW: The opening of Train's controversial horse-drawn tramway at Birkenhead. He can be seen on the top deck at the far left.
Courtesy of the National Tramway Museum Photographic Collection, Crich, Derbyshire.

MAJOR WINTHROP'S NEW NOVEL,
EDWIN BROTHERTOFT, by the late **THEODORE WINTHROP,**
1 vol., 16mo., uniform with "Cecil Dreeme" and "John Brent."

☞ *Just published, and for sale by all Booksellers. See next page.* ☜

THE AUGUST ATLANTIC.
THE ATLANTIC MONTHLY for AUGUST, 1862,
is now ready, with contributions from EMERSON, WHITTIER,
WINTHROP, the "COUNTRY PARSON," and other popular writers.

☞ *For sale everywhere. See next page.* ☜

VOL 6.

NO. 135.

VANITY FAIR

Saturday,
JULY 26,
1862.

PUBLISHED EVERY SATURDAY, AT 116 NASSAU STREET, N.Y.

PRICE TWO DOLLARS PER ANNUM—SINGLE COPIES SIX CENTS.

The G. F. TRAIN:
GOING IT LIKE THUNDER, WITH BULL ON TRACK.

Published for the Proprietors, by LOUIS H. STEPHENS, at 116 Nassau Street, N. Y.

The July 26, 1862 issue of "Vanity Fair" depicting
"The G.F. Train: Going it like Thunder, with Bull on track."
Collection of Dr. Edmund B. Sullivan.

LEFT: Cassius Marcellus Clay was Minister to Russia and a prominent anti-slavery campaigner who advised President Lincoln on issues of emancipation and its implication for the Union cause at the time of the Civil War. About 1863 Train and Clay opposed one another publicly in debates on the issues; Train feared that Clay's plans would be disastrous for the Union.

Collection of Robert Sterling.

RIGHT: Train's letter to Abraham Lincoln, sent September 25, 1862, declared his change of mind and support for the Emancipation Proclamation. The text reads:

"Revere House
Boston
Sept. 25, 1862

Dear President of the United States
   Your Proclamation is the cleverest document issued this century.
I understand it. God bless the nation."

From The Abraham Lincoln Papers at the Library of Congress, courtesy of the Collections of the Library of Congress.

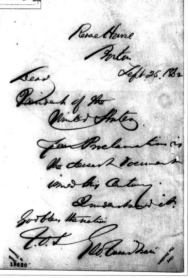

TERRIBLE EFFECT OF MY FIRST BOMBSHELLS IN BOSTON.

A lithograph apparently circulated by Train himself on his return to Boston from England.
The cast of characters were, apparently, prominent Massachusetts abolitionists – with the exception of Train.
FROM LEFT: William Lloyd Garrison, founder of the American Anti-Slavery Society; Senator Henry Wilson;
Thomas Higginson, Colonel of the first Black Regiment in the Union Army; Train; Charles Sumner, a leader
in Congress among opponents to slavery and reputedly the first statesman to urge emancipation;
John Andrew, Governor of Massachusetts; Henry Ward Beecher, the clergyman and publicist;
and, perhaps, New York politician Boss Tweed in the background.

Courtesy of the Boston Public Library.

𝕷etter from 𝕲eorge 𝕱. 𝕿rain.

DANVILLE, Pa , October 29th, 1864.

To the Editor of The Age, Philadelphia.

SIR :—The AGE OF TREASON has arrived. Many thanks for your complimentary editorial. A column just before election is appreciated. You open with "The Abolitionists have drawn a prize in the political lottery." That's so! You close with "What has happened to change his opinions?" Let me reply. I supposed the Democratic party would have had sense enough to come over to me. How could they expect me to come over to the T. P. platform? It had three planks: STATE RIGHTS, that is SECESSION; FREE TRADE, that is DESTRUCTION; REPUDIATION, that is INFAMY.

My impeachment of the President was made at Chicago the night before the nomination ; and when you put up the man who recommended the illegal acts alluded to, I thought it was time to change. WISE MEN change their opinions; FOOLS NEVER DO. If the Convention had followed my lead, and nominated JNO. A. DIX, you would not now be dependent on the defeat of our armies to elect your man. I told Barlow and Gen. Ward that my hot shot would go through their " Alabama" candidate, and I am glad to see that they are the chief point of the "AGE." Fire a stone into a pack, and the hound that is hit is sure to howl.

The difference between us is, you have party on the brain—I have country. You cheer when gold goes up—I hiss. You despond when Sheridan beats Early—I cheer. You want to throw poor men out of employment by free trade—I want to give them higher wages by protection. You go for the English candidate—I for the American. You prefer the Jews—I the Gentiles. YOU RECOMMENDED THE SURRENDER OF YORK—I would have died first! Your party has no opinions—mine has. You say "I was not a member of the Chicago Convention"—I say YOU are a LIAR, and say it offensively. But (as I am not a proud man) if I have offended you by my recent course, I am willing to accept your apology, for

> While the Union lamp holds out to burn,
> The vilest traitor may return.

YOURS, &c.,

GEORGE FRANCIS TRAIN.

JOHN L. KIRKE, Printer, No. 43 South Eleventh Street, Philadelphia.

ABOVE: The excursion to mark the crossing of the 100th Meridian by the Union Pacific in 1866. Train is seated; his wife, Wilhelmina, is behind him chatting to William C. Durant.
Courtesy of the Union Pacific Historical Collection.

LEFT: Train had his tongue firmly in his cheek when he autographed this photograph on May 6, 1870, for the Editor of the *New York Tribune*: "Hon. Horace Greel[e]y (the name caller) – If you feel sorry, I'll forgive you."
Courtesy of Brown Brothers.

Train's cousin, George Pickering Bemis, served as 'Passepartout' on the first journey
around the world in eighty days in 1870.
From J. Sterling Morton, The Illustrated History of Nebraska *(Vol. II, c. 1906),*
courtesy of the Omaha Public Library.

> *foreign traders, revealed the existence of an enormous, and profitable commerce."*

Both men were in popular demand by the resident foreigners, who in those days of infrequent communications were always eager to entertain visitors who brought news from home. Deciding where to dine soon became a task in itself. One day Train ended up with eleven invitations; Green had thirteen. Green suggested that there was only one thing to do: they would have to find out who among their potential hosts would have the best dinner for them. He led Train around to the rear of the residences, where a high wall separated the gardens from the native city. There Train discovered that the Chinese cooks customarily hung up whatever game, poultry or anything else that they were preparing for meals. Gazing on this array, the pair could tell what each household was going to have for dinner. After a leisurely stroll through the alley, they selected a house which had some lovely pheasants and salmon displayed behind it.

"The owner of that house shall have the honor of being our host," said Green. Train wryly said that he approved this choice "both then and after the dinner, which was an excellent one, at which the golden pheasants were the *pièce de résistance*".

Since Canton was the first Chinese city that Train had the leisure to investigate in detail, he was eager to satisfy his curiosity and explore. The fact that the inner city was forbidden to foreigners on point of death was well known to Train. Despite this and the fact that six Englishmen had been killed shortly before Train's arrival for daring to disobey, the ban did not put him off. It only made him more determined to get inside the walls. Against all advice he calmly walked in through the open gates. He had hardly sent foot inside the forbidden city when all hell broke loose.

All around him wild cries erupted. Men came running towards him shouting: "Fan-kwai!" – foreign devil. At once he realised that he had stirred up a hornet's nest. Looking around swiftly, he saw that the entrance gate was still open. Train instantly realised his one chance of survival depended on escaping through the gate before the angry mob could cut his retreat off. He plunged towards it and only avoided being set upon by the skin of his teeth. "If the stop-watch could have been held on me, I am sure I should have established a record for a short-distance sprint."

The next time Train visited Canton was in 1870. The gates were open and the walls no longer kept the foreign devils out. The American merchant Nye, who was known as the Napoleon of China because of his gigantic enterprises, gave Train a guided tour of the city. Train could hardly believe his eyes when one of the natives came up to them in the street and offered to sell them a rat, "a big fellow still alive," Train recorded.

"I asked if it was to be eaten, and the Chinaman said it was. 'But it is not cooked,' I objected. 'I am not going to begin on live rats.' The Chinaman said he would prepare it — the rat cooked and served to cost me two cents. I told him to go ahead. To my surprise he took a little stove from under his arm, lighted a fire, and in a few minutes had the rodent roasted to a crisp. I was astonished — and ashamed — to see how nice it looked. It did appear toothsome. I said to the Chinaman, 'Now, you can eat it.' He did, and with great gusto and smacking of the lips. So he got his rat and my two cents, also."

Not everything about China amused George. He was disgusted to find out how a favourite snack of his, Canton ginger, was processed. Since childhood Train had been "outrageously fond" of it, and had always indulged in large quantities of it whenever he had the opportunity. Now that he was in its place of origin, he jumped at the opportunity to find out how it was manufactured. After making some inquiries, he was able to arrange a visit to a factory on Ho-nan Island. The factory, as well as most of the so-called island, was built on piles. Alarm bells began sounding in Train's mind. His worst fears were confirmed when he asked the factory people where they got the water needed to make the syrup for the preserves. They looked at him as if he was demented, replying: "Water! Why, we are right over the river!" Train must have felt ill at the thought of what he had been eating with such relish all those years.

"Yes, they were right over the river," he lamented, "the dirtiest and most villainous river in the world. The sewage of the dirtiest city in China — which is saying about all that can be said on the subject — is emptied into this river. I need not say that I did not eat any of the Canton ginger then, and I have not eaten any of it since."

Train decided to drop in to Shanghai on his way to Japan, despite both the foreign and native Canton merchants' advice to avoid it. Train admitted that this was the type of advice that only made him more resolute to follow his initial path. He took passage in a P. & O. boat, the

Erin, and supposed, of course, that he would have a state room. It turned out that a great Chinese mandarin, Li Hung-chang, going from Hong Kong to Shanghai, had already taken the cabin. Pinyin Li Hongzhang, to call him by his correct name, was a leading Chinese statesman of the nineteenth century, who would make strenuous efforts to modernise his country. When Train encountered him in 1856, he was on his way to achieve his first success by crushing the Taiping rebellion as commander of the imperial army. Train must not have been too disappointed; after all, now he would be able to see, and perhaps even meet, this great personage who controlled China's destiny. Before long he had his opportunity.[10]

It was Train's custom, while at sea, to exercise by walking briskly up and down the deck. He was taking his daily exercise while the mandarin settled on board ship. Every time Train passed the cabin, he noticed Li Hung-chang watching him closely. A bit bewildered and puzzled by Train's actions, the mandarin observed Train's movements curiously, as if he was "some strange animal". After a while his curiosity got the better of him. He called the first officer and asked what Train was doing.

The officer replied, "Walking up and down the deck."

"But why does he do it? Is he paid for it?"

The officer told him it was for exercise.

"What is that?"

The officer explained it to him, but Li Hung-chang could not understand why anyone would want to do such a thing unnecessarily. He could not believe that a sane man would waste energy for no purpose. Li Hung-chang scornfully pointed to Train and gave his verdict: "Number one foolo."

At Woosung Train saw six armed ships used to transport cargoes of opium from Calcutta and Bombay to China. A sudden realisation of the meaning of this traffic came to him. "[I]t will never be forgotten in China, or anywhere else, that England went to war with China to force China to permit the shipment of opium into that country to ruin millions of lives and impoverish millions of families." His revulsion grew as he remembered with shame that one of his early private ventures through Enoch Train & Co. had been smuggling a small amount of opium into China. While it had all seemed innocent enough in faraway Boston, he now realised the devastation caused by the drug in China and deeply regretted his actions.

While Train was in Shanghai the Chinese authorities displayed heads of rebels hanging from the city's walls, like gruesome trophies, as an example to all those who contemplated opposing Manchu rule. "These hideous trophies of the war," he commented, "were the most impressive things that I saw in Shanghai."

[1] Rev. C. Stuart Ross, "Two American Types that Left their Stamp on Victorian History" in *Victorian Historical Magazine* (July 1919), Vol. VII, No. 8, p. 126.

[2] Quoted in E. Daniel and Annette Potts, eds, *A Yankee Merchant in Goldrush Australia* (Heinemann, Melbourne, 1970), p. 132.

[3] *Ibid.*, p. xix.

[4] November 6, 1855.

[5] February 27, 1856.

[6] Quoted in Willis Thornton, *The Nine Lives of Citizen Train* (Greenberg, New York, 1948), pp. 57–58.

[7] Quoted in George Francis Train, *Spread-Eagleism* (Derby & Jackson, New York, 1859), pp. xxx–xxxi.

[8] *Argus*, November 6, 1855.

[9] New York *Herald* article, reprinted in George Francis Train, above, n. 7, p. xxxii.

[10] "Li Hung-chang" in *Encyclopedia Britannica* (15th edition, Chicago, 1994), Vol. 7, p. 321.

Train booked passage bound for Shimoda and Hakodate, Japan. He intended to continue to Yokohama, and establish a branch of Train and Co., Melbourne. However, the Crimean war upset his plans, with the result that it would be several years before he did visit Japan.

At this point, Augustine Heard invited G. Griswold Gray, of Russell & Co., and his guest George Train, to accompany him to Fu-chow on one of his ships, the *John Wade*. Train was delighted and looked forward eagerly to seeing more of China. As it happened the trip turned out to be more adventurous than even he expected. As they were sailing down the Chinese coast, a typhoon suddenly struck, toppling over *John Wade*'s masts and sails. Besides this, they had other problems. Neither the pilot from Shanghai nor the pilot from Fu-chow spoke the other's language. Finally, they overcame these difficulties, and got into a boat to complete the forty-mile journey up the unfamiliar River Min in total darkness. To make matters worse, the river was infested with pirates.

After a troubled night on the river they finally reached Fu-chow. Immediately on landing, Gray, Train and Heard took sedan chairs for a tour through the city. As they were passing through a very narrow but important street, their coolies were suddenly set upon and overturned. The trio scrambled out of the chairs, alarmed, and asked what the matter was. They learned that the Viceroy was passing through and everybody and everything had to give way for him and his entourage. Although his companions stepped out of the way, Train's blood was up: "I resented being upset in the street, like so much refuse, in order to have the filthy thoroughfare cleared for the passage of a mere Chinese viceroy."

George had a small American flag in his pocket, carefully wrapped around its little pole. With a great deal of ceremony he took it out and waved it in the air triumphantly, daring the Viceroy's servants to interfere with his right to pass through the streets of Fu-chow. It had an instant effect. At once he noticed that the Chinese fell back on recognising the flag. The coolies got back on their feet and once more took hold of the poles of the chairs. The viceroy passed by, disdainfully pretending not to have noticed the incident. In a few minutes the way was clear again.

Train sailed from Hong Kong to India on an opium steamer, the *Fiery Cross*. He had a letter of introduction to George Ashburner in Calcutta. On his arrival Ashburner insisted that Train stay with him as a guest. Train spent three days living like royalty. Normally a person for whom the best was never good enough, Train was highly impressed by Ashburner's lavish hospitality and commented approvingly: "It is only man in the Orient who knows how to live fast and furious and get every enjoyment out of his little span of life."

Fourteen servants were specially assigned to take care of Train's every need. Train's "little army" comprised four designated chair, or palanquin, carriers, with an additional relay team in reserve, a man especially to serve Train at a table, a punka man to pull the string of his personal fan, and "a man for every other detail of living".

There was always something to do and see in Calcutta. Amongst other activities Train was taken to see the sights of the city. It seemed to Train that much of his sightseeing was limited to the city's more gruesome attractions, such as the Black Hole[1] and the burning ghauts, where dead bodies were cremated. By his own calculation, he saw five hundred funeral pyres burning there. Train innocently enquired of an attendant whether only men were cremated. By way of reply the man took a long hook, thrust it into one of the fires, pulled it back and raised the charred leg of a man. Immediately, watchful birds of prey pounced on the smoking flesh and swiftly carried it away. These birds were performing a necessary function by removing unburned corpse parts, keeping down disease. Always a practical thinker, Train noted that it only cost half a cent to cremate a body.

Train should have learned his lesson when he found out how Canton ginger preserves were manufactured and not dared to enquire the origin of any other of his favourite foodstuffs. But he was very fond of shrimps. He was taken to the fishing grounds at the mouth of the river. There he saw an unbelievable sight, far worse than Chinese ginger preservation methods: millions of prawns scavenging around the neverending supply of dead bodies that floated down the Ganges. Train's reaction to the fact that he, and no doubt countless other unsuspecting shrimp lovers, had in fact been unwitting cannibals though once removed, was uncharacteristically understated: "This was enough for me. I stopped eating shrimps in India, as I had stopped eating Canton ginger preserves in China."

His second day in Calcutta saw Train attending a "brilliant" reception given by the retiring Governor-General, Lord Dalhousie, for his successor, Lord Canning. It made a lasting impression on Train, not least because he met and observed the cream of the British administration mingling with some of their most daring enemies, "who were even then plotting revolution and bloodshed". Amongst others Train was introduced to both the outgoing and incoming Governor-Generals.

The voyage from Calcutta to Suez was almost devoid of incident. They put in at Madras, "a barren, flat, and dismal place", to take on passengers, then sailed for Point de Galle, Ceylon. Two thousand miles further, as they were nearing Aden, Train began to look forward to completing this leg of the voyage that would bring him a little closer to home. He usually slept with the bulkhead open opposite his berth. One night he felt something slap him in the face. As he was alone in the room, he did not know what to make of it. As there was no light, he could not investigate. As soon as he fell asleep he received another slap. In the morning, he found the cause of his discomfort. Nine flying fish lay dead in his berth.

There was not a lot to see in Aden. It was another dismal spot. "The most barren and gloomy place" Train had ever seen, in fact. They hurried up the Red Sea to Suez, then made the 84-mile overland crossing to Cairo, accompanying a six-hundred camel caravan. Train and his five companions travelled comfortably in coaches. Although they were journeying in considerable style, Train got a fair idea of the unforgiving nature of the Sahara. Just before they reached Cairo there was a cry from one of the coaches for them to look up at the sky. "There were masts, minarets, and the whole city, in fact, painted on the sky."

Actually, they were only half way to Cairo. Train had seen his first mirage. Finally arriving in Cairo, Train checked in to Shepheard's Hotel, and immediately arranged to go out to the pyramids, ten miles outside the city. Fifty donkey boys competed with one another to get his custom. Train's initial start was not an immediate success. The first thing his donkey did was to accidentally step in a gopher-hole and stumble. Before he knew what was happening, Train found the donkey rolling over him in the sand. Years later he noted: "Travelers now go out in trolley-cars, eat ice-cream and drink champagne under the shade of the pyramids, and a splendid hotel stands alongside the Sphinx." Train was convinced the moment he saw the pyramids that they were huge grain stores, made from massive blocks of an ancient kind of concrete, not tombs for the Pharaohs of Egypt.

The pyramids were the most astonishing thing he had seen in his life. It took three Arabs to get Train to the top of one of the pyramids: two to push and one to pull. Half-way up, one of the Arabs went on strike for more money. Although others might have found it wise to pay up at that location, Train had other ideas and held his ground, shouting at the man until he consented to go further.

He was pleasantly surprised to find a modern railway in Cairo and the party took the train for Alexandria. From there they sailed for the Holy Land, landing at Jaffa. One of Train's travelling companions, the Reverend J.R. MacFarlane, chaplain of Madras, wanted to see Jerusalem, so the group accompanied him on donkeys through the beautiful, but desolate, countryside.

> "One of these mules had irreverently been named Christ and the other Jesus. To the perfect horror of the clergyman – until he understood that the men could say nothing else in English – the names of the donkeys were spoken with every crack of the whip all the way to Jerusalem."

A few weeks before, Bedouins had killed several travellers. No-one was under any illusions as to the safety of their journey. Continuing on through the Valley of Jehoshaphat, they reached a plateau. Jerusalem could be seen in the distance. While they were admiring the city's beauty, someone spotted half a dozen horsemen galloping from the city and shouted: "There are the Bedouins!" Abram, their interpreter, knew better and reassured them that the men were only "barkers" for the hotels of Jerusalem, looking for customers.

In order to move around Jerusalem at night, Train and MacFarlane arranged for the chief of police to act as their guide and bodyguard. It was Train's objective to show his friend the nightlife of the region, and they explored by candlelight. When they went into a dark alley, their guide's suspicious movements alerted Train. He was puzzled why a policeman was so careful where he went.

When they got to the door, the policeman tried to shut it, but Train quickly put his foot in the way. Sensing something was very wrong, he asked MacFarlane if he was armed. His companion replied that he had a Madras dagger. MacFarlane was already in the room, but Train pulled him out. "Those are Bedouins," he warned. "I could see their pistols and swords." Train's intuition probably saved their lives. He was aware of at least sixteen people who had been killed in Nablus in 1855–56. The chief of police was the gang's leader. Train says that he immediately reported this to the American consul, who acted to have the men captured. After Train and MacFarlane left the country, the gang members were executed.

Train rushed onwards through Syria, Smyrna, Constantinople and down the Bosphorous into the Black Sea towards the Crimea. A huge fleet of allied ships was anchored at Sebastopol port. He was delighted to meet many old friends and see several of the ships that he had been instrumental in building. These ships, the *Great Republic*, the *Monarch of the Seas* and the *Ocean Queen*, were active as transports in the Crimean war for the French and British. Train observed that they were packed into the port so tightly that none would have been saved if a fire broke out.

Despite this unexpected pleasure, Train kept his sights fixed on his main objective. Immediately he got a horse and rode out to Balaklava to see if there were any leftover munitions for sale. He had hoped that there would be piles of surplus materials lying about in the Crimea to be sold by the victorious allies for a song. Unfortunately for Train, the armies (English, Russian, Turkish, French and Sardinian) had taken all their supplies away with them, so there were no business opportunities about to interest him. Undaunted by this disappointment, he decided to see the after-effects of the war for himself. In due course he was "astonished at the magnitude" of the devastation caused by the Crimean war, which was started by Britain and France to prevent Russian dominance in the eastern Mediterranean.

When Russia went to war against the ailing Ottoman Empire and victory looked almost certain, Britain and France had to do something to keep Russia in check. They and the ambitious new state of Sardinia tactfully came to the Ottoman Empire's rescue and declared war against Russia as a means of preventing the unpalatable Russian expansion.[2] The war lasted three, long years until Russia was finally defeated. The conclusion of the Crimean war marked the end of Russian dominance in the region. The military campaign itself was notable for the stubbornness, gallantry and appalling disregard for casualties on both sides. The scandalous treatment of the troops, in particular the wounded, depicted by war correspondents stirred Florence Nightingale and Henri Dunat into action, perhaps the only positive results of the war.

Train saw it all with his own eyes and was horrified. He viewed the ruins of Sebastopol, which had been heroically defended for over a year, and automatically made a rough estimate of the costs of reconstruction. The miserable conditions of more than two hundred square miles of Allied soldiers' camps shocked him: "The British troops were in rags and tatters. Their new uniforms had not arrived, and their shoes were worn out."

Train made inquiries and soon found out that a ship full of shoes had lain in the harbour for the previous six months without being unloaded. The war was so badly conducted that provisions, uniforms and supplies were sent even after the war was over. The London *Times* war correspondent, William Howard "Bull Run" Russell, exposed this terrible mismanagement and blundering.

Twenty of the various participating countries' officers, under the directions of a French commander, held a banquet for Train one evening. Several times he almost provoked them into fighting. The Russians were delighted to see the Allies bickering amongst themselves and helped Train stir things up by provoking the parties. It was obvious that the alliance was very fragile. Train wrote:

> "The French and English are not friends. Peace has been confirmed, and now we begin to see the national antipathies come out. I know it must be so. Centuries of enmity cannot be cemented so soon. Officers and soldiers here are full of recriminations, and it is painful to see how soon they have forgotten that they have fought and bled together…".[3]

Train had travelled to the Crimea, ostensibly to make money out of the debris of battle. What he saw, even after the fighting was over, taught him something. Brooding over the ruins of Sebastopol, he wrote:

> "Directly and indirectly, a million of men have gone, in the awful moment of crime, to meet their Maker. The heads of families numbering five millions have been lopped off, and orphans and widows, beggars and cripples are once again added to the swelling list. Never before has been recorded such terrible mortality. The recital of the facts sickens the heart. So much misery! And what has been accomplished? Nothing. Europe is darker than ever before, and clouds heavy and sombre hang over her convulsing politics, concealing under the deceptive garb of peace the thunderbolt that is ambushed within."[4]

Train continued his journey home, shaken by the "horrible desolation" he had witnessed. In London, on May 22, he wrote a vivid summary of his six-month journey from Australia, before he left to sail from Liverpool to America. In it he concluded regretfully:

> *"Wherever I go, money is the ruling power, the passion giving birth to all the forms of crime. In this respect there is a wonderful resemblance... all seem to look out for self, number one, before the million; the Jew and the Gentile, the Catholic and the Protestant, the Christian and the Infidel, the Greek, the Turk, and the followers of Bhudah and Confucius are not so different as one might suppose, for in self-preservation and love of money there's a wonderful likeness to us all."[5]*

Now twenty-seven years of age, Train could truthfully say that he had travelled all over the world. He arrived in New York in July 1856, having been away since February 1853, to be greeted by a wave of publicity. The New York *Herald,* for instance, which had published much of Train's correspondence, carried sixteen columns (about three pages) of material devoted to his tour of the world in one issue. Train's trip was a sensation and made a public figure out of him. James Gordon Bennett senior, owner of the *Herald*, held a reception for him, sounding Train out as a possible candidate for Congress. Uncharacteristically, Train declined to take up this suggestion, saying that he intended to return to Australia to cultivate his business interests there.

He quickly travelled onto Boston, where his wife and daughter were waiting for him – but so were the police. Train was arrested on Barings' behalf, supposedly over credit used by Train in Australia. He was adamant that Barings' credit facility had been returned to them unused. Train "escaped" his first jail, when Enoch Train and Donald McKay guaranteed an eighty thousand dollar bail bond. The prosecution was never carried through. The matter was apparently a case of poor bookkeeping, rather than deliberate fraud. Train later commented: "This was my first false arrest and legal prosecution. From this time for many years I kept getting into jail, for no crime whatever."

Freeman Hunt, the pioneer of business journalism in America, was the editor of the *Merchants' Magazine*, to which Train had contributed an extensive article on the commerce and resources of Australia. Hunt included parts of some of Train's letters home in a book called *An American Merchant in Europe, Asia and Australia*. Train dedicated it to his uncle:

"To Enoch Train, Esq., of Boston, these inklings from foreign lands are respectfully inscribed in grateful remembrance of his many acts of kindness, by a graduate of his counting-house."

At Hunt's suggestion, Train returned to Europe with his family. For the next year he sent back letters on the state of society and finance in London, Paris, Rome, and Venice. Because of Train's informative letters on Australia, Asia and Europe, he became known as America's first foreign correspondent. He praised Melbourne, which continued to grow, concluding that "no other place can rival it... no more flourishing place... no more richer place... no such go-aheadative place" existed elsewhere.[6] In Paris he attributed "the present firmer tone of the money market" partly to the "opportune arrivals of Australian treasure ships".[7]

The more he saw, however, convinced him that a worldwide financial crash was imminent. He was soon proved right. Speculative enterprises in Europe and America alike brought down many firms. James Maguire, a prominent Boston merchant, later wrote to his son in Melbourne in 1857 with "very bad news from all Europe in regard to business and finance".

"It would seem," he observed, "as if Train was nearly right in his predictions that the whole of Europe was rotten."[8]

---

[1]   The "Black Hole" was a small, airless dungeon (24ft x 18ft) where 69 British men were left to die during the Nawab of Bengal's occupation of Calcutta in 1756. Few survived.

[2]   Fenton Bresler, *Napoleon III, A Life* (HarperCollins, London, 1999), pp. 279–281.

[3]   From a letter of April 30, 1856, reproduced in George Francis Train, *An American Merchant in Europe, Asia and Australia* (Putnam, New York, 1857), pp. 324–325.

4   *Ibid.*, p. 341.

5   *Ibid.*, p. 353.

6   George Francis Train, *Spread-Eagleism* (Derby & Jackson, New York, 1859), pp. 80–81.

7   George Francis Train, *Young America in Wall Street* (Derby & Jackson, New York, 1857), pp. 30–31.

8   James Maguire to James Frank Maguire, Boston, November 24, 1857, Vol. 23, Maguire Collection, Baker Library, Harvard Business School, Cambridge, Massachusetts.

The Trains arrived in France at the start of the golden age of the second empire, which reached its peak in 1860. The country became an international superpower under the rule of Napoleon III, a benevolent dictator whose social and economic reforms enabled France to blossom culturally and economically, until its catastrophic defeat by the Germans at Sedan in a needless war in 1870. One of the period's most important contemporary historians, Frédéric Loliée, summed up the time as it must have appeared to Train and countless others: "It was the golden age of the Second Empire, at the height of its prosperity, a honeymoon for speculation… Foreigners flocked to the capital dazzled by the gaiety of Parisian life."[1]

Train thought he had seen the world, but soon discovered how little he knew compared to others. The family quickly established themselves in some style at the Grand Hotel de Louvre in the newly-improved but long-fashionable Rue de Rivoli. They immediately set about their principal objective, namely learning some European languages. This was due to Train's observation that German merchants first learnt the languages of the people with whom they wished to trade. At first the Trains studied Italian and French simultaneously. Then they progressed to Portuguese and Spanish. Train had already been taught a smattering of German by refugees of the 1848 revolution.

Naturally, they moved in the most glittering circles possible. Prince Galitzen of Russia gave a dinner for Train at the Café Philippe, where he met some of the other resident Russian nobility. "These men were the cleverest I have ever seen," he declared. "All were good linguists, artists, statesmen, soldiers, men of the world." At Prince Czartoryski's he met some leading Polish revolutionaries, who were plotting against Russia. One of these, a man of about eighty, spoke memorable words to Train about the stubbornness of man and history:

> *"In my teens I went to St. Petersburg, saw Alexander and told him the condition of Poland. I asked him what he was going to do. He*

asked me what I should recommend. 'There are two ways of governing Poland,' I said; 'through interest or through fear.' Fear was the policy adopted. When I was forty, I again went to St. Petersburg. Nicholas was Czar, and he repeated the same question. I again answered, 'through interest or through fear.' When I was sixty I met another Emperor, and the same question was put to me, and I made the same reply. Poland is partitioned... and we are now only a memory."

Train laid the foundations for a later enterprise, the building of the Great Western Railway, when he met the Spaniard, Leon Lillo. Through him Train met many Spanish notables and members of the ruling family. The most important contact Train made through Lillo's connections was the acquaintance of José de Salamanca y Mayol, who was financial adviser and banker to Queen Cristina of Spain. Train continued to clock up highly impressive social acquaintances. He went on to meet the great Italian "tragedienne", Ristori, at the residence of her husband, the Marquis del Grillo. At the Count de Rouville's house he met several of the leading figures of the Second Empire, including Count de Morny, the Minister for War, Persigny, the Foreign Minister, and Mocquard, the Emperor's private secretary. Another time, at Triat's Gymnase, he met some of the people who were later responsible for organising the Paris Commune (the communist takeover of Paris) in the turbulent period following the Francoprussian war.

These social triumphs were eclipsed in the winter of 1856–57, when the Trains received an invitation to a ball at the Emperor's residence, the Tuileries. The engraved card was a foot square and bore the seal of the Second Empire. Even Train, who was always well dressed, did not have anything suitable to wear. He hired what he later labelled a "flunkey suit... a sort of mongrel affair", a mixture of civilian and military dress that was to serve him as a court costume, while his wife wore a more conventional evening dress.

Though the Tuileries was very large, he related that the four thousand or so guests found themselves packed like sardines into the rooms. There was an orchestra reputedly conducted by Johann Strauss. The guests were a splendid mixture of the cream of society: "ambassadors in their regalia, regimental officers in their different uniforms, and the aristocracy in their robes", as well as Algerian officers and, of course, foreign notables who happened to be in Paris – such as George Francis Train.

Their patient wait while queuing in diplomatic order to be presented to the royal couple was deemed worthwhile when their turn finally came. Empress Eugenie seemed particularly courteous to Train, complimenting him in English: "You speak French very fluently."

Train replied: "When I am able to speak French, your Majesty, as well as you speak English, I shall be willing to trust myself in that language. In the meanwhile, let me ask you to talk as you prefer."

Everybody around seemed surprised that the Empress talked with him longer than was normal for such greetings, especially since he was a foreigner and newcomer. Train always spoke very highly of her: "She was very gracious, and made me feel as much at home as if I had been in my own family."

The highlight of the evening was yet to come. A wave of silence enveloped the hall, usually alive with the hum of people. All eyes turned to the great folding doors at the end of the hall, where a lady soon appeared. Train looked on as the Emperor's current favourite, Countess Virginie Castiglione, upstaged the Empress with her spectacular entrance. Her presence caused a tremendous sensation.

The Countess was a woman of outstanding beauty. Princess Pauline Metternich, wife of the future Austrian ambassador to Paris, described her in her diary:

> *"The Countess was clad in a white tulle gown covered with huge long-stemmed roses, her head unadorned, her beautiful hair plaited in the form of a diadem. Her waist was that of a nymph. Her shoulders, neck, arms, hands — she was carrying her gloves — as though sculpted in pink marble.*
>
> *Her décolleté though exaggerated did not appear indecent, so much did this superb creature resemble a classical statue. Her face was striking. A perfect oval, a complexion of unrivalled freshness, dark green cloudy eyes crowned by brows that could have been traced by a miniature brush, a little nose, definite yet of absolute regularity, teeth like pearls. In a word, Venus come down from Olympus. I've never seen such beauty as hers, and never will again...".* [2]

No doubt the other guests were equally captivated by her beauty. Her brazen presence at court electrified the atmosphere. The silence was quickly broken as the stunned multitude came to their senses and started to speculate on her appearance at court. It was widely believed that she was present under the instructions of her cousin, Count Camillo Cavour, Prime Minister of Piedmont, in order to win over the Emperor to the cause of a United Italy. They were not far wrong. Early in February 1856, Cavour cheerfully wrote to his Deputy Foreign Minister:

> *"I have enrolled the beautiful countess in the service of Piedmont. I have told her to flirt with and, if necessary, seduce the Emperor. I have promised that, if she succeeds, her brother will get the post of secretary in our Embassy at St Petersburg. She has already begun to play her part discreetly yesterday at the Tuileries."*[3]

In fact, her mission was not so much as to try to influence Napoleon III, but to report back his opinions on Italian unification and, only if possible, push him in the right direction. The Emperor had always been sympathetic to their cause and did later help the Italians drive out the Austrians, but more than a year after he broke off his affair with the Countess.

After the Countess had made her spectacular entrance, it was clear that the Empress was put out. The following day the Empress went to England and stayed with Queen Victoria for three weeks. It certainly was a night to remember for the young American couple. Train also remembered the night for another reason:

> *"I suddenly felt some cold substance going down my back. Putting my hand to my neck, I found there a cupful of ice-cream that an Algerian officer had dropped, with the usual 'Pardon monsieur'. I assured him it was all right, but the ice-cream gave me a decidedly boreal feeling."*

That winter Train kept busy by showing William H. Seward, later Lincoln's Secretary of State, around Paris. Amongst other things Train even arranged for Seward to meet Lamartine, the French poet, novelist and politician; he acted as a translator for them, since he was now fluent in French.

When France and Piedmont went to war against Austria, Train tried to use his connections for the benefit of Napoleon III, to help supply him with steamers to transport troop provisions. In the end, Train's efforts were wasted when peace was declared.

All these distractions did not prevent Train doing his duty to investigate and report the financial health of Europe. During his stay he wrote a series of financial articles for Freeman Hunt's *Merchant's*

Magazine, which were later published in book form under the title *Young America in Wall Street*. As early as November 1856 Train was predicting a worldwide financial meltdown – a catastrophe of which the world had never seen the like. His articles of that period reported faithfully on the overheating economies of the world, but his warnings fell on deaf ears. All of his fears were realised in the events that unfolded that following year.[4]

Train also made observations on another phenomenon that was becoming widespread. It was obvious to him that the day of personal financial empires owned and controlled by individuals was over. They were being superseded by corporations bringing together different sources of capital and groups of shareholders. Train saw that the men who controlled these corporations would wield enormous power. He mused: "When you reflect, you find but a few men rule the world…" and pointed out that the governments these men controlled went to war suddenly against other countries and made peace as quickly for their own selfish national interests.[5]

> "I wish they would turn their talents to something useful, such as cutting that Siamese band at Darien, making islands of the two Americas, as France and England propose to do with Africa and Asia, by channeling a road to Suez."[6]

He was envisioning a great canal across Panama half a century before its construction.

After spending nearly eight months in France, the Trains decided to continue their travels through Europe. In his hotel in Rome, Train paused to jot down his last observations on France. In particular, he singled out the Crédit Mobilier's hold on the French economy and the fact that it seemed uncontrollable. Once again, he reiterated his belief that a financial crash was imminent: "thinking men will assure you that everything is sound! (to be sure, the more *hollow* the more *sound*)."[7] A few months later he was proved right.

While the Trains were in Rome a delegation of secretive Italians paid George a visit. Train did not know what was going on when they hailed him as their "Liberator". There were a great number of liberators in Italy in those days and he supposed that they had mistaken him for Garibaldi, Mazzini, Orsini, or some other Italian deliverer. He was taken aback when they corrected his assumption, insisting they knew who he was: "Citizen George Francis Train."

What was even more startling was that they asked him to go with them. Italy was drowning in political conspiracies at the time and Train had misgivings: "Things were pretty black in Italy just then, and I did not desire to be mixed up in 'revolutions', or liberty movements, or conspiracies."

Driven by his curiosity, but obviously not by common sense, he chose to accept their assurances that it would be all right. Leaving his family in the hotel, Train accompanied the delegation through dark alleys to some secret meeting place. He claimed he was told "more things about the revolution than I cared to know or to remember. It was not a healthful kind of knowledge to carry about Italy with one".

The strangers were obviously members of the powerful Carbonari, a secret society dedicated to the creation of a unified Italy and to expelling all foreign occupiers. It was a modern resistance movement. Members were sworn to secrecy in mystical initiation ceremonies. They operated in small cells numbering a few individuals, so anyone infiltrating the organisation could discover at best a few names. It attracted huge support from Italians of all classes, all liberal patriots.[8]

It is possible that the Carbonari had heard of Train's connection with the Australian miners' revolt, though more likely it wanted to use his position as an influential foreign correspondent to highlight their cause before the world, just as their latter-day counterparts use journalists to put their side across in the media. It always was a mystery to Train why these people – the Carbonari, La Commune, Chartists, Fenians, Internationals – regarded him "as a leader of revolts... as if I were ready for every species of deviltry. For fifteen years five or six governments kept their spies shadowing me in Europe and America."

Probably motivated by this incident, the Trains left Rome for Venice. They were delighted by this "glorious city in the sea". They also toured other parts of Italy, such as Florence, which Train considered "rich in natural beauty if not in historical association" and of which he became particularly fond.[9] From Trieste the family made their way to fashionable Vienna.

It was typical of Train to move between extremes of society, attending a secret Carbonari meeting one week and a gathering of their oppressors, the crown heads of the Austrian Empire, next. They arrived in Vienna just in time to see the spectacles in honour of the Centennial Anniversary of the High Order of Maria Theresa, Empress of Austria, pageantry of such magnificence that "no person now living will probably ever see again".[10] A century later, Train was proved correct: the Empire had been dissolved for over forty years.

He managed to wrangle a prestigious invitation to the apartments of the Empire's Minister of War to view a midnight serenade by Imperial bands. From here the Trains watched a torchlight procession attended by as many as one hundred thousand spectators. The atmosphere must have been fantastic. "The square was jammed with humanity," Train related. Just like a "Boston Common scene at the fireworks, on the Fourth. The martial music filled the air, and you heard the notes for miles outside." Train was also invited to a military review the following day. Although he had seen huge displays by the French army in Paris, nothing could have prepared him for this astounding military spectacle. Unusually, Train was "awed into silence" by its grandeur.[11]

The day was rounded of with a "glorious pageant at the theatre". Once again Train was on hand to witness "the last act in this splendid drama". Admittance to the theatre was by royal invitation only and these, naturally enough, could be neither bought nor sold. Thousands were turned away disappointed. Train, of course, once again made use of his connections to get seats. He and his wife arrived early and gathered together with the cream of the Austrian Empire. Soon the venue was packed to capacity, without one seat to spare. It was with smug satisfaction that Train described the extraordinary scene:

"The wealthiest dignitaries of the land were there – distinguished statesmen, grey-headed generals, the hope and pride of the aristocracy, came in their coroneted carriages; all the Esterhazys and Metternichs of Austria were there, each endeavoring to outshine the others in the richness of their dress, the brilliancy of their diamonds, and the number of their decorations. Hungarian chiefs, in that beautiful hussar dress, and Bohemian jagers, and the uniforms of all the princes, gave a scenic effect to the house.

The imperial box contained all the living members of the grand and kingly house of Hapsburg; the Emperor's mother, the boy Emperor, almost beardless – his young and beautiful Empress, her sisters, brothers – all the royal family, blazing with diamonds and the choicest gems."[12]

The evening's entertainment was also quite spectacular. It consisted of scenes from the Empire's history performed by a vast array of participants. The highlight of the show was the unforgettable sight of a battlefield brought to life by hundreds of actors. It was a perfect but sanitised rendering of the real thing, introduced to the audience by the sounds of battle: artillery fire and clashing weaponry, right down to "the shrieks of dying soldiers, the wild strains of martial music, the rattling of musketry, [and] the trumpet-toned voice of command". When the curtain rose, the audience immediately felt that they were in the middle of a battlefield. As Train breathlessly related, there were:

> "Hundreds of men and officers in all and every attitude, advancing, retreating, dying, dead; horses plunging into action, regiments at the cannon's mouth, bayonets, the cut, the thrust, the cry of the last moment before eternity — it was a tableau never to be forgotten."

It brought the house down. As soon as the curtain fell, a spontaneous roar of cheering swept through the theatre as each and every member of the audience stood up and directed their approval towards the Emperor.[13]

Dashing to Liverpool, the Trains arrived just in time to meet the *Niagara*, a U.S. warship sent to take part in a new British-American effort to lay an Atlantic cable. Commander Pennock, who served under Captain Hudson on the *Niagara*, was Train's cousin. Train arranged a banquet in their and the other ship's officers' honour, at Lynn's Waterloo Hotel, a favourite resort of American sailors.[14]

Captain Hudson had received a letter from the Grand Duke Constantine of Russia, the Czar's brother, who had been at Dover in his yacht, the *Livadia*. The note thanked him for allowing three Russian officers to witness the cable-laying ceremonies. Train instinctively sensed an opportunity to visit Russia in a semi-official capacity and gain access to distinguished Russian society. He offered to personally carry Captain Hudson's reply to the Grand Duke. Hudson replied that no answer was required, reminding Train that the Grand Duke had returned already to St Petersburg. But Train would not be put off and finally persuaded Hudson that courtesy dictated the necessity of a reply; George declared that he would be happy to deliver it personally to the Grand Duke in St Petersburg, as he was planning to visit that city. Train even went as far as suggesting the phrasing of the letter.

He wasted no time and quickly set off for Russia. Along the way he arranged to write foreign correspondence for the *Times*. When he reached St Petersburg, he was informed that the Grand Duke had left the city for his country residence at Strelna. Train did not know how far away Strelna might be, but immediately arranged to travel there.

With Captain Hudson's letter in hand, Train explained his mission and was allowed through the numerous sentry points guarding the approaches to the palace. His luck held and he was received by the Grand Duke. From then on Train's needs were attended to by the Grand Duke's aide-de-camp, Colonel Greig. Train was made welcome by his hosts, who ensured that his visit to Russia passed without a hitch. Moscow impressed Train more than any other European city: "It seemed to belong to quite another world and to a different civilization. There is something primitive and prehistoric about it – elemental in its somberness and in its grandeur." He was received by the Emperor's brother-in-law, Prince Dombriski, and was greatly surprised to see a portrait of Napoleon hanging in the Kremlin.

The Grand Duke also arranged a visit to the Nijnii Novgorod commercial fair. The city was a thousand miles east of Moscow on the Volga, quite remote from Western eyes. It was the traditional trading place between the merchants of Asia and Europe. Train reported that over $50,000,000 worth of goods were traded here over a six-week period. He also noted that the effects of global trade were present: "Even in this primitive market the expanded credits, and the golden mines of California and Australia, have raised the prices of all kinds of commodities." [15] Train was delighted by what he saw. He called his time in the wonderful city of Nijnii Novgorod "a marvellous experience" and considered that it was well worth a trip around the world only to see it.

Some time afterwards, when Train was in England, he received a letter from the Russian ambassador enclosing a letter from Colonel Greig. He said that the Grand Duke had read Train's book, *Young America Abroad*, with interest. The Grand Duke, he said, was "greatly pleased" with Train's descriptions of Russia and his exposure of the Crimean fiasco, and also with Train's future predictions for his country. The Russian Government invited Train to visit the Amur, Petropauloffski and the Vladivostok regions, and to make a report concerning the prospects of eastern Siberia. They proposed to make all the arrangements for him so that he could travel in "luxury and leisure". Surprisingly, Train declined to accept their offer. He reasoned:

> "I have ever preferred to follow my own ideas rather than those of others. I desired to pursue original lines of investigation, to go over new routes of travel and of trade, to explore corners of the world that had not been worn into paths by the myriad feet of travelers. I have always felt hampered in trying to carry out the suggestions of others. I have found that there is but one course for me, if I am

to succeed, and that is to follow my own counsel. I must be myself, untrammeled, unfettered, or I fail. If I had gone to Eastern Siberia for the Russian Government, I might have succeeded in the way the Government expected; but the chances, I consider, would have been against me. If I had gone there at my own motion, I might have created a sensation by exploiting that vast and magnificent region, which must soon play a tremendously important part in the history of the world."

Eighteen fifty-seven was a memorable year for Train in many ways. The great financial panic that he had forecast the year before finally broke, forcing him to change his plans to return to Australia. In his absence, his company had been managed by George Starbuck, junior, and had apparently not performed as well as in its first year of operations. At the beginning of that year it had ceased to act as agent for the White Star Line. It had also received unpleasant publicity as a result of a lawsuit to recover outstanding rent from the chartering of a vessel called the *Amelia*.[16] Added to this, market conditions were no longer appealing enough to encourage Train to return to Australia.

By the time of his arrival back in America in late October and the publication of *Young America in Wall Street* financial chaos was sweeping the world. In the introduction to his book Train explained the investigative work he had undertaken throughout the previous year that had led him to conclude that a dreadful worldwide financial crash was imminent. The more he had examined the state of financial affairs in the major global economies, the more convinced he had become:

"The moment I examined the statistics I thought I saw breakers ahead... I came to the conclusion that the panic of 1857 must be more terrific than anything before!... The most surprising thing to me is, that an intelligent community, a mercantile people, could march on with a steady tramp to the brink of a precipice, blindfold their eyes, recklessly advance, deliberately step over, and fall into an almost universal bankruptcy, without being aware of it themselves!... Like a ship under full sail, the compass of sound sense gone, and no officer in command, no wonder the ship went upon the rocks!"[17]

Like Train's earlier book *An American Merchant in Europe, Asia and Australia* (also known as *Young America Abroad*), which was widely praised by the press, *Young America in Wall Street* was highly respected on both sides of the Atlantic.[18] Although it did not bring the kind of money he had made as a merchant, it did result in a steady stream of commissions from Hunt and others for foreign correspondence in a similar vein. Critics, sometimes dismissive of the literary worth of Train's various writings, universally acknowledged their informative content. Encouraged by the success of his books, Train "threw off" numerous letters and articles as he travelled. He began to be known as the embodiment of "Young America" – a term which signified Train's hopes for the future. In his preface to another eclectic collection of his foreign correspondence, letters, and speeches, published in early 1859 under the title of *Spread-Eagleism*, he defined "Young America" as: "a nation, and signifies progress… the vanguard of change – the coming age." To him, the movement advocating free trade and economic expansion represented an optimistic future for America.[19]

Train's books greatly enhanced his reputation. He was especially highly regarded in British financial circles. One review of *Young America Abroad* and *Young America in Wall Street* by the *Illustrated London News* must have been a favourite of Train's, since he reprinted it in *Spread-Eagleism*.[20] It was a particularly insightful analysis of Train and his books, and recognised that Train's "sober" assessment of the facts had been ignored by men who should have known better. While the *News* cautioned that Train was one of the most vocal proponents of the emergence of America as a world power, it acknowledged that:

> "[W]hen it is a question of commercial enterprise and speculation, he is as sensible, as respectable, and as full of worldly wisdom, as a Rothschild, a Baring, or any greyheaded father of the Exchange. On questions of banking and currency, and the legitimate operations of commerce, he enunciates his maxims like an old fogy who knows all the ins and outs of trade… No fine-spun and high-sounding theories… can influence his sober judgement."

This approbation was not unqualified, however.

> "If, in addition to his genius for statistics and his wonderful memory for facts, Mr. Train had literary ability and experience equal to the knowledge which he has gained by the acute and diligent study of men, he might rise to considerable distinction in literature as a writer on economic and commercial subjects. At present his style is not only redundant but harsh, and betrays in every page how much

*better he can think than write, and how much polish the diamond
still requires before ordinary eyes can recognize it to be a diamond
at all."*

The reviewer, quite rightly, considered *Young America Abroad* to be the
better book and praised Train's ability to carry the reader "by 'express'
all over and all around the world, till we toil and pant after him in vain,
and shut the book for want of breath to be whirled along so rapidly".
Indeed, George was sometimes called "Express Train", although the
sobriquet was not always intended as a compliment.

Train's familiarity with the countries he wrote about showed and
was acknowledged, as was the fact that he was apparently:

*"hand-in-glove with Russian Grand Dukes; on friendly terms with
Ambassadors and Plenipotentiaries; knows Kings and Emperors...
His modesty never stands in his way or operates in the slightest
degree to his detriment; and his impudence — if the word be not too
harsh for a degree of conceit and self-assertion which is linked with
a great deal of good feeling and good fellowship — never degener-
ates into repulsiveness. Mr. Train, in fact, may be looked upon as a
not unfavorable representative of what the Americans have themselves designated 'spread-eagleism'. At a 'spread-eagle' speech he
has few superiors, and brings down by the vehemence of his manner and the evident sincerity of his convictions the applauses of
auditors who in cooler moments would pronounce his speeches to
be, in American parlance, gas, or, in vulgar English, bosh... We
doubt whether we shall hear much more of Mr. Train as a maker of
books. He has, we believe, a better business to attend to, and one for
which nature has more eminently qualified him. As a maker of
speeches, and a steady, active man of business, long may he flourish!"*

To have wanted to republish this article in his book, Train's ego must
have been very robust indeed.

---

[1]   Quoted in Fenton Bresler, *Napoleon III, A Life* (HarperCollins, London, 1999),
      p. 301.
[2]   *Ibid.*, p. 288.
[3]   *Ibid.*, p. 290.

4   George Francis Train, *Young America in Wall Street* (Derby & Jackson, New York, 1857), pp. 20–22, 24.

5   *Ibid.*, p. 92.

6   *Ibid.*

7   *Ibid.*, pp. 121–123.

8   Fenton Bresler, above, n. 1, p. 89.

9   George Francis Train, above, n. 4, pp. 149–158.

10   *Ibid.*, p. 164.

11   *Ibid.*, pp. 164–165.

12   *Ibid.*, pp. 166–167.

13   *Ibid.*, pp. 167–168.

14   George Francis Train, *Spread-Eagleism* (Derby & Jackson, New York, 1859), pp. 63–73.

15   George Francis Train, above, n. 4, p. 282.

16   E. Daniel and Annette Potts, eds, *A Yankee Merchant in Goldrush Australia* (Heinemann, Melbourne, 1970), p. *xxii*.

17   George Francis Train, above, n. 4, pp. *vi–xi*.

18   *Ibid.*, pp. 399–406; George Francis Train, above, n. 14, pp. *v–vii*.

19   George Francis Train, above, n. 14, pp. *viii–xiv*.

20   *Ibid.*, pp. *xv–xxiv*.

EIGHT

A Railroad Fit for a Queen

It had been in Train's mind for some years to build a railway connecting the Eastern and the Mid-Western States. It seemed to him that the obvious solution to this problem would be to persuade Queen Maria Cristina of Spain to finance the project.

The Queen could truly be said to have had a turbulent royal career, having been deposed and restored to the unstable Spanish throne on several occasions. Whether on or off the throne, however, she was a very rich woman. When Florida was sold by Spain to the United States, Cristina, deeply conscious of the insecurity of her throne, had shrewdly left large amounts of cash in the Bank of the United States – something for a rainy day, as it were. When President Jackson liquidated that institution, she accepted an arrangement whereby she received extensive Pennsylvanian property in lieu of her funds.[1]

Her representatives, John and Christopher Fallon – Spaniards of Irish extraction – had control of almost forty thousand acres. They had produced painstaking plans for development of these lands for both the Queen's and their own benefit. There was coal on the land and, it was believed, iron ore and ceramic clays. It was also heavily forested. The Fallons anticipated massive development in the near future that would provide the infrastructure to exploit the region's full potential.

The only hindrance to their grand scheme to develop the full potential of the lands was a lack of access. Fortunately, the Atlantic and Great Western railroad was steadily making its way westward over the Appalachian mountains toward the Great Lakes and the Mississippi and was nearing the Queen's lands. It was to connect the western terminus of the Erie railroad in New York State with Cincinnati, where another line led westward to St Louis. This connecting link had been on the cards for a while. Short sections of it had even been completed, but lack of funds had always prevented a dedicated major construction to complete the line. It had proved to be an impossible task to raise enough money in the United States. Funds would have to be sought abroad.

Train surmised that the possibility of the Queen's participation in the project was not entirely farfetched. After all, the proposed route of the line would pass close by her Pennsylvanian coal lands, which could have obvious benefits for her; she was the logical source for funds for the line. It was lucky for Train that he had made several useful Spanish contacts some years before in Paris. Most importantly, these had included Don José de Salamanca, the Queen's banker.

Train himself was not without connections. He was acquainted with several Liverpool bankers, including James McHenry, the Queen's British agent. He had already, Train soon found, been appointed general European agent for the Atlantic and Great Western.[2] This did not demoralise Train. He knew that scheme was large enough to handsomely reward both their efforts.

Dashing back to Europe again, Train put his plans before the Queen's husband, the Duke of Rianzares, and her secretary, Salerno. It was promptly agreed that Train should take the Queen's assistant secretary, Don Rodrigo de Questa, back with him to America, to inspect the property incognito. Train was to be his interpreter and guide. Numerous misunderstandings arose on the voyage to America because of de Questa's lack of English. Once he tried to order fish for breakfast. He could not think of the English word, so he tried the French word for fish, "poisson". Needless to say, the astonished steward thought that he was trying to order poison and reported the incident to higher authorities. Fortunately, Train was on hand to sort the matter out and de Questa finally got his fish. The Spaniard resorted to using sign language for the rest of the trip when ordering food to avoid a repeat of the incident. This had its own drawbacks. Train observed: "When he wanted eggs, he would flap his arms together and cackle like a hen that has just laid an egg." The steward laughed "until he almost had a fit". Poor de Questa gave up eventually and made do with whatever food was put in front of him.

Finally arriving in Philadelphia, the gentlemen went on to Lock Haven, Pennsylvania, the headquarters of the Fallons, and introduced themselves as foreigners who were interested in mines and in coal lands in particular, concealing their identities as representatives of the Queen. It was quickly apparent that the brothers were living a luxurious ducal lifestyle in the wilderness with, Train remarked, "something of a court around them".

John Fallon gave the visitors a guided tour of the forty thousand acres under their management. It was obvious that the lands were highly valuable and that the proposed railroad project would benefit the area immensely, by improving access to exploit its valuable natural resources.

Train and de Questa returned to Philadelphia, sought legal advice there, and sailed back to Europe to report to the Queen's bankers. In London they met with McHenry and found that all previous attempts to sell the railroad's securities there had failed. The general rating of American internal improvement loans was poor abroad; successive British losses in such investments had alienated the financial community there. Only the previous year, several Pennsylvania counties had refused to honour their railroad bond repayment commitments. This had even further undermined demand for Atlantic and Great Western bonds in the London market.

It was clear to all that Queen Cristina's money could provide the solution to the railway's financial difficulties. Train, McHenry and de Questa went on to Paris to seek the backing of Don José de Salamanca. They pointed out the mutual benefits of the railroad and the Queen's lands, reasoning that the Queen's investment would be logical. Salamanca was tempted, but did not commit himself there and then. Some time later he invested heavily in the ill-fated railway. All he received in return was the gratification of seeing a small New York town named in his honour: Salamanca.[3]

Train did not give up easily. Back in London McHenry and Train succeeded in interesting the banking house of Kennard. The bankers sent an engineering representative, T. W. Kennard, to accompany them to America in the autumn of 1858 and to inspect the proposed route. In New York meetings were held with potential investors at Train's usual headquarters there, the plush St Nicholas Hotel on Broadway. They were shown maps of the route and the plans were fully explained. Then the investors and promoters left for Olean, where they met the contractor in charge of the railroad.

The whole party took wagons for Jamestown. Over a three-week period the group journeyed along the proposed 400-mile route of the railroad as far as Dayton, Ohio. They stopped at all the important towns along the route to hold meetings and drum up support for the project. One such meeting was held at Mansfield in November 1858 "to meet the president, directors, and agents for foreign bondholders of the Atlantic and Great Western Railroad". The committees of the three states involved were present: New York, Pennsylvania, and Ohio. Eclipsing the other speakers present, Train galvanised the audience with his enthusiasm. He announced to the crowd that "the road" was to be built with the assistance of Queen Maria Cristina of Spain and the banker Salamanca.

In later years, Train practically claimed exclusive credit for the financing of the Atlantic and Great Western. But that evening in Mansfield he was more modest, giving primary credit to McHenry and others: "McHenry made his arrangements with Salamanca, two of the ablest men in Europe. Two cargoes of iron are already in New York, and two installments of money are here, and I have bills of lading in my pocket of five more cargoes on the way."[4] Train was more of a catalyst than an active player in the affair. That was the way he preferred to operate. He was the perfect choice to lead the public relations campaign, and the general public held him in high regard.

Train went back to Europe to buy rails for the new road and negotiated several contracts pledging a rate of two million dollars of railroad bonds for one million dollars' worth of iron. Train's own egotistical account of some of his transactions on behalf of the railroad are certainly dubious.

When at last Train secured a million-dollar loan from Salamanca by pledging two million dollars' worth of the road's bonds as security, his troubles were not yet over. No British financial institutions were willing to accept any Spanish credit at the time, so Salamanca's notes were effectively worthless in London. This was a major problem since the bonds had to be exchanged in that city: the iron for rails had to be bought in Britain. Train was prepared for this difficulty. He went to a banker friend in London called Marshall and tried to get him to discount fifty thousand dollars of the Salamanca notes. When Marshall refused them as Train expected, he put his plan in motion. He asked Marshall if he could tell him, as a favour, what Spanish bills were worth, if they could be used. Marshall replied that they would be worth six per cent. Train immediately telegraphed McHenry in Liverpool, saying that "Marshall will not touch this paper under six per cent".

This was true of course, but Train "forgot" to mention that Marshall had refused to touch it on any terms. Train directed McHenry to see if he could persuade a large financier there named Moseley to handle it at five. McHenry soon replied that while Moseley would not handle the paper at less than Marshall, they would take it at six per cent. In his autobiography Train proudly related that the railway was built on this simple deception. Whatever way this transaction might be viewed today, it must even then have been considered morally questionable.

Train had no written contract with McHenry, but only a verbal understanding that he was to receive stg£100,000 as commission for his help. As a down-payment, Train requested that McHenry give Willie U.S. $100,000, a fraction of the full amount. This he did, and the money was put in a trust for her. It is clear that Train had a close relationship with McHenry. Train's first son, born in 1856, was named after himself, but his second, born at about the time of these negotiations, was named Elsey McHenry Train.

Despite Train's talk, it was really McHenry who was close to the Queen. He even loaned his house in Kensington to her during one of the periods when she was pushed out of Spain. On one occasion McHenry even helped to engineer an almost bloodless revolution to bring her back to the throne.[5] Yet, although Train played a secondary role in the railway's development, it was an important one. He and McHenry seem to have fallen out over what Train believed he was owed for his efforts. McHenry finally settled the matter in 1866, but not without being pursued for the debt.

McHenry was entertaining Sir Morton Peto and other British bankers at a lavish fifteen-thousand-dollar banquet at Delmonico's restaurant.[6] Train was apparently not invited. He saw the occasion as a good opportunity to collect his dues, so he sent his lawyer, Clark Bell, to McHenry to present his claim. Train recorded that McHenry was so alarmed at the possibility of being arrested in front of his guests that he settled on the spot, giving his payment notes for the balance due Train.

Train's story cannot be relied on entirely, as ten years later he maintained that McHenry still owed him large sums. Train also added that the presentation of McHenry's notes for payment in London a little later caused a panic and the failure of several large banking houses, including that of McHenry.

"This showed to me," he declared, "the real shallowness and insubstantiality of the great world of finance. It is built upon straw and paper. The secret of its great masters and 'Napoleons' is nothing but what is known among other gamblers as 'bluff'." This was something he was now qualified to speak of, since his stroke with the Spanish credit in London.

As for the railway, it proved to be a terrible failure. It went into receivership three times in thirteen years, before its eventual success as part of the Erie railroad.[7]

1   Irving Wallace, *Square Pegs* (London, 1968), p. 56.

2   Willis Thornton, *The Nine Lives of Citizen Train* (Greenberg, New York, 1948), p. 90.

3   Irving Wallace, above, n. 1.

4   George Francis Train, *Spread-Eagleism* (Derby & Jackson, New York, 1859), pp. 163–164.

5   Willis Thornton, above, n. 2, p. 95.

6   The wealthy elite of the nineteenth century met at Delmonico's, perhaps the most famous restaurant of the time.

7   Irving Wallace, above, n. 1.

While he was acting as a public relations officer and financial broker to the Atlantic and Great Western Railroad, Train was also working on a project of his own. When he had been in Philadelphia in 1858 he had seen and noted the success of the horse-drawn street railway, what we would call the tram network. It struck him how convenient the system was for the populace and wondered why London, with a much larger population, had not adopted such a system. At that time Philadelphia and New York were the only places in the world with street tramways. Train studied painstakingly the details of their construction and operation, with a view to replicating their success in England.

Previous efforts by others to establish horse-drawn tramways in England had all failed dismally in the face of strong opposition, but Train did not let that get in the way of his plans. Despite these early setbacks, the principle behind trams was a good one, with several advantages over traditional forms of transportation. Metal wheels turning on smooth tracks built into the road were much easier to pull than carriages running on uneven road surfaces. Principally this meant that two horses could pull a tram carrying around fifty passengers, which was almost double the capacity of horse-drawn omnibuses. As a result, trams were much cheaper to run and more comfortable.[1]

In 1858 Train threw his heart and soul into a daring effort to become the pioneer of British street railways. First he went to Liverpool, as it was the city with which he was most familiar. Not unreasonably, he felt that it offered him his best chance of success. Since it was the world's leading seaport, he had the mistaken view that it was a progressive city. The municipal authorities there would not even consider his proposal. They were as narrow-minded and short-sighted as they had been almost a decade before when Train had to force them to adopt new practices at Liverpool port. Although others might have lost heart when faced with this attitude, Train quickly made a new plan of action.

Through his past shipbuilding involvement he had become acquainted with John Laird, "the progressive and energetic ship-builder" who was chairman of the Commissioners of Birkenhead, directly across the Mersey from Liverpool. A few years later Laird would build many of the Confederate blockade-runners, such as the *Alabama*. It occurred to Train that Laird would be an easy convert, since he was a forward-thinking individual and would have enough sense to appreciate the merits of tramways. Moreover, Train proposed to build a tramway entirely at his own expense, to pave a certain number of streets which the line passed through, and still charge lower fares than the omnibuses. In the event that the line did not satisfy the Commissioners, Train promised to remove the tracks and restore the streets to their previous working order, again at his own expense. Laird was indeed sympathetic to Train's generous offer and with his influence the Birkenhead Board of Commissioners consented to allow Train to proceed with his plan. Train rushed to complete the tramway before further opposition, particularly before other transportation companies prevented him.

The grand opening of the first tramway line measuring a mile and a half for the Birkenhead Street Railway Company (Liverpool) was held on August 30, 1860. At ten in the morning the first cars were wheeled out onto the track, two horses were yoked to each, and the first run began. It was a success from the start, as Train had envisaged. Crowds stood on the streets to watch the experiment and the new cars proved to be highly popular. The opening was celebrated by Train with a lavish invitational luncheon banquet. Twelve hundred people were invited, including thirty European monarchs plus assorted peers, members of Parliament and even the Pope! Though no monarchs attended, many other prominent people came, about three hundred and fifty altogether.[2]

Train was highly flattered to receive praise for his efforts. He was delighted when the tramway met with widespread critical approval. For example, the *Times* commented that "Birkenhead witnessed yesterday the formal inauguration of an undertaking which in this country wears all the aspect of novelty".[3] It sketched briefly previous, unsuccessful efforts to replace crowded and uncomfortable omnibuses for transport like Train's "large and roomy coaches gliding rapidly and with an equable motion over little strips of iron".

"It remained for a citizen of the United States to infuse renewed hopes into the supporters of the scheme. To Mr. G. F. Train of Boston,

the introduction of street railways is mainly to be attributed. But
five short months have elapsed since he laid the proposals on the
subject before the Commissioners of Birkenhead. Two months later
found those proposals accepted. Yesterday saw them carried into
practical effect."[4]

Though the *Times* felt that the coaches were "fitted up in a style more luxurious than tasteful", it still conceded that "travelling by one of Mr. Train's carriages, as contrasted with one of our ordinary omnibuses, is like quitting a narrow and confined room for a commodious and well-ventilated apartment," and cautiously predicted that "on the whole nothing could to all appearance be more successful than this experiment of Mr. Train's on British soil". It concluded that it had "no reason to doubt" that Train would be successful in similar undertakings.

The Birkenhead tramway was an immediate success with the public. Train viewed it as a stepping stone to achieve his aims. Buoyed by his achievement, Train dusted off his plans to build similar tramways in Manchester, Glasgow, London, and in all major British cities. He extended his operations to London right away, even though a French firm had failed to set up a tramway modelled on American lines there not three years earlier. Ultimately, it failed because of financial irregularities and stiff nationalistic opposition to such an intrusion.[5]

In London, however, opposition was much more forceful and vocal. Every one of London's six thousand omnibus drivers was Train's bitter enemy. He soon found out that they were a highly organised and unrelenting lobby group. Due to the nature of their job, they could reach the masses in a way that Train could only dream of. They fought against Train at every level of local government. Their influence even reached parliament itself. Not only did Train have to contend with this, but also with the huge task of getting all the necessary franchises. Since every parish in London was virtually a separate municipality, this presented itself as nearly impossible. Only a patient person with a defined strategy would be able to negotiate this task.

Sir Benjamin Hall, the Commissioner of Works, consistently opposed his plans. Train had to appear before the Metropolitan Board of Aldermen with his models, maps and drawings ready for inspection. They questioned him about the tram's construction and operation, the effect its presence would have in the narrow streets, on other traffic, the danger of accidents, and so on. One particular peer present was a determined enemy of tramways. As he cross-examined Train, he glared at him through a monocle. When the board was examining Train on how he would lay track up Ludgate Hill, where the street was very narrow, the man again fixed Train with his glittering monocle and asked:

"Suppose that when I go down to the Mansion House in my carriage, one of my horses should slip on your d[amne]d rail and break his leg – would you pay for the horse?"

"My Lord," replied Train without missing a beat, "if you could convince me that your d[amne]d old horse would not have fallen if the rail had not been there, I certainly should pay for it."

The audience came over to Train's side. Despite the peer's best efforts, the hearing was a success and Train received permission to lay a tramway track from Hyde Park to Bayswater. Although only a short distance of a couple of miles, the precedent was set in the heart of London. It would be vital that this concession succeeded if he was to achieve his aims. The first line was opened along Bayswater Road on March 23, 1861. It is said that Dickens and Thackeray were among the spectators. A second followed from Victoria Station to Westminster Abbey on April 15, and a third from Westminster Bridge to Kennington Gate on August 15.[6]

Ironically, Train's difficulties were only beginning. The omnibus drivers were determined not to give in without a struggle. Train's tramways had a step-rail which he based on the Philadelphia type and patented in April 1860. It was of rolled iron, weighing fifty pounds per lineal yard. It was almost exactly the same gauge as the wheels of the omnibuses and the omnibus drivers soon found that by suddenly wrenching their vehicles out of the tracks, they could break off a wheel and cause accidents, to the detriment of the tramway's reputation. Train reported that "they would drive across again and again and take the rails in the most reckless way, in order to catch and twist their wheels. They were very often successful, and there were many accidents of this sort."

Strange as it must sound, Train's most influential and implacable enemies were not the omnibus drivers. The well-to-do and influential residents of the areas chosen for the lines hated the tramways because of the hazard and inconvenience they represented. The tramway lines were not flush with the road and the gentry's carriages were jolted when they crossed the rails.

The two groups – gentry and omnibus drivers – were a formidable combination. The ordinary working people, who found Train's tramways a cheap and comfortable means of transport, sided with him. Exactly the same groups of people had opposed the trams when they were first introduced in America. The opposition became more and more bitter, until finally Train was convicted of maintaining a nuisance. He was fined five hundred pounds, but resolutely refused to pay it on a point of principle. He was promptly thrown into jail, not to be released until he complied. At first he was held in Sloman's sponging house and then in the White Cross Street jail, as a debtor. But this was not the end of his problems.

Tragically, a young boy was killed in a tramway accident; Train, as the promoter of the conveyance, was arrested – apparently while still in debtor's prison – and charged with manslaughter. He maintained that the accident was entirely unavoidable and not the tramway's fault, but there was uproar against him. In order to appease public opinion, Train paid for the boy's funeral "and did everything that could possibly be done to pay, in a material way, for his death". The manslaughter case was heard in June 1862. According to one account, Train would have been convicted, only for the fact that he defended himself in court.[7]

Feeling against him was also fuelled by the fact that by now he was known for making speeches in favour of the American Union cause. Precisely the same upper circles of British society which opposed his tramways as an obstruction to their carriages were now doubly offended, as they supported the Southern states.

A Bill to authorise tramways was defeated in Parliament by a few votes and Train had to abandon his efforts in London. By June 21, 1862, the three lines had ceased operations. Practically all of the Train tramways in London were soon removed. Not until 1870 were trams in operation again, permanently, in London. However, Train's failure in London was partially offset by his success elsewhere. He built several miles of tramways through the pottery-making countryside of Staffordshire. He also built a tramway in Darlington.[8] A new kind of flat rail caused no obstruction to other road vehicles and helped matters. These northern lines were a longstanding success.

Train also tried to build tramway lines in Glasgow, but his Bill for parliamentary authority was opposed by the city officials and was lost. He received permission to build them in Birmingham but, due to other circumstances – namely his efforts to defend the American Union – he was unable to carry this out, so the corporation built the lines itself.[9] He also claimed to have built lines in Geneva and Copenhagen.

One authority on the subject summed up Train's considerable contribution to public transport in England, writing that:

> "His cars were the best and most comfortable road vehicles that had

been used... His innovations included uniformed staff, 'straphanging', cheap fares, extensive use of prepaid (metal) tickets sold at a discount... improved ventilation, and greater facility for boarding and alighting."[10]

Oddly enough, the first set of rail lines were invented by one Benjamin Outram a century earlier (hence the word "tram"), who put down a railway line to haul coal wagons. This led to the ironic rhyme:

> "Trams are trams and trains are trains
> And never the twain shall meet
> While trains run on the railway lines
> And tramcars in the street.
> But, strange to say, they both are liked
> By history's twisted chain.
> For trains were built by Mr Tram
> And trams by Mr Train."[11]

---

[1] http://www.ltmuseum.co.uk

[2] "Mr Train and Europe's First Tramway" in *The Cheshire Magazine* (Issue 1). See http://www.cheshiremagazine.com

[3] August 31, 1860. The *Times* was on other occasions one of Train's most severe critics.

[4] *Ibid.*

[5] E. Daniel and Annette Potts, eds, *A Yankee Merchant in Goldrush Australia* (Heinemann, Melbourne, 1970), p. *xxii*.

[6] Staff correspondent of *The Christian Science Monitor*, "Tram Tales Twined", from an unidentified newspaper cutting in the Carleton Simon Papers at Albany University, New York.

[7] A.C. Edmunds, *Pen Sketches of Nebraskans* (R&J Wilbur, Omaha, 1871), p. 15.

[8] E. Daniel and Annette Potts, eds, above, n. 5.

[9] Albert Shaw, *Municipal Government in Great Britain* (T. Fisher-Unwin, London, 1895), p. 190.

[10] Charles E. Lee, "The English Tramways of George Francis Train" in *Journal of Transport History* (1953), Vol. I, numbers 1 and 2, quoted in E. Daniel and Annette Potts, eds, above, n. 5.

[11] Staff correspondent of *The Christian Science Monitor*, above, n. 6.

TEN

A Yankee Patriot in a Hostile Nation

If he had stayed out of politics and stuck to business, as he had done in Australia, George Train might have achieved more support from the influential section of British society in his efforts to establish his tramways. However, with an American civil war imminent, he was left in the unenviable situation of having been born and bred in Massachusetts. Train was a staunch Union supporter. His wife, on the other hand, was pro South.[1] As he declared himself, he was a fervent patriot:

> *"Love of country was always stronger in me than love of money, and I let slip no opportunity to defend the cause of the Union and to prove to the English of the upper classes that they were mistaken in supposing that the Confederacy could succeed."*

As a businessman trying to establish an enterprise in Britain, he must have realised the importance of keeping a diplomatic silence on American political conflicts. This was particularly so since it was obvious, to him at least, that though Britain proclaimed its neutrality in the conflict, it was decidedly pro South and connived with the blockade runners that continued to trade there.

But Train's battle to establish his tramways in Britain was only a minor skirmish compared to another battle he fought against the British establishment on behalf of the Union cause in the civil war.

On July 5, 1858 he made a speech at a banquet to celebrate the 82nd anniversary of American Independence. Responding to a toast of "Young America and Old England – divided in 1776, united in 1858", Train outspokenly condemned Britain's prejudiced view of America and its people, pointing out that socially, commercially, financially, and politically, America was grossly misrepresented in England. As an example, he stated that Britain was not qualified to comment on supposed American filibustering since it was the "King of Filibusters". Essentially,

Train's speech was about the need for recognition of America as an equal. He concluded: "Natural ties should make us natural allies."[2]

In most quarters in both countries the speech was well received. One exception was the Foreign Affairs Committee of Sheffield, which took particular exception to Train's "justification of American filibustering". This resulted in an exchange of strongly worded letters throughout July. Train responded that America's policy was peace, not filibustering, and should not be unjustly labelled by the actions of individuals in Cuba and South America.[3]

Just before war came, Train published a pamphlet called *The Facts; or, At Whose Door Does the Sin (?) Lie?* in New York, Liverpool, and London. It was mostly a collection of letters he had written to the Liverpool *Northern Daily Times*. "Who profits by slave labour?" the pamphlet asked. "Who initiated the slave trade? What have the philanthropists done?" A well-researched summary of the slave trade pointed out that it was the British who had brought the slave trade to America. "Every bale of cotton, every hogshead of sugar England buys is a premium on slavery," Train heatedly argued, pointing out Britain's indefensible position. While they paid lip service to the abolition of slavery, Britain continued to be a huge consumer of slave-grown cotton, coffee, sugar, rice, grain, and tobacco.[4] None of the unpalatable challenges he made on any of these questions increased his popularity.

To his detriment, Train continued to antagonise the very people on whom his business success depended, and then ended his sermon in *The Facts* with a suitably dramatic flourish:

> *"Dissolve the Union! Never! When the sun shines at midnight, the moon at mid-day — when Nature stops a moment to rest, or man forgets to be selfish — when flowers lose their odor, and trees shed no leaves — when birds talk and animals laugh — when impossibilities are in fashion, the Union may be broken!"*[5]

When the war finally erupted, Train quickly became one of the most outspoken defenders of the Union cause in Britain. He was up against a powerful enemy: "the element in England that took sides with the South was tremendously influential." Train had already felt the effects of that power through the defeat of his tramway projects. He later reckoned that his personal convictions cost him dearly and destroyed his chances of making a fortune, perhaps as much as £5,000,000, on his various tramway projects. Before taking part in this desperate effort to stem the tide of British opinion and to defeat the efforts of British traders profiteering by selling goods to the South, he placed his wife and children on board a steamer bound for New York, where they would be out of harm's reach.

Now free from distractions, Train rushed to defend the Union even more fervently. Seeing how public opinion lay, he spoke in public halls in its favour. He also condemned the blockade-runners. His pursuit of a characteristically enthusiastic campaign was bound to lead to his businesses suffering from the adverse backlash.

However strange it must seem, he was filling a vacuum. The Union desperately needed a spokesman at that time, since it was in essence without an ambassador; the incumbent was passively waiting his replacement after the change of administration in Washington. The Confederacy was confident that its nationhood would be recognised, since British industry badly needed cotton. They believed that the European nations would fight the North, if necessary, to get cotton from the South for their industries. France was openly hostile towards the North.

Without official encouragement or support, Train publicly defended the Union cause. One of his first acts was to start the *London American* newspaper to present the Union point of view to the British. He appointed as editor John Adams Knight, who was assisted by Train's own secretary, George Pickering Bemis. Offices were established at 100 Fleet Street, in the heartland of the British newspaper industry. The facade of the building was decorated with American flags, leaving no-one in any doubt which side he supported. The paper, of course, was a pro-Union mouthpiece. Its motto was: "The Union, the whole Union, and nothing but the Union."

Train made numerous speeches for the Union. They were later reprinted in America in pamphlet form, with the proceeds going to the support of the *London American*. Train also had a more subtle approach in his campaign to sway British public opinion. For some time, he had been hosting lavish Sunday breakfasts for powerful and influential members of British society in his home. In the past these had been used to enhance his personal and business profile, in order to further his tramway interests and raise his reputation in business. It is no small credit to his brilliant and original scheme that he was quite successful in rounding up his targets.

Train used a simple but ingenious tactic to lure them to his gatherings. In keeping with his policy of getting nothing less than the best, he had a rakish photo of himself taken by John and Charles Watkins,

"Photographers to Her Majesty". On the back of these cartes-de-visite was printed the following invitation:

"16
St. James's St
S.W.

Come and meet a dozen
live men at my round
table breakfast next
Sunday at eleven.

Repondez s'il vous plait."

Turnouts were always impressive in terms of numbers and celebrities. His novel champagne breakfasts attracted curious members of Parliament, city officials, authors, journalists, and other distinguished notables.[6]

In February 1861, before the outbreak of civil war in America, Train drew quite a distinguished crowd to a dinner at Fenton's Hotel in St James's Street. The group included ten members of Parliament, Viscount Bury, Lord Colville of Culross, the illustrator and etcher George Cruickshank, Z. Pearson, Esq., Mayor of Hull, Sir F. Slade, Bart., Q.C., and the journalist and writer George Augustus Sala. The novelist Anthony Trollope was also present. The occasion was the celebration of the 129th anniversary of the birthday of George Washington. Train shamelessly used the occasion to promote his viewpoint.

Although he was not opposed to slavery as much as he was against the break-up of the Union, he declared that "Next winter the slaves of the South will be much better fed than the free operatives of Manchester."[7] Train was never anything other than a diehard Union supporter and swore that "should any one of [its States] leave the... American Union, in less than twenty-four hours I will become an English subject."[8] When war actually came, it was naturally more difficult to get members of Parliament to attend his breakfasts; yet, on June 19, a celebration of the anniversary of the Battle of Bunker Hill drew a quite good crowd of notables.

Train made no effort to conceal the fact that he was seeking to promote the Unionist cause. He warned his guests that their conversation was being taken down and that any or all of it might be printed in the

London American. He dominated conversations with sermons in favour of the Union cause.

As the year progressed, things looked bad for the Union side. The Civil War's first major battle ended in disaster for the North, when Confederates routed overconfident Union forces at Bull Run. After this major defeat the general opinion in England was that the North wouldn't fight. The Union was becoming increasingly difficult to defend.

Train deployed another brilliant strategy. He spoke in many cities for the benefit of local charities. In this way the selected charities gained financially and his reputation was elevated. More importantly, he gained a wider audience to put his views to, one that he would not have reached otherwise.

Train was also doing something else that was perhaps even more important than his Union speeches. He kept a close eye on smugglers' boats preparing to take supplies past the Union blockade of Southern ports. He reported their movements back to the North. He revealed details of these activities in an open letter to the New York *Herald* in November, pointing out that these ships carrying contraband goods for the Southern war effort against the Union were openly loaded in British ports with the full connivance of the authorities. Although this was yet another example of the British establishment's tacit support for the South, it only strengthened his belief that the ordinary working people were on the side of the Union. "England's neutral position is contemptible," declared Train. "I have seen one, two, three vessels load under my very face with cannon, rifles, shoes, and blankets for the Southern conspirators."[9]

Train utterly condemned Britain's actions. He named dates and places, ships and captains, cargoes and owners. He also reported that he had personally gone to the commander of the U.S. war steamship *James Adger* at Southampton and provided him with information about the *Gladiator*, an English steamer that was about to depart loaded with six hundred cases of rifles, gunpowder, shoes, blankets, cannon, and other war provisions for the Confederacy. His letter was widely copied on both sides of the Atlantic. It did not make him very popular with the British press.[10]

About the same time, Federal warships removed two Confederate agents off the *Trent*, a British steamer, as prisoners of war. This incident nearly resulted in war between the United Sates and Great Britain. On December 18, while defending the Union actions at Tunstall-on-Trent during a speech on the *Trent* affair, Train was badly heckled. A member of the audience stood up and read parts of Train's letter to the *Herald* aloud, virtually accusing him of being a Union spy. Despite the odds against him, Train came out well against a hostile audience. He stood his ground that evening, but he soon had a change of mind.[11]

A few weeks later he took part in a debate in London on the subject "Whether England is justified in Going to War on the *Trent* Affair or Not?" He gave an amazing performance, publicly admitting he had been wrong to defend the *Trent* seizures, and urged that the two Confederates be released. At that moment, unknown to Train, Washington was preparing to do a U-turn and do just that.[12]

In the middle of the *Trent* crisis some official demanded that the Stars and Stripes be removed from the front of the *London American* building. Train referred the matter to Sir Richard Mayne, Commissioner of Police, and ascertained that official policy did not sanction the demand. The flags remained as a tribute to Train's resolve and Mayne's non-partisanship.

Though Train never got physically involved in the war, he fought a valiant verbal battle to defend the Union in his own way. Apart from writing numerous letters to newspapers and delivering speech after speech, he also attacked individuals such as the Confederate Commissioner William Yancey. The famous London *Times* war correspondent William Howard Russell was also assailed by Train in a pamphlet which accused him of been a drunken hack out to profit from his position as a newspaper correspondent. Train called him "Munchausen Russell" and "The English Libeller". It was an unfair attack on Russell, due in part to his critical but accurate view of the Federalist rout at the first battle of Bull Run.

Next Train went after Thomas Colley Grattan, a writer and diplomat who Train believed had denigrated America in his book, *Civilized America*. In letters first published in the Liverpool newspapers and later reprinted as a separate volume, Train methodically rubbished Grattan's work:

> "*Americans deserve better treatment from the late British Consul at Boston. He accepts their hospitalities, and abuses their courtesy; he laughs at the guests, sneers at the host, and finds fault where others praise… Every American who has read it is furious; and, as several have asked me to review it, I have looked over its pages, and must say I am surprised to find anything so illiberal emanating from so distinguished a source.*"[13]

It was all the more disappointing for Train because Grattan was a friend of his. "I know him well, and like him much; but he has gone so far out of his path to abuse America and the Americans, more especially the American ladies, he must pardon me if I forget our old acquaintance, as I become indignant at his uncalled-for comments. My country first; friends afterwards."[14]

Train accused Grattan of having lost money in speculations in the States, losses which he hoped to recoup through book sales. There was probably some degree of truth in this. Train concluded his dissection of his former friend's work by saying that "Mr Grattan has shown neither love, wisdom, or knowledge, in 'Civilized America.'... If Mr Grattan feels really sorry for having abused us, I forgive him... but it is the very meanest thing of all to accept hospitality and slander him who gave it. If I have been personal, I regret and retract it. If I have offended the author of 'Civilized America,' I am man enough to accept *his* apology."[15]

Train received as good as he gave from the British press, but after the *Trent* affair public opinion was almost universally virulently anti-American and Train's activities provoked attacks from "all the penny-a-liners from Aberdeen to Dover". Representative of the savage attacks was one appearing in the December 11, 1861 edition of the London *Morning Chronicle*. It was a bitter tirade against the Union and, in particular, Train:

> "There is a man now lodging in St James's street who, uniting in his own person everything that is ridiculous in the general demeanour of a Yankee, is enjoying our hospitality and availing himself of our generosity to act the spy and to insult us in the most ribald journals of New York. This individual is Mr. George Francis Train, somewhat notorious in connection with the tramway nuisance in our public thoroughfares." [16]

What was worse, it contained a barely veiled threat of physical violence towards him and rounded off with:

> "Mr. George Francis Train, his photographs, his speeches, his breakfasts, his cards, his omnibuses, his slang, his petitions, his puffs, have long been standing nuisances; but we can put up with a nuisance. Putting up with a spy is a very different matter." [17]

It was a particularly vicious attack, made worse by the fact that Train had bought the London *Morning Chronicle* and another paper, the *London*

Spectator, on behalf of the French Emperor Napoleon III in 1858. When the Italian war ended, the papers passed into other hands and the *Chronicle* went on to make what Train called "a most savage attack" on him in relation to the tramway debate, taking the omnibus drivers' side. Now it was attacking him for exposing the blockade runners.

In direct contrast to what was happening in Britain, Train was inversely popular in the United States. He was widely praised by the American press for his efforts. One commentator summed up opinion perfectly: "Seldom has a man been so successful in touching the heart of a great people as has Mr Train that of the Americans."[18] In response to a letter from ninety-five of the leading citizens of his home state, Massachusetts, that praised his patriotic actions, Train replied nobly: "I am proud of Boston — proud of Massachusetts, but never before have I felt so proud of being a citizen of the United States of America."[19]

In another instance, a public meeting in Philadelphia[20] passed resolutions and a testimonial signed by a long list of prominent citizens lauding "The Eloquent Champion of the American Union". Train replied to William D. Kelley, the Philadelphia member of Congress who had forwarded the testimonial, with sincere thanks:

> *"My Dear Sir:— When it comes to pass that a prophet becomes known in his own country — the wealth of censure is usually in striking contrast to the poverty of praise — commendation stimulates the mind to higher aims, but how few have the generosity to bestow it! — I have been so misunderstood — so misrepresented — so abused in this country simply for being true to my own, it pleases me to bask in the sunshine of your good will."* [21]

Train admitted that he had acted impulsively to defend the Union, but felt that it was pride that had inspired his conduct. Then, noting without any irony that "this is the first time I ever had occasion to write a political letter", Train let them know what was really on his mind:

> *"Observing that the riflemen* [sic] *aims above the mark he intends to hit, I point to the White House with the intention of lighting on the floor of Congress. Start fair and wonders are easily accomplished."* [22]

1. Edmund B. Sullivan, "George Francis Train: Knight of the Rueful Countenance" *The Rail Splitter* (April 1999), Vol. 4, No. 4.

2. George Francis Train, *Spread-Eagleism* (Derby & Jackson, New York, 1859), pp. 102–129.

3. *Ibid.*, pp. 134–144.

4. George Francis Train, *The Facts; or, At Whose Door Does the Sin (?) Lie?* (New York and London, 1860), quoted in Willis Thornton, *The Nine Lives of Citizen Train* (Greenberg, New York, 1948), p. 110.

5. *Ibid.*

6. Edmund B. Sullivan, above, n. 1.

7. George Francis Train, *Young America in Wall Street* (Derby & Jackson, New York, 1857), p. 340.

8. George Francis Train, *Train's Union Speeches* (T.B. Peterson & Brothers, Philadelphia, 1862), p. 31.

9. Quoted in Willis Thornton, above, n. 4.

10. George Francis Train, above, n. 8, pp. 50–51.

11. *Ibid.*, pp. 63–68.

12. *Ibid.*, pp. 68–70.

13. George Francis Train, *George Francis Train, Unionist, on T. Colley Grattan, Slanderer* (Lee & Shepard, Boston, 1862), p. 7.

14. *Ibid.*, p. 8.

15. *Ibid.*, pp. 47–48.

16. George Francis Train, above, n. 8, p. 82.

17. *Ibid.*, p. 83.

18. *London American*, May 21, 1862, reprinted in George Francis Train, above, n. 8, p. 57.

19. *Ibid.*, p. 61.

20. December 23, 1861.

21. Letter dated February 18, 1862, published by the *London American*, February 19, 1862, and reprinted in George Francis Train, above, n. 8, p. 85.

22. George Francis Train, above, n. 8, p. 85.

ELEVEN

"Thank God I am again in a civilized country!"

Even in jail Train could not be stopped from broadcasting his message. He preached to his fellow prisoners on "The Downfall of England" and continued his campaign. It's not clear how he managed to be released from debtors' prison despite his refusal to pay the fine. Perhaps by now the authorities realised that keeping Train locked up was more hassle than it was worth. On August 16 Train wrote triumphantly: "My friends insist upon my coming out. Claims all withdrawn, and I am off next week for America!"[1]

It was clear to Train by now that his tramway dreams were in ruins and his effectiveness in lobbying the Unionist caused had been severely diminished by the bitterness directed against him by the press. The jail sentence probably had been a welcome break for him. He was safe there, and untouchable. For a long time the dilemma of his situation had been a heavy burden to him. Sending his family out of harm's reach must have given him some relief.

The realisation that his views had probably put him in danger was always at the forefront of his thoughts: "The intense strain wore upon me to such an extent that I had an attack of insomnia, and almost lost my senses at times." He never went out unarmed, relying on a small cane for protection. He carried it under his arm, gripping it tightly so that he could whirl it around quickly if he was attacked from the rear.

Newspaper articles like that of the particularly vicious *Morning Chronicle* were enough to convince him that he was not safe. He had enough sense to realise that it was time to return home. Somehow it came to his intention that a vessel called *Mavrockadatis* was acting suspiciously. Train came to the not unreasonable conclusion that she was a blockade-runner "loaded with supplies for the Confederates, and that as soon as she was clear at sea she would make for a Southern port or for some rendezvous with a Confederate ship". He was convinced that its stated intention to sail to St John's, Newfoundland, was a ruse, and decided to try and frustrate these supposed blockade-runners any way he could. He decided to sail with the ship and wisely booked a passage under the name of "Oliver".

In his memoirs he also gave another reason for sailing on that ship. When the blockade-runner finally reached its Southern destination, besides frustrating its mission, Train intended to go directly to the leaders of the Confederacy in Richmond to see if anything could be done to end the war.

Leaving aside the fact that Train sailed with two contradictory aims, it is difficult to believe his uncorroborated assertion that he had an arrangement with President Lincoln and Secretary Seward to see what he could negotiate with the Confederate President Jefferson Davis that might end the devastating war.

However, it is not beyond the limits of plausibility that Train was associated with Davis, because Train's wife was a distant relative of his. Several other attempts had been made officially and unofficially. Train himself was convinced he could persuade Davis that they could expect no help from France and England and that in view of the North's considerable resources it was a hopeless struggle. He was sure he could show the Southern leaders that they would obtain far better terms now, rather than after a long and harrowing war.

Train had his own reasons for wanting to get home, too. Louisville was the heart of Confederate spy and smuggling activities. "A considerable number of women... many of them of high position in rebel society, and some of them outwardly professing to be loyal, were discovered to have been actively engaged in receiving and forwarding mails," the Judge Advocate General revealed in a report.[2] Train must have been concerned about what his Southern-sympathising wife was up to; certain rumours had already reached him suggesting that her support constituted more than just words.

In any case, all Train's alleged plans and hopes came to nothing. It turned out that the *Mavrockadatis* did indeed sail straight for Newfoundland. Seeing all his plans thwarted, Train took stock of his situation and made new ones. Though he only stayed in Newfoundland for one day, he was able to gather enough information to write a history of the colony. On his way home to Boston from St John's, Train travelled by way of St John's, New Brunswick. He stopped at Portland, Maine, and took the time to meet Curtis Guild of the Boston *Commercial Bulletin*. Guild was so impressed with Train that he agreed to publish his

Union speeches as well as his *History of Newfoundland*. Train was paid ten dollars a column for the history, which he later said was the only pay that he ever received from a newspaper or periodical for his work.

As he approached Boston, the *Daily Evening Traveler* heralded his imminent arrival:

> *"We observe that it is announced that this irrepressible Union ora-tor and embodiment of Young America is now en route for Boston and will arrive on Friday. The Prince of Wales' suite of rooms are reserved for his reception at the Revere House."*[3]

Everywhere he went Train was greeted by huge crowds of people cheer-ing him and demanding that he talk about his experiences in England. Train could be forgiven for believing that he was the "most popular American in public life."

Crowds flocked to Tremont Temple to hear Train on September 13. After being introduced by Mayor Wightman, Train began with a cry: "Thank God I am again in a civilised country; thank God I am again in a Christian land!" He passionately denied that England could be consid-ered the "mother country", insisting that "there is not more than one-tenth English blood among us". He called for a boycott of English goods and for Americans to ignore British opinions. "Let us think for our-selves," he concluded dramatically, "for we are a superior race."[4]

Train lost no time in getting into trouble. A mass meeting was held on October 6 at Faneuil Hall in response to Lincoln's September 22 Emancipation Proclamation. Senator Charles Sumner spoke in its sup-port. Though Train was pro-Union, he also was stubbornly anti-aboli-tion, but he went along to see what was going on. It was immediately obvious to Train that:

> *"Sumner was not a very effective speaker before mixed audiences, and could not have stood up for twenty minutes in the halls of London, where the greatest freedom of debate is indulged in, and where every speaker must be prepared to answer quickly and to the point any question that may be hurled at him, or to reply with sharpness and point to any retort that may come from the crowd that faces him."*

In short, poor Sumner was no match for Train. Sumner had hardly spo-ken for fifteen minutes when he challenged anyone to question him. Considering Sumner's poor speaking abilities, Train was astonished at the man's invitation. Of course, Train knew there was a chance he only meant it rhetorically, "but in England it would have been taken up at once, and Sumner would have been routed. The temptation was too much for me." To the apparent astonishment and embarrassment of Sumner and the committee on the platform, Train rose and said: "Mr. Sumner, when you have finished, I should like to speak a word."

As Sumner finished and was about to leave, Train climbed the platform. The moment he attempted to speak, the committee signalled to the band and the music drowned him out. When the committee members made a rush at Train in a valiant effort to stop him, a farcical confrontation followed and several members found themselves pushed off the stage. Train was arrested and taken to the Court Square police station and confined in the captain's private room. A large crowd had gathered in front of the police station demanding Train's release. When it had dispersed Train was allowed to leave, but he was furious at his treatment and immediately wrote a proclamation, "God Save the People!", which was published by Curtis Guild of the *Commercial Bulletin*. Train was smart enough to realise that this type of public speaking was his strength, despite the *Boston Transcript's* conclusion: "If these individuals were in the interest of any political party, they sadly damaged it by their rowdy conduct."[5]

He made a contract with Guild for a series of lectures in the North and West. His first lecture was given in the Academy of Music, New York. The general subject was the abolition question, as it related to the war between the States. Cassius M. Clay, of Kentucky, was chairman, much to the audience's disapproval, owing to his anti-slavery campaigning. Train was appalled at the audience's reaction and took charge of the meeting himself, urging them to be respectful:

> "I see that you do not like Mr. Clay; but he should have a fair chance. If Mr. Guild will arrange for a meeting at Cooper Institute to-morrow night, I will debate with Mr. Clay, and you can then fire at me cabbages or gold dollars, as you like. I propose the following subject for the discussion: American Slavery as a Stepping-stone from African Barbarism to Christian Civilisation; hence, it is a Divine Institution."

It was a smart move on Train's side. He had delivered a speech on the very same topic in London on March 12 and 19 earlier the same year, which had been published in pamphlet form.[6] Train had also corresponded with Victor Hugo on the subject.

Train related that the next evening, at Cooper Institute, a large audience packed the hall from door to stage. About $1,300 was taken at the box-office. He recalled that the following day's papers allotted several columns to the debate and that the London *Times:*

> "...considered it sufficiently important, even to Englishmen, to give a long account and editorial comments. It said that the honors of the debate had been with me, and gave a specimen of my repartee, which, it said, had swept Mr. Clay off his feet.
>
> Mr. Clay had referred in his speech to an interview he had had with President Lincoln, who was then hesitating as to issuing the Proclamation of Emancipation. Mr. Clay said, 'I told the President that I would not flesh my sword in the defense of Washington unless he issued a proclamation freeing the slaves.' My reply was: 'It is fair to assume that, in order to make Major-General Cassius M. Clay flesh his sword, the President will issue the proclamation.' There was loud laughter at this."

Actually, Clay was quite close to the President and advised him on the issues of emancipation and its implications for the Union cause. Three months later the President issued the Emancipation Proclamation.[7]

A few weeks after this debate Train wrote rather immodestly to a sympathetic group in London, saying:

> "I speak to four or five thousand at a time, and take $500 to $1,500 for an hour's talk... I am smashing up the Abolition Party here... I am too young to take Charles Sumner's place in the Senate, [he was 33] else I would be elected by acclamation."[8]

Not everybody shared in Train's self-belief. The Cleveland *Leader* was probably more accurate when it stated:

> "He told the English some sharp truths during and after the Trent excitement, for which we gave due credit, but since his return to this country he has given daily recurring proofs of his total absence of both decency and common sense. He is afflicted with diarrhea of words more than any person we have ever known." [9]

Throughout his time in London Train supported the Union as well as strongly defending slavery. At first glance this stance seems contradictory, but it was one shared by others. About this time President Lincoln told Horace Greeley of the *Tribune*:

> *"My paramount object in this struggle is to save the Union and is not either to save or destroy slavery. If I could save the Union without freeing any slaves I would do it; and if I could save it by freeing all the slaves I would do it; and if I could save it by freeing some and leaving others alone I would also do that...".*[10]

Like Lincoln, Train was prepared to accede to the South's demands on slavery if it meant that the Union could be saved. While they both wanted to save the Union at any cost, Train was indifferent to slavery, but Lincoln hated it.

As the war dragged on, Train's attitude changed dramatically. Horrified by its effects on the country as a whole, he began to search for some way to end it; some way both parties could settle their differences peacefully and stop the needless destruction of the country. As a measure of how desperate Train was, he even considered proposing that America embark on a foreign war as a means of restoring unity to the country. Later on in the year he proposed a plan for restoring the Union by assuming the Confederate debt and by paying to free all slaves.

Shortly after the debate with Clay, Train went to Washington where he dined with President Lincoln and several members of his cabinet at Secretary Seward's home on the momentous night of September 17. It was a pleasant affair, with the diners vying with each other to tell the most humorous anecdotes. Train was asked to describe some of the scenes of his recent travels. He told them about Chinese dinners and such like, to great amusement and laughter.

> *"In the very midst of the uproar the door was burst open, and Secretary Stanton appeared, his face white with emotion. In a choking voice, that was scarcely audible and would not have been heard had not every nerve in our bodies been strained to catch the momentous words we expected, he said: 'A battle is raging at Antietam! Ten thousand men have been killed, and the rebels are now probably marching on Washington!'"*

Stanton was quite wrong when he said that the rebels were endangering Washington. In fact, the battle ended as a stalemate in military terms. Despite this, it was a turning point in the Civil War. For some time the Confederate's string of successes had lowered the North's morale. As a result, President Lincoln had been forced to keep his Emancipation Proclamation on the backburner for fear of being seen to be seeking to enlist the support of slaves in what looked like an increasingly hopeless cause. When he reluctantly shelved the Proclamation, he did so vowing to issue it after the first Union victory.

He had to wait a while. Instead of victory, setback after setback followed. Finally the Confederates, under the command of General Lee, met a numerically superior Union force under General McClellan at Antietam Creek in Maryland on September 17, 1862. The battle raged all day long, resulting in roughly 11,000 casualties on each side and no decisive victory. The next day General Lee felt it prudent to withdraw; victory was McClellan's, at least superficially. Although little was achieved militarily, the North triumphed enormously in propaganda terms and much-needed new life was injected into the Union cause. The Union victory at Antietam, however slight it was, finally allowed President Lincoln to issue the Emancipation Proclamation on September 22, decreeing the freedom of all slaves in territory still in rebellion on January 1, 1863. For these two reasons it was one of the most important battles of the Civil War.

President Lincoln's momentous declaration introduced a new moral right into the war, possibly preventing any foreign intervention on the South's behalf. In one step he had cleverly taken the moral high ground. At the beginning of the war the North had fought to preserve the Union and the South had been portrayed as the underdog struggling to win its recognition as an independent nation. A victory for the North would mean the abolition of all slavery, while a Southern victory would ensure its continued existence.[11] A few days after Lincoln issued the Proclamation, Train wrote him the following congratulatory letter:

> "Revere House
> Boston
> Sept 25. 1862
>
> Dear President of the United States.
> Your Proclamation is the cleverest document issued this century.
> I understand it.
> God bless the nation
>
> Y.O.S.
> Geo. Francis Train"[12]

In a speech at Philadelphia, Train made a bitter attack against the English, calling them cowards, and even went as far as to insinuate that Lord Palmerston had poisoned Prince Albert as part of a plot to get the crown for himself. Needless to say, this crazy and entirely unfounded allegation provoked the wrath of Fleet Street, who had not forgotten Train; on October 25 *Punch* launched a counter-attack:

> *"The notorious Train, the would-be introducer to this side of the Atlantic of Yankee street-railways, Yankee puffs, and Yankee log-rolling having got off the rails here, gone to smash, and been taken back from White Cross Street to the United States for repairs, has been blowing off steam at Philadelphia, which condenses into a stream of dirty water aimed at England and the English...*
>
> *From this it is plain that the Train we had considered shivered to smithereens is on the rail again, with a vengeance. It is evident that, however familiar with smashes, neither this Train nor its Yankee drivers, have any notion of a break [sic] or it would have been pulled up short in its rabid and random career."*[13]

It also included an epigrammatic rhyme that Train no doubt appreciated; he was in the habit of writing his own witty poems and sending them out to friends and newspapers.

"A LITTLE QUESTION

The ribald bankrupt Yankee Train,
Declares us English fools and knaves;
Sneaks, who when struck won't strike again,
Gluttons and blockheads, brutes and slaves.

Swears that Lord Palmerston would make
His way, by poison, to the Crown;
But Train has hopes that Pat will wake,
And tread the English tyrant down.

The fool were fun, if not so coarse,
So were the patriots of the North
Who cheered and cheered till they were hoarse
The idiot trash he bellowed forth.

> We've crawled, no doubt, we Saxon worms,
> And have been trampled for our pains;
> Is it worth while to keep on terms
> With friends who cheer such terms as Train's?" [14]

Many people who had applauded Train's heroic defence of the Union in England and welcomed such a prominent supporter home must have wondered why the healthy 33-year-old had not enlisted in the war on his return. Years later Train defended his pacifist stance:

> *"I took no part in the war on the battlefield, because as soon as I looked into the causes of the war and its continuance, I saw that it was a contract war. I came back to this country fully expecting to serve. I had been assured of a high commission; but could not conscientiously take part in a struggle in which thousands of lives were being sacrificed to greed. Such was my honest belief, and such was my course."*

Train's actions, or lack of action, led to the Union defender being labelled as a "Copperhead" – someone who opposed the war and aided the South. His conciliatory attitude towards the South landed him in trouble in several other places besides Boston. He was shot at in Dayton and arrested in St Louis by General Curtis. An attempt to assassinate him was again made at Alton in Illinois and he was attacked by a bayonet in Davenport.[15]

At the same time, Train had not forgotten his political ambitions. He was out of his depth, though, and had not got a clue as to how to go about kick-starting his political career. He was too impatient to start at the bottom of the political ladder and work his way up. Instead, he spoke of vague plans to run for the Presidency in 1864. In any case he had no practical plan of action for any political career. In a letter to Francis O. J. Smith, a Maine politician and campaigner for peace on any terms, Train's political naivety is all too clear.

> *"Parker House,*
> *Boston, Nov. 6, 1862.*
>
> *Dear F. O. J. S.:*
> *Hurrah for our side. Hurrah for the next U.S. Senator from Maine!*
> *New York, New Jersey, and the West! and hurrah for the 53,000*

Traitors *in Mass. I did my best, but the forces of the people's party had not your brain nor pluck nor that of*

Sincerely,

Geo. Francis Train

Much love to the babies and regards to the Fair Nellie F.O.J.S. Come and see me at the St. Nicholas, N.Y."[16]

---

[1] Quoted in Willis Thornton, *The Nine Lives of Citizen Train* (Greenberg, New York, 1948), p. 126.

[2] *Report of the Judge Advocate General* on "The Order of American Knights" (Washington, 1864), quoted in Willis Thornton, *ibid.*, p. 128.

[3] Quoted in Willis Thornton, above, n. 1, p. 129.

[4] *Ibid.*

[5] *Ibid.*, p. 131.

[6] George Francis Train, "Train's Speeches in England on Slavery and Emancipation; Also his great speech on 'Pardoning of Traitors'" (Philadelphia, 1862).

[7] It was said that Clay took up so much of Lincoln's time with his advice on the war that the President decided the Union cause would benefit by Clay's absence: Clay was sent to Russia to serve as U.S. Minister there. See David Herbert Donald, *Lincoln* (Jonathan Cape, London, 1995), p. 413.

[8] Quoted in Willis Thornton, above, n. 1, p. 131.

[9] *Ibid.*, pp. 131–132.

[10] "Lincoln" in John A. Garraty and Mark C. Carnes, eds, *American National Biography* (Oxford University Press, Oxford, 1999), Vol. 13, p. 670, citing Basler, Vol. 5, pp. 388–389.

[11] Paul S. Boyer, ed, *The Oxford Companion to United States History* (Oxford University Press, Oxford, 2001), p. 131.

[12] George Francis Train to President Abraham Lincoln, September 25, 1862. The letter is now in the Abraham Lincoln Papers at the Library of Congress, Washington D.C., U.S.A.

[13] *Punch*, October 25, 1862, courtesy of *Punch* magazine, London.

[14] *Ibid.*

[15] "George Francis Train" in Thomas W. Herringshaw, *Prominent Men and Women of the Day* (A.B. Gehman & Co., New York, 1888).

[14] Quoted in Willis Thornton, above, n. 1, p. 134.

The Transcontinental railroad's importance to the development of America cannot be underestimated. It was certainly one of the greatest industrial achievements in American history. Some historians believe its creation surpassed the importance as a development of the atomic bomb or the Apollo moon flights. What is certain is that, along with the telegraph, it made the creation of modern America possible. It acted as a backbone – a vital part of the country enabling a unified nationwide economy and culture to emerge and flourish.

The story behind the railroad's development is almost the stuff of legend, with larger than life characters determining the fate of a nation. It has all the ingredients of a bestseller and numerous scenarios that even the most imaginative and creative novelists would be hard pressed to dream up. It was a great race, where thousands of men battled with merciless weather, torturous country, hostile Indians and one another against a backdrop of financial and political intrigue in high places.

Although Train dramatically claims that he first suggested its construction as far back as the mid-1850s, he certainly had no monopoly on the idea. As early as 1832, many wanted to connect California with the rest of the Union. In the 1840s a passable wagon road, known as the California Trail, was established. A wealthy merchant named Asa Whitney relentlessly campaigned for such a railroad in the 1840s, writing and broadcasting pamphlets. In 1845 he determinedly lobbied Congress for a grant of land that would enable him to start the road. He asked modestly for a strip of land sixty miles wide along the proposed route from Lake Michigan across Dakota, Wyoming, Idaho and Oregon to the Pacific.

Not surprisingly, Congress turned Whitney down flat. He gained a reputation as a crazy visionary. He lost his entire fortune promoting his "wild" scheme and wound up making a living selling milk from his own dairy in Washington. Perhaps a more modest proposal would have been accepted, or at least considered, since it must have been clear to Congress that the idea had some worth. Other visionaries met the same lack of success. D.C. Josiah Perham, a wool merchant who invented the railroad "excursion trip", pushed vainly for what was popularly nicknamed the "Perham's Peoples' Pacific".

Another visionary, Theodore Dehone Judah, also had a wild scheme for a railroad across the desert and over the Rockies. He was more successful than the others. In time he became the chief engineer, lobbyist, railroader and surveyor for the Central Pacific. He did a great deal to make the transcontinental railway a reality, but sadly never lived to see it completed.

By 1850 it was becoming increasingly obvious that a railroad was necessary to bridge the gap between the eastern and western United States. In early 1851, J.J. Warner's *Report on Railroads to the Senate of California* stated:

> "[A] Railroad, from some point on the Mississippi, or its tributaries, to some point on the bay of San Francisco, is the best route that can be adopted for the purpose of securing the Commerce of China and India... to open a great national highway from California to the Atlantic coast, [and] would be a greater defence and protection than all other military works. It would also be the means of great daily intercourse between the East and West coast of this Republic... to prevent those sectional feelings which have ever been the destruction of wide-extended governments... [I]t is the duty of this Legislature to encourage the speedy building of a Railroad from the Atlantic to the Pacific, across the territory of the United States."[1]

The December 1, 1851 *Report of the Superintendent of the Census to the House of Representatives* was pessimistic:

> "The routes proposed in this great work are almost as numerous as the persons who claim the merit of having first suggested and brought forward the scheme of thus completing the chain of railroad connexion between the Atlantic and Pacific coasts of the Union. Although the importance of such a work to the prosperity of the nation cannot be doubted, there is reason to suppose that many years will elapse before the resources of the country will be found sufficient for its accomplishment. No scientific survey of any

*route west of the frontier of Missouri has been made, but it is not
probable that any could be found that would bring the line of travel between the Mississippi and the ocean within the limit of 1,600
miles. The natural obstacles to be overcome are the Rocky mountains and the Sierra Nevada, the deserts between the Missouri and
the former chain, and those of the great basin, the flying sands, and
the want of timber. Further explorations may lead to the discovery
of means to overcome these difficulties... The only question, then,
affecting the probability of the construction of the Pacific railroad
is that of practicability. This can only be determined by thorough
surveys of some or all of the routes proposed, from the valley of the
Rio Grande, the Arkansas, the Missouri, and the upper Mississippi.
If this road were completed, and the route continued westward by
steamship to Calcutta, it would reduce the time required for the
circuit of the globe, by the American overland route, to ninety-three
days."* [2]

Almost two years later, the project looked to be a certainty at last.
Putnam's Monthly Magazine wrote in November 1853:

*"A railroad from the Mississippi to California or Oregon is a
foregone conclusion. Stupendous as the enterprise seems, rivaling
in grandeur and surpassing in usefulness any work that the
genius of man has hitherto undertaken... it has been decided that
it must be built. Mr [Asa]Whitney, pioneer of the scheme, said
long ago that it should be... the Memphis and St Louis
Conventions have said that it should be; and the newspapers have
said it must be, which settles the question. Surveying parties,
appointed by the Government to explore the routes are already on
the ground...".* [3]

By now people realised just how important good transport links were
to provide them with the means to develop the vast, previously
untouchable, hinterlands. When the British tore up his tramways, Train
responded in kind by promising that he would build a railway across the
Rocky Mountains and the Great American Desert, which would ruin
the old trade routes across Egypt to China and Japan. He pointed out
that such a route would be far shorter than the old one, and would see
a flow of traffic across the American continent for Asia. Years earlier he
had written about the Panama Railroad across the Panama isthmus,

wondering why a transcontinental railway had not been constructed. "If private enterprise has done all this, what may not Government accomplish in carrying out... [the] grand project of joining [by rail] the Atlantic and Pacific Oceans?"[4]

Joseph C.G. Kennedy, Superintendent of the 1860 Census, reported to Congress that:

> "Previous to 1850 by far the greater portion of railroads constructed were in the States bordering the Atlantic, and... were for the most part isolated lines, whose limited traffics were altogether local... [T]he internal commerce of the country was conducted almost entirely through water lines, natural and artificial, and over ordinary highways.
>
> The period of settlement of California marks really the commencement of the new era in the physical progress of the United States. The vast quantities of gold it produced imparted new life and activity to every portion of the Union, particularly the western States, the people of which, at the commencement of 1850, were thoroughly aroused as to the value and importance of railroads."[5]

There were three main events that led to the construction of the Pacific railroad. First, California and Nevada's population increased, owing to the vast riches from the gold rush in northern California and the silver strikes in Nevada. This resulted in the building of the railroad through Nevada and also towards Sacramento in northern California. Second, Congress had many options of routes to consider due to new surveying technology and the rise in the number of railroad specialists. Third, the secession of the South from the Union in the Civil War removed the Southern politicians in Congress that were lobbying for a southern route and allowed the North to build the railroad without their interference.

The North's principal reason for building the railroad was to bind California to the Union so that it would not secede or be taken over by England. They also hoped "to facilitate the movement of troops, guns, and supplies over the plains in a continuing war with the Indians".[6] Even before the war the project had such a high degree of support in Congress that Senator Butler of North Carolina had declared: "The Pacific Railroad project comes nearer a subject of deification than anything I ever heard in the Senate."[7]

The Civil War brought the great railway debate to a conclusion and finally Congress passed the Pacific Railway Act in July 1862, incorporating the Union Pacific Railroad Company to build west from Omaha, Nebraska, and the Central Pacific Railroad Company to build east from Sacramento, California, until the two met. It also permitted a telegraph line to be built adjacent to the tracks, empowering each railroad: "to lay out, locate, construct, furnish, maintain, and enjoy a continuous railroad and telegraph with the appurtenances...".[8]

It was an enormous undertaking. Whatever way one looked at it, even the least expensive proposed routes amounted to one year's Federal budget. Huge public subsidies were provided, since it was clear that it would be impossible to raise the huge sums of money needed from private investors alone. The Union Pacific Railroad had an authorised capitalisation of $100,000,000 of stock in 100,000 lots of $1,000 face value. No individual was to hold more than two hundred such shares. This requirement in itself must have acted as a deterrent to private investors in the early stages, since it limited their control on the railroad. The government offered to underwrite $50,000,000 of bonds to be issued in sections. Whenever $2,000,000 had been subscribed and ten per cent of that amount had actually been paid in, the corporation was to be organised.

Congress guaranteed that the Central Pacific and the Union Pacific would end up racing each other by offering government bonds and land grants for every mile of track each company built. The Pacific Railway Act gave each company government-guaranteed bonds issued at a rate of $16,000 for each mile of track laid in the flat plains, $32,000 for each mile of track laid in the Great Basin, and $48,000 for each mile of track laid in the mountains. It also provided for each company to receive ten sections (6,400 acres) of public land grants, mineral rights excluded, on each side of the track for each mile of track built. The faster and further the competing railways were laid down, the more they gained. This government provision attracted several powerful investors.

In 1864 a second Pacific Railway Act was passed increasing the land grants for each company to twenty sections per mile. In total, the companies received thirty-three million free acres of land. The second Pacific Railway Act also gave the companies rights to the iron and coal deposits on the land granted and moved the federal loans to second-mortgage status so that the Union Pacific and Central Pacific could issue first-mortgage bonds for sale to private investors.

Train jumped at the chance to have a hand in organising and building the Pacific Railroad. He addressed meetings, appeared before Congressional committees, lobbied individuals and pitched the scheme to potential investors. Despite the liberal government inducements, investors were initially very slow to come forward. Perhaps it was this reluctance that encouraged Train to maintain until the day he died that he virtually financed the railroad single-handedly. He says he personally approached some of the leaders of the financial world in New York, such as Commodore Vanderbilt, Commodore Garrison, William B. Astor, Moses H. Grinnell, Marshall O. Roberts, and others, and told them of his plans, trying to enlist their support and capital. They refused point blank. One of these financial barons (Train refrained from ever saying who) advised him:

> *"Train, you have reputation enough now. Why do something that will mar it? You are known all over the world as the Clipper-Ship King. This is enough glory for one man. If you attempt to build a railway across the desert and over the Rocky Mountains, the world will call you a lunatic."*

Train's claim that the $150,000 which he pledged to the railway was "the pint of water that started the great wheel of the machinery" was definitely an exaggeration. It should be remembered that only ten per cent had to be paid up front in cash; in other words, fifteen thousand dollars. In reality, the prescribed two-million-dollar level of stock subscription was not reached until October 30, 1863, and only two hundred thousand dollars of that was actually in cash, mostly put up by Thomas Clark Durant. Other subscribers included Samuel J. Tilden, Thurlow Weed, Augustus Belmont, and Brigham Young (whose son, Joseph, helped to survey one of the routes through the mountains).[9]

Although Train's claim that he "organised the Union Pacific" was also far off the mark, he was an important part of the team. He worked closely with his friend Thomas C. Durant, the railway's real builder and its chief manager during construction. Train's great achievement was as a sort of public relations guru. At that he was peerless. He galvanised the press and they, in turn, public opinion. He also, in part, created the Crédit Mobilier as a means of financing the railway. A few years later this organisation caused a major scandal, after Train had been squeezed out, but without it construction of the railway might have been substantially delayed.

While in France, Train had studied the new methods of finance devised by Émile and Isaac Perrère: "These shrewd and ingenious men, finding that old methods could not be used to meet many demands of modern times, invented entirely new ones which they organized into two systems known as the Crédit Mobilier and the Crédit Foncier." In essence, the new practices were based on the premise of sourcing capital from the public in small amounts rather than from a few rich individuals. Though this is common now, it was a revolutionary concept then. Train was determined to introduce this new style of finance into America. Now he had his chance. It was a perfect means of financing the railway.

He found that a Bill had been passed in Pennsylvania in 1859 allowing an institution called the Pennsylvania Fiscal Agency, owned by Duff Green, to hold a general licence to place loans, market stocks and conduct a general banking business. Further examination proved that it was perfect for his needs. Train, acting as agent for Durant and Oakes Ames, bought the charter of this corporation for $26,645. He immediately resold it to them, after getting its name legally changed to Crédit Mobilier of America, at a cost of $500. For this transaction, Train received $25,000 in cash and a similar amount in stock in the new company. Durant became principal stockholder and president.[10] Train took no actual part in running it, nor was he involved in the controversy involving it years later.

Characteristically, Train preferred to make the deal, take his profit or commission, and leave the actual operation to others. Nevertheless, he was a key instigator of corporate development in America. Neither of the vital jobs of financial or practical administration in the building and operating of the railroad had any appeal to Train. He was not one of the practical railroad-builders. It was Durant who actually drove the construction onwards. Train was a gifted public relations man, an effective motivator of the masses – the spark that lit the fire.

In October 1863 the Union Pacific was formally incorporated under the terms of the previous year's Act. General John Adams Dix was elected President, and Durant Vice-President. General Dix was a veteran of the War of 1812, a man of known quantity, who actually had railroad experience as president of the Chicago and Rock Island. Dix had added a creditable Civil War record to his good work as Secretary of the Treasury. By all accounts he was an honest and straightforward fellow. Perhaps if he had been able to play an active role in the railroad, some of the later scandals might have been avoided. But, like most of the key players in the project, he preferred to stay in the East, where the Union Pacific offices were "probably the first in New York, beautiful with paintings and statuary, and enlivened with the singing of birds".[11]

As a result, when breaking of ground for the first mile of the Union Pacific west of the Missouri took place at the village of Omaha on December 2, 1863, the only one of those closely connected with its financing to be present was George Francis Train. That afternoon, amid great excitement and before a large crowd from Omaha and Council Bluffs, the great undertaking was formally dedicated:

> "...with all the pomp and ceremony that the importance of the event demanded. After invoking a divine blessing for the success of the enterprise, Governor Saunders stepped forward, grasped a spade, and amid the thunder of artillery and the deafening cheers of the enthusiastic assembly, removed the first spadefull of earth... The ceremony closed with addresses of a most eloquent and enthusiastic character."[12]

Train made the concluding speech. In itself, it was a significant event. He played to the crowd, saying that he just happened to be in the vicinity and thought he would attend. It would have been nearer to the truth to say he would not have missed the ground-breaking ceremony for the world. Train predicted the railroad's completion by 1870 (it was finished actually in 1869) and forecast a brilliant future for Omaha and the Northwest.

> "The official business is over, and as I happen to be lying around loose in this part of the country... it gives me a chance to meet some of the live men of Nebraska at the inauguration of the grandest enterprise under God, the world has ever witnessed.
>
> America is the stage, the world is the audience of to-day. While one act of the drama represents the booming of the cannon on the Rapidan, the Cumberland, and the Rio Grande, sounding the death knell of rebellious war, the next scene records the booming of cannon on both sides of the Missouri to celebrate the grandest work of peace that ever attracted the energies of man. The great Pacific Railway is commenced, and if you knew the man who has hold of the affair as well as I do, no doubt would ever arise as to its speedy completion. The President shows his good judgment in locating the road where the Almighty placed the signal station, at the entrance

of a garden seven hundred miles in length and twenty broad...

> *Before the first century of the nation's birth, we may see in the New York depot some strange Pacific railway notice:*

> *'European passengers for Japan will please take the night train.*
> *Passengers for China this way.*
> *African and Asiatic freight must be distinctly marked: For Peking via San Francisco.'*[13]

The crowd hung on every word he spoke. No doubt Train savoured the moment for many years to come.

> *"The Pacific railroad is the nation and the nation is the Pacific railway. Labor and capital shake hands today... The two united mark the era of progress... Congress gives something toward building this great national thoroughfare — not much, but something; say a loan of government credit for thirty years, for $16,000 a mile and 20,000,000 acres of land. But what is that in these times?...*

> *My idea is that the shares, $1,000, are too high. They should be reduced to $100, and subscriptions should be opened in every town of five hundred inhabitants. Let the laboring man have one share; make it the peoples' road in reality...*

> *Immigration will soon pour into these valleys. Ten millions of emigrants will settle in this golden land in twenty years. If I had not lost all my energy, ambition, and enterprise, I would take hold of this immigration scheme, but the fact is I have gone too fast, and to-day am the best played-out man in the country."*[14]

There was laughter. Standing there listening to him speak, nothing must have seemed impossible to his audience. It was "the finest address I have ever heard on such an occasion. He was more of a success in this line than in the practical details of railroad-building," wrote J. Sterling Morton, one of those present.[15] On the day following the ground-breaking *The Nebraskan* gave a none-too measured assessment of Train. "The raciest, liveliest, best-natured and most tip-top speech ever delivered west of the Missouri," it called his address.

> *"An encyclopedia of knowledge, a walking library, a modern miracle, is George Francis Train. Is he played out? Has he gone to seed? What is to be the future of his brilliant talents? These are questions*

*that Train should seriously and solemnly ponder. He has visited all
the countries of the world, and having a prodigious memory, has
probably the largest fund of available practical knowledge of any
man in America. And he is still a young man — 33 years. The Train
of ideas sometimes lacks the coupling-chains."* [16]

Papers around the world were not so kind. They ridiculed him as either
a madman or a visionary. Among those newspapers was the *Hong-kong
Press*, which said that it was generally thought that Train was a little "off"
during his visit to China in 1855–56 and that this speech predicting a
railway across the Rocky Mountains clearly proved that he was both
visionary and mad. On his journey around the world in 1870, a year
after the completion of the railway, Train went out of his way to pay a
visit to the editor of the paper:

> *"I stepped into the office of the Hongkong paper and asked for the
> editor. When he came out, I asked him to show me the file of his
> paper containing my Omaha speech. He brought it out, and we
> turned to the column. 'Do you know Train?' he asked me. 'Why, I
> am Train,' I said, 'and it seems that you did not know me in Hong-
> kong in '55–'56. I have just come through the Rocky Mountains
> over that road."*

The newspaper's editor was, in fact, close to the truth. As events
showed, for the first time in his life, Train was in danger of going off the
tracks completely.

---

[1]   Quoted in Rebecca Cooper Winter, "Eastward to Promontory":
    http://www.cprr.org/Museum/Eastward.html#Construction of the CPRR

[2]   *Ibid.*

[3]   *Ibid.*

4   George Francis Train, *Young America in Wall Street* (Derby & Jackson, New York, 1857), p. 332.

5   Quoted in Rebecca Cooper Winter, above, n. 1.

6   *Ibid.*

7   Quoted in Willis Thornton, *The Nine Lives of Citizen Train* (Greenberg, New York, 1948), p. 140.

8   Quoted in Rebecca Cooper Winter, above, n. 1.

9   Willis Thornton, above, n. 7, p. 141.

10 Wesley S. Griswold, *A Work of Giants* (Frederick Muller, London, 1962), pp. 101–102.

11 Willis Thornton, above, n. 7, p. 144.

12 Harrison Johnson, *Johnson's History of Nebraska* (Henry Gibson, Omaha, 1880), p. 116.

13 Joseph Nichols, *Condensed History of the Construction of the Union Pacific Railroad* (Kloop, Bartlett & Company, Omaha, 1892), pp. 51–53.

14 *Ibid.*, pp. 55–58.

15 J. Sterling Morton, *Illustrated History of Nebraska* (Jacob North & Co., Lincoln, c. 1907).

16 December 4, 1863, reproduced in Willis Thornton, above, n. 7, p. 146.

Train was his own worst enemy. When he started to dabble in politics and various political causes, he neglected his various business enterprises. Train's first real dalliance with American politics came about in 1864, at the Democratic convention of that year. The party had split into rival factions in 1860. Party members who wanted to carry on the war had gone to the Republican convention in Baltimore and helped to nominate the Union candidate, Lincoln.

A "Radical-Democratic" convention had already been held at Cleveland and had nominated General Fremont on an anti-administration ticket. The remainder of the Democratic Party, and a disgruntled group calling themselves Peace Democrats, assembled at Chicago. Their opponents called them "Copperheads" because some wore copper pennies as identity badges. This soon became the generic name for any Northerners who opposed the war. They had a more conciliatory attitude towards the South than the Republicans.[1]

Although a majority of Peace Democrats supported the war to save the Union, a strong and active minority openly came out against it, asserting that the Republicans had provoked the South into secession and were now waging the war in order to establish their own dominion, suppress civil and State's rights, and impose racial equality; they argued that military means had failed and would never restore the Union. For any number of reasons besides these, they opposed the war and wanted a compromise. Disturbed by the infringement of civil liberties and the needless bloodshed, they believed that a negotiated settlement was preferable to war.

The party was strongest in the Midwest, an area with strong ties to the South. The Lincoln administration's treatment of dissenting voices provoked strong feelings of resentment, as did the Emancipation Proclamation. The Peace Democrats' fortunes fluctuated as the war progressed. When things were going badly for the Union, larger numbers of people were willing to contemplate the prospect of making peace with the South; when things were going well, their support fell away. They had to defend themselves constantly against charges of disloyalty to the Union. Revelations that some members had ties with pro-South secret societies, such as the Knights of the Golden Circle, led to the entire party being tarred with the same brush.[2]

Actions of opponents to the war were a huge problem for the Lincoln administration. They aided the South by discouraging enlisting in the North, opposing the draft, and even helping Confederate prisoners to escape. Their candidate had little chance of winning the presidential election and *Harper's Weekly* was right when it wrote in 1864 that "it matters little who is nominated there, because the convention represents opposition to the war, and its candidate cannot escape the fate of his position".[3] They were all labelled Southern sympathisers and accordingly despised by the public.

The most prominent Copperhead leader was Clement L. Vallandigham, a recently returned exile, who was immediately elected as the Ohio delegate to the convention. This resulted in the branding of the whole proceeding as a Copperhead event. Train, armed with a proxy from Nebraska, hoped to nominate General Dix for President and Admiral Farragut for Vice-President, but he was not permitted to take his seat. Undeterred, Train set up his own headquarters at the Sherman House Hotel and began to proclaim his views, opposing both McClellan and Lincoln in various articles, pamphlets and newspapers. His response to a hostile editorial in a Philadelphia newspaper was vehement:

> "Many thanks for your complimentary editorial... You open with 'The Abolitionists have drawn a prize in the political lottery.' That's so! You close with 'What has happened to change his opinions?' Let me reply. I supposed the Democratic party would have had sense enough to come over to me. How could they expect to come over to the T.P. [Treason Party, i.e. the McClellan Democrats] platform? It had three planks: STATE RIGHTS, that is SECESSION; FREE TRADE, that is DESTRUCTION; REPUDIATION, that is INFAMY... Fire a stone into a pack and the hound that is hit is sure to howl."[4]

Train made a particularly arch comment about the out-of-office politicians:

> "Why wax they so exceeding wroth?
> Their feet are not inside the trough." [5]

The Chicago *Tribune,* loyal to Lincoln, attacked Train viciously as "a singular gaseous compound of vulgarity, vanity, and stupidity, done up in no attractive form and labeled 'George Francis Train.'... a peripatetic humbug."[6]

The New York *Evening Post* also described his political activities, but in words which raise suspicions that he wrote the report himself:

> *"Mr. Train worked alone. He seemed an island. But a floating island. Delegates came and went. One day the convention was in his hands. Then Dean Richmond and August Belmont would roll out their five thousand dollar checks... There are witnesses all over the country who will do Mr. Train the justice to say he did his best to preserve the democratic party from destruction... Bulletin after Bulletin, and Manifesto after Manifesto, were thrown off, written by Mr. Train while the room was full of people... Here are a few of the most important Mottoes, Squibs and Pasquinades. . .".*[7]

The telltale style and phrases, such as the "floating island", strongly suggest that Train was trying to run the convention while covering it for the *Evening Post* at the same time.

An almost daily flood of Train's words was reported in newspapers, leaflets, and his widely-distributed "manifestoes". The most important of these, which he published himself, proclaimed the "impeachment" of President Lincoln for the widening of his executive powers.[8] Among the list of charges were indictments that Habeas Corpus had been suspended and that freedom of speech and of the press no longer existed. For these and other offences, Train impeached President Lincoln on general grounds of "Perjury".

There was an element of truth in Train's accusations. Many Americans were disturbed by the curtailment of civil liberties by the Lincoln administration, including prominent citizens such as former President Franklin Pierce, who as early as 1862 said that he hoped the next campaign would be waged "on the great issue of Executive usurpation against the Constitution, against freedom of speech and of the press, against personal liberty".[9]

As the convention progressed with its nomination of General George B. McClellan, it became clear to Train that he could not hope to influence it, so he returned to what he excelled at, namely drawing a crowd and holding them in his grip. A group of Irish delegates from the West who, like Train, were excluded from the convention, gathered in front of Sherman House and shouted for Train. He fed their appetites:

> "They bought us out with British gold... Thank God, I am no politician. I have not the heart to sell the noble Irish race out to that base Government that has treated them like dogs for a thousand years. Oh! Irishmen, sons of Erin, I sympathize with your misfortunes.
>
> Delegates from the territories! mark every man in the Convention! Put these words with a red hot iron on his forehead — Sold out for thirty pieces of silver!"[10]

Disregarding Train's protestations that he was not a politician, The New York *Evening Post* paid tribute to his political skills: "one of the most conspicuous and active of the politicians at Chicago was the celebrated Mr. Train..."[11] Overall, however, Train's efforts were not very successful. For a start, he was even more bitterly opposed to McClellan than he was to Lincoln. Train considered himself anti-Copperhead, as shown by his introduction to an anti-McClellan speech, which he distributed later:

> "Mr. Train's single-handed fight against the Copperhead party at Chicago... is talked over every table in the nation. He beat the English on his Horse Railways, which makes him one of the richest men in the country, and he is breaking up the Copperheads, which makes him one of the boldest champions of Liberty in the land."[12]

Despite his best efforts he continued to be called a "damned Copperhead" owing to his other actions and public statements. Originally, the term "Copperhead" was used to describe a person who actively sympathised with the South and worked in the North for the benefit of the South. As the war progressed, it became a derogatory label for anyone who criticised the war effort in any way. Train was even ordered out of St Louis by General Curtis.

The Copperhead Vallandigham ruined whatever chance McClellan might have had. The party adopted a stance calling the war an experiment and a failure. Some extreme Copperheads even planned armed uprisings. Although McClellan won the nomination easily, repudiated Vallandigham's platform and openly declared his support for the war effort, the damage was done. The country was in no mood to be told that so many had been killed in a vain cause – the Democrats were facing defeat.[13]

Train not only demanded that McClellan step down, but issued a call for another convention in his Fifth and Last Manifesto:

> *"On the 19th of October, the day Cornwallis surrendered to Washington, at the Academy of Music in New York, at the great People's Convention, (adjourned from Buffalo 22nd September), the Council of the Eagles will nominate, and the Eagles in November will elect under the Constitution, the next President of the United States; under this regulation – Equal Justice to all, Favors to Friends Alone."*[14]

This convention never came about, but that did not deter Train from running for the office of President. He campaigned against the leading candidates, Abraham Lincoln and George McClellan, as an Independent. He kept heckling McClellan, in particular, through letters published in the daily newspapers. "Your election on the platform they have placed you on is impossible," began a typical open letter.

> *"There is one way you can show yourself a patriot and help save the Union. Retire in favor of the coming man, and accept the position of Secretary of War or Lieutenant-General of the American Army. Otherwise you destroy yourself forever, and carry down with you the largest load of passengers that ever entrusted their fortunes on board of one ship."*[15]

As the letters and speeches appeared, they were collected in widely circulated pamphlets that intrigued but sometimes puzzled voters. The Owl Club of Rahway, New Jersey, for instance, wrote to Train on September 23:

> *"We have noticed your course at Chicago, and believe that you are working out an idea for the benefit of all, yet we do not understand your motive in opposing Mr. Lincoln one day and General McClellan the next. Are you in the field with another candidate?"*[16]

The Club invited Train to speak to them and enlighten them. He accepted gladly, in words that hinted at his eagerness to be elected President.

"I am breaking out all over with ideas of what should be done, and I shall feel better by having an earnest talk on passing events. This time I shall not come out to laugh and joke, as I did before, but to ask your serious attention to my plan for setting up and commencing anew. I will speak on this condition and no other. That is, independent of party action. *Our ship is in the breakers. The Life Boat! The Life Boat!"* [17]

Some time later, Train did speak in New Jersey. The lecture was a great success, despite the fact that the audience was populated by leading figures of the opposing parties he attacked.

Just as Train had predicted, McClellan barely carried a state, but he polled a very respectable 1,802,237 votes against Lincoln's 2,213,665. This outcome was an accurate reflection of a large segment of the population's concerns and McClellan did surprisingly well. If Train got even a single vote, it is not recorded. The failure had no lasting effect on him, however; among the guests at President Lincoln's Inaugural Ball on March 6, 1865 were "the rich eccentric, George Francis Train and his beautiful wife". [18]

While the attendance of a Copperhead – a peace monger, a man who had openly opposed Lincoln and actually brazenly demanded his impeachment, and then had the audacity to enter the Presidential race against him – and his beautiful wife, a known southern sympathiser, if not an activist, may have raised a few eyebrows amongst Train's fellow guests, he was not bothered with the irony. George Francis Train was among the powerful movers and shakers of the nation, where he felt he belonged.

Train became involved in politics again in October 1865. This time he showed his support for an independent Ireland by speaking to a Fenian convention in Philadelphia. Once again Train was drawn to the political underdog: first it had been the Australian miners, then the Italian Carbonari, and now the Fenians. He never passed up on any opportunity to speak, anywhere, at any time, and on almost any subject. Standing before a crowd was like an addiction.

On the evening of Wednesday, October 18, 1865, Train spoke before the assembled "Fenian Congress" and the "Fenian Chiefs", an audience of six thousand people at the Philadelphia Academy of Music. The "distinguished lecturer" was introduced by Lieutenant-Colonel Roberts, President of the Central Council.

"Ladies and gentlemen: –, I have the honor to introduce to you this

evening the distinguished lecturer, who speaks as a free, enlight-
ened American citizen, in behalf of Irish Republicanism.
[Applause.] He is the embodiment, I trust in Heaven, of the senti-
ment that animates the heart of every true American, for liberty in
every quarter of the globe. Allow me to introduce to you George
Francis Train."[19]

When the deafening cheering subsided, Train stepped forward, dressed in "lavender kids, white vest, dress coat, and brass buttons",[20] with his hat in his hand. For the next two hours he spoke on "Irish independence and English neutrality", adding his support to the cause. He also predicted another rebellion in Australia before rounding of his speech with a rally cry of "Ireland for the Irish!" His speech went down well with the receptive audience and all proceeds were donated to the Irish cause, as were the monies raised from publication of the speech in pamphlet form.

---

[1] http://www.civilwarhome.com/copperheads.htm

[2] "Copperheads" in *The Reader's Digest Family Encyclopedia of American History* (Reader's Digest Association, New York, 1975), p. 296.

[3] *Harper's Weekly*, September 3, 1864, quoted in Willis Thornton, *The Nine Lives of Citizen Train* (Greenberg, New York, 1948), p. 149.

[4] From a letter to the editor of *The Age*, October 29, 1864, in the American Memory Collection, Library of Congress.

[5] From a letter to "Gen. Geo. B. McClellan, the War Candidate of the Peace Platform", printed in the New York *Evening Post*, dated September 19, 1864, reproduced in *George Francis Train in Cleaning Out the Copperheads follows up Geo. B. McClellan with a Sharp Stick* (American News Co., New York, 1864), p. 7.

[6] Willis Thornton, above, n. 3, p. 150.

[7] Special Correspondent, "Geo. Francis Train in Chicago" in the *Evening Post*, dated September 4, 1864, reproduced in *George Francis Train in Cleaning Out the Copperheads follows up Geo. B. McClellan with a Sharp Stick*, above, n. 5, p. 2.

[8] George Francis Train, *Geo. Francis Train's Great Speech on the Withdrawal of McClellan and the Impeachment of Lincoln* (American News Co., New York, 1864), pp. 12–14.

[9] Willis Thornton, above, n. 3, p. 152.

[10] "Speech to the Irish who surrounded the Sherman House and called for Mr. Train when shut out of the Convention" reproduced in *George Francis Train in Cleaning Out the Copperheads follows up Geo. B. McClellan with a Sharp Stick*, above, n. 5, p. 4.

[11] New York *Evening Post*, September 7, 1864, reproduced in *George Francis Train in Cleaning Out the Copperheads follows up Geo. B. McClellan with a Sharp Stick*, above, n. 5, p. 5.

[12] *George Francis Train in Cleaning Out the Copperheads follows up Geo. B. McClellan with a Sharp Stick*, above, n. 5, p. 2.

[13] "Copperheads" in *Dictionary of American History* (Charles Scribner's Sons, New York, 1976), Vol. 2, p. 222; "McClellan" in *American National Biography* (Oxford University Press, Oxford, 1999), Vol. 14, p. 865.

[14] Willis Thornton, above, n. 3, p. 154.

[15] See above, n. 11.

[16] George Francis Train, above, n. 8, p. 2.

[17] *Ibid.*

[18] Margaret Leech, *Reveille in Washington, 1860–1865* (Eyre & Spottiswoode, London, 1942), p. 372.

[19] George Francis Train, *Speech of George Francis Train on Irish Independence and English Neutrality* (T.B. Peterson & Brothers, Philadelphia, 1865), p. 20.

[20] *Ibid.*, pp. 20–21.

FOURTEEN

"A man who might have built the pyramids"

"Have the men of high character and of a national reputation, whose names were at an earlier period connected with this enterprise, been here, animated by a commendable public spirit and by motives of patriotism, to ask us to pass this bill? I have not heard of such men being here for that purpose, but on the other hand the work of 'putting the bill through' has gone into the hands of such men as Samuel Hallett and George Francis Train...".[1]

The remark was a kind of backhanded compliment from Congressman E.B. Washburne of Illinois. Train, sitting beside Collis P. Huntington in the gallery, proudly congratulated himself on what Washburne had intended as a denunciation. He knew the other man mentioned by the Congressman, Hallett, as a successful railway builder. Train had had several meetings with Hallett's associate Edmund Clarence Stedman, who had publicised Hallet's achievements in various papers.

Train was certain he could do the same for the Union Pacific's chief driving force, T.C. Durant. He knew that Hallett and Durant had merged their interests, and that Stedman was writing articles for them on the Crédit Mobilier. More and more, Train's abilities as an effective lobbyist and publicist were put to good use by his associates, as their face to Congress and the public.

The building of the Transcontinental railroad had progressed slowly during the Civil War. Only a few farsighted people could see the validity of it. However, by May 1864, the time of Washburne's angry congressional outburst, the war had highlighted the importance of the railroad to the country's future.

In 1864 a second Pacific Railway Bill was debated and passed. It increased massively each company's land grants and mineral rights, and allowed them to raise more capital from investors. It also allowed for the capitalisation of 1,000,000 shares of $100, instead of 100,000 shares at $1,000. Perhaps someone had paid attention to Train's speech at the ground-breaking ceremony the year before, and agreed that the shares were too expensive at $1,000 each for the normal working person to acquire. At $100 there was a better chance of truly making it the "people's road". This is not entirely unlikely, since Train had become one of the most successful lobbyists for the Union Pacific, which was well able to match the efforts of its rival, the Central Pacific, in Washington.

The crucial 1864 Act, which Train had helped to lobby successfully through Congress, gave a much-needed boost to the project and allowed its construction to finally begin on a large scale. Previously, Durant and Oakes Ames had kept the work going with their own money, but this barely covered the cost of preliminary surveys. Only small amounts of construction had been carried out. The 1864 Act made the railway a very tempting prospect and investment soon rolled in.

By 1865 the capitalisation of Train's creation, the Crédit Mobilier, was increased to $2,500,000. The dominant Union Pacific stockholders were also its major shareholders and they used their position to award Crédit Mobilier extremely lucrative contracts for construction work on the line. A major scandal ensued: Train was lucky he had been bought out by the bigger shareholders.

The Crédit Mobilier, envisaged by Train as a financial body, became a construction company, which allowed these dominant investors and their associates, including several key congressmen, to line their pockets with profits at the railway's expense. This set the stage for one of the greatest financial scandals of the nineteenth century.

The construction of the railroad was fascinating. In effect, it was the last great building project to be done mostly by hand. The difficulties were enormous. A brilliant engineer, General Grenville M. Dodge, tackled the actual engineering problems. He had been interested in the project before the war, and had even advised Lincoln about it. Lincoln had Dodge discharged from the army so that he could help create the railway. Along with Durant, Dodge became a major driving force behind its construction.

The job was organised on a semi-military basis. All the construction parties were well armed and were ready for action at a moment's notice. Since many of the workers had fought in the Civil War, they became an experienced army capable of defending themselves from hostile Indians. As the road slowly began to snake westwards, Indian parties often attacked with some degree of success and did everything they could to hinder, if not destroy, the railway that threatened their traditional hunting grounds. Prairie fires were constant hazards, as were floods. In the spring of 1867, floods washed away a good portion of the railroad's completed track.

The first part of the race was to the hundredth meridian, since the first railroad to reach that point would be given the right to connect with the Central Pacific. It was steadily building eastward from Sacramento. Fortunately, the Union Pacific beat its rivals to it and secured its future.

Train, who had been invaluable in the early stages of the railroad, found himself edged out of the picture, as realists like Durant, with achievable and definable goals needed for the railway's completion, took over and drove the project forward. "Doc" Durant, a controversial figure who had helped to build the Michigan Southern, was a very capable, but ruthless man. Ames, a member of Congress from Massachusetts, had become rich and earned the nickname "the Shovel King" by making and selling shovels.

Even while Train was helping to lobby the crucial Act of 1864 through Congress, it must have been plain to him that he was being squeezed out, as his usefulness was coming to an end. A letter, in the Union Pacific Museum at Omaha from a R.W. Lattimer, shows how precarious Train's personality had made his situation precarious:

> *"My dear Train:*
> *I inclose you a letter of introduction to Col. Larned from Col. Davis. I did not mention the matter to Durant and told Col. Davis not to do it.*
>
> *Col. Davis says with me, that Larned is the best man you can get to take hold with you in 'Fiscal Agency.'*
>
> *Now for goodness sake, stoop a little to the* Conqueror.
>
> *Present this letter as soon as possible, let the Eagles… and all the others alone for the moment, and deal with Larned in a plain, practical manner such as you can do to* perfection. *Don't tell him how you intend to operate it, but ask him for his plan how it should be managed. Col. Davis thinks Larned has no superior."*[2]

The "Fiscal Agency" Lattimer refers to is the Crédit Foncier, through which Train planned to build a great chain of cities across the continent from Boston to San Francisco. Train saw the development of the Union Pacific railway as a catalyst for the development of western America.

This was indeed a farsighted view. In a few years the well-developed American railway network allowed the rapid delivery of inexpensive grain and produce to ports. From there it was shipped around the world with devastating impacts on other countries unable to compete with the cheap imports.

Once again falling back on his observations in France, Train set up another corporation to which he persuaded the Nebraska legislature to give general powers "to make advances of money and credit to railroad and other improvement companies". He called it the Crédit Foncier of America. Albert D. Richardson, author of *Beyond the Mississippi* wryly commented that Nebraska had given it "nearly every power imaginable, save that of reconstructing the late rebel States".[3]

Through the Crédit Foncier, whose name he also borrowed from a French firm, he worked on the real estate side of the railroad expansion. The government gave the railroad company land rights the width of forty miles on either side of its corridor and allowed it to sell off the lands to settlers and developers. Many of the men who had invested in the railroad were persuaded to put money in the Crédit Foncier as well.

Albert D. Richardson met Train in Omaha in 1864 and was highly impressed:

> *"[H]e is trying to build a belt of cities across the continent. At least a magnificent project. Curiously combining keen sagacity with wild enthusiasm, a man who might have built the pyramids, or been confined in a strait-jacket for his eccentricities, according to the age he lived in, he observes dryly that since he began to make money, people no longer pronounce him crazy! He drinks no spirits, uses no tobacco, talks on the stump like an embodied Niagara, composes songs to order by the hour as fast as he can sing them, like an Italian improvisatore, remembers every droll story from Joe Miller to Artemus Ward, is a born actor, is intensely in earnest, and has the most absolute and outspoken faith in himself and his future."*[4]

Another man, George D. Prentice, had a different viewpoint:

> *"A locomotive that has run off the track, turned upside down, with its cow-catcher buried in a stump, and the wheels making a thousand revolutions a minute — a kite in the air, which has lost its tail — a human novel without a hero — a man who climbs a tree for a*

bird's nest out on the limb, and in order to get it saws the limb off
between himself and the tree — a ship without a rudder — a clock
without hands — a sermon that is all text — a pantomime of words
— an arrow shot into the air — the apotheosis of talk — the incar-
nation of gab. Handsome, vivacious, versatile, muscular, as neat as
a cat, clean to the marrow, a judge of the effect of clothes, frugal
in food and regular only in habits — a noon-day mystery — a solved
conundrum — a practical joke in earnest — a cipher hunting a fig-
ure to pass for something; with the brains of twenty men in his head
all pulling in different ways; not bad as to heart, but a man who
has shaken hands with reverence."[5]

Train came to be closely identified with Omaha. In 1864 he shrewdly
bought five hundred acres of cheap land in the south-eastern part of
what is now Omaha, extending from the Missouri River to Twentieth
Street, south of the newly-built tracks of the Union Pacific. For years it
was known as "Train Town". He also bought eighty acres in what is now
the north-east corner of the city, which he proudly named the Crédit
Foncier Addition. Train's property was an incredible investment and an
example of a shrewd businessman at work. While others were too
short-sighted to see that Omaha had a bright future ahead of it, Train
put his money where his mouth was and bought these well-situated
properties that would inevitably rocket in value when the railway
opened and bring new vitality to Omaha. All Train had to do was sit
back and watch his property soar in value as the frontier town became
a thriving city — but patience went against everything in his character.

The Union Pacific Headquarters in Omaha was the town's leading
hotel, the Herndon House. Train often stayed there during the railroad's
construction and while he was working on his property interests. One
day in 1867 he was entertaining a group of very prominent friends from
the east there, among whom were members of Congress. While they
were eating their breakfasts of prairie chicken and Nebraskan trout, a
storm suddenly erupted, shaking the hotel like a leaf. Their table was
near a window with large panes of plate glass, which Train feared would
not withstand the tremendous pressure of the winds. Seeing the panes
quivering, Train called to a huge waiter and ordered him to stand with
his back to the broken window pane, offering to pay him ten cents a
minute.

Mr Allen, manager of the Herndon, resented the outside order to
his employee, not to mention what seemed to be an insult to a newly-

freed Negro, and he hurried over to the table to protest. Train kept his calm and dismissed the man's allegations. "I think I am about this man's size. I will take his place." Train ordered the waiter away from the window, took his place and stayed there until the storm subsided, whereupon he sat down and calmly continued eating his breakfast. Inwardly, Train was seething with rage at having his ethics questioned and planned to get even.

Following breakfast Train calmly walked across the street to a vacant lot facing the hotel and asked who owned it. A messenger was sent for the man in question, who soon arrived. Train asked his price. It was $5,000. Train wrote a cheque for the amount and handed it to the man, who in turn transferred the property's deeds to Train on the spot. Having concluded this bit of business speedily, Train next summoned a local contractor called Richmond.

"Can you build a three-storey hotel in sixty days?" Train asked.

After some hesitation, the contractor replied that it was only a question of money.

"How much?" asked Train.

"One thousand dollars a day."

Train agreed and quickly sketched a rough plan of the hotel on the back of an envelope. "I am going to the mountains, and I shall want this hotel, with 120 rooms, complete, when I return in sixty days." When he duly returned in sixty days the completed hotel awaited him. It was named The Cozzens House after its first manager, to whom Train rented it for ten thousand dollars a year. It stood as one of Omaha's showplaces until it was demolished in the 1940s.[6]

Advertisements with a distinctive Train touch appeared all over the country for the Crédit Foncier:

> *"Prosperity, Independence, Freedom, Manhood in its highest sense, peace of mind and all the comforts and luxuries of life are awaiting you… Throw down the yardstick and come out here if you would be men. Bid good-bye to the theater and turn your backs to the crowd in the street!*
>
> *How many regret the non-purchase of that lot in Buffalo, that acre in Chicago, that quarter-section in Omaha? A $50 lot may prove a $5,000 investment.*
>
> *Paris to Pekin in Thirty Days!*
>
> *Passengers for China this way!… The Rocky Mountain excursion of statesmen and capitalists pronounce the Pacific Railway a*

great fact... The Credit Mobilier a National Reality, the Credit Foncier an American Institution!" [7]

Late in 1866 the Union Pacific decided to celebrate the passing of what was once the Holy Grail of the railway, the hundredth meridian, with a massive party for anyone who was anybody and whose presence would give the railway a publicity boost. Newspapermen, officials, dignitaries and notables of every kind were invited to attend the spectacular celebrations. Somewhere between one hundred and fifty and two hundred prominent citizens attended. Train was press relations officer and looked after all the newspapermen; he was assisted by Winnie and her maid.

The people assembled at Omaha where the Union Pacific gave them the full, red-carpet treatment. A special train was waiting to allow the party to view the railway's progress in the lap of luxury. Every need and whim was catered for and a whole array of entertainments kept the passengers amused. Some of the passengers were even provided with rifles so that they could shoot antelope and buffalo at their leisure as the train rolled across the prairie.

Their first stop was Columbus, a new town in which Train had a paternal interest. He was optimistic that it would become the nation's new capital inside ten years. In the evening a lavish dinner was served, which, like all the other meals served on the trip, was an extraordinary affair with no expense spared. [8]

The next day the hospitality train continued on and reached its destination at the hundredth meridian, 247 miles west of Omaha. Once again a massive party was held. There was a dance, more band concerts, swimming in the Platte, and buffalo hunts for those who wanted them. In the evening there were fireworks, ceremonies concerning the founding of a new city, and a lecture on phrenology with none other than the fine and handsome head of Train as its subject. He had already consulted the greatest phrenologists in London, all of whom had assured him that he was a genius.

Early the next morning Dodge secretly hired a band of Indians to stage a mock raid on the camp, to the shock and disbelief of the revellers. The Indians then staged a war dance. The trip was commemorated in its own paper, *The Railway Pioneer*, which was printed on a portable press and distributed to the party. On the way back to Omaha Durant organised a spectacular sight for the party's entertainment: a prairie fire twenty miles long. Of course, the biggest thrill of all was to witness the railroad progress rhythmically a few miles each day.

The journey went to plan perfectly and the guests had a marvellous time. They sang the railway's praises to all and sundry when they returned home. "The excursion of statesmen and capitalists", as Train called it, fully merited his advertisements' claims that the Union Pacific was a true wonder. The trip was so successful that it was repeated at various intervals during the railroad's construction.

Though it had shoved him into the background as a public relations expert, the railroad still had use for Train's extraordinary persuasive powers. The Union Pacific turned to Train in November 15, 1867 to help them out of a tricky situation.

All the transcontinental routes had bypassed Denver at that stage and the city was feeling left at the post without any prospect of a connection to the important railway. Train was despatched on a delicate mission (one for which his unique talents were perfectly suited) to address a meeting of the Denver Board of Trade. He was unstoppable as he worked the audience. As soon as he had them in the palm of his hand, hanging on his every word, he got down to business. He pointed out that the Kansas Pacific was too far from Denver, but the Union Pacific was only a hundred miles away. While neither railroad could be expected to deviate from its route to build to Denver, he suggested that the good people of Denver build their own link to the Union Pacific.

Train's speech and its compelling logic went down well with his audience and drew cheers from the exited crowd. This was the reaction that Train had anticipated and he set the next step of his plan into motion. Although he had professed to have spoken on the spur of the moment with no idea of what his subject might be, he pulled a list of Denver citizens' names out of his pocket and proposed that his audience organise themselves to build the railway at once; he suggested a provisional board of directors be formed from the list there and then.[9]

Work on the line was started soon afterwards. With his mission accomplished, Train left Denver the same night and had nothing more to do with the line. With one electrifying speech delivered with lighting force effect, Train had motivated an entire community into action. As a token of their gratitude, the people of Denver presented Train with a set of moss-agate jewellery, which he treasured as a memento of his evening's work.[10]

---

[1]   Quoted in Willis Thornton, *The Nine Lives of Citizen Train* (Greenberg, New York, 1948), p. 159.

2 *Ibid.*, p. 163.

3 Quoted in George Francis Train, *My Life in Many States and in Foreign Lands* (D. Appleton and Company, New York, 1902), p. 292.

4 *Ibid.*

5 Quoted in A.C. Edmunds, *Pen Sketches of Nebraskans* (R. & J. Wilbur, Omaha, 1871), p. 7.

6 Willis Thornton, above, n. 1, p. 172.

7 Reproduced in Willis Thornton, *ibid.*

8 Stephen E. Ambrose, *Nothing Like It in the World* (Simon & Schuster, New York, 2000), p. 186.

9 Glenn Chesney Quiett, *They Built the West* (Appleton-Century, New York, 1934), p. 159.

10 *Ibid.*

In the autumn of 1867 Susan B. Anthony and Elizabeth Cady Stanton travelled from New York to Kansas to canvass for women's suffrage. Acting on the advice of a friend in St Louis, they decided to see if they could get George Francis Train to support their cause. He was in Omaha organising another railway excursion for the press when he received their message: "Come to Kansas and stump the state for equal rights and female suffrage. The people want you. The women want you."[1] A week later Train responded:

> *"Right, Truth, Justice is bound to win. Men made laws, disfranchising Idiots, Lunatics, Paupers, Minors, and added Women as junior partner in the firm. The wedge once inserted in Kansas we will populate the nation with three millions voting women. Shall be with you as soon as our Editorial Party have shot their Buffalo, and seen the Rocky Mountains. Nebraska already allows women to vote in School Committee. If women can rule monarchies they should vote in republics."[2]*

Susan B. Anthony replied the same day: "God bless you. Begin at Leavenworth Monday, Oct. 21st. Yes with your help we shall triumph."[3]

After arriving in Kansas, Train spent the last two weeks before the November referendum campaigning for women's rights alongside Anthony. Elizabeth Cady Stanton made another circuit in the company of a former governor.

This was the first determined and organised attempt to extend suffrage to women. Two propositions were to be voted on: the first, to remove the word "male" from the state constitution; and the other, to remove the word "white" (in other words, to allow women and non-white persons to vote). While many supporters of black male suffrage tended to be sympathetic to the women's suffrage cause, they hesitated to openly campaign for it in case it distracted from their own campaign.

Train's help was sought because it was next to impossible to get any other well-known men from the east to support either cause.

Starting in Leavenworth, Train and Anthony made a whirlwind campaign through Lawrence, Olathe, Paola, Ottawa, Mound City, Fort Scott, Humboldt, Leroy, Burlington, Emporia, Junction City, Topeka, Wyandotte, and back again to Leavenworth for the referendum on November 5.[4] At the end of their trip Train carefully compiled all the newspaper reports of the tour, added his own comments, and published the lot in pamphlet form.[5] From this one can get some idea of the hectic nature of the duo's barnstorming jaunt. They usually spoke at a town a day, sometimes even two.

Anthony, a seasoned campaigner, arranged to rent halls along the route and organised all of the advance publicity. All Train had to do was show up and warm the crowd for her. Usually he went and sat at the back of the venue and had something to eat while she addressed the crowd. He normally stayed at the town hotel, if there was one, but she could normally rely on the hospitality of a local supporter. Their campaign only seems to have had one major mishap: on one occasion they lost their way to a venue and ended up arriving at 11:00 p.m.

Train and Anthony drew good crowds. They got on together and the partnership worked well. As the campaign progressed, each came to hold the other in high regard. Later, when Anthony was describing their two-week journey to an audience in Buffalo, New York, she turned to Train next to her on the platform and asked him if he had ever kept any account of the miles they had travelled. "We were together, Miss Anthony," he replied. "It did not seem long to me." The audience laughed and cheered at his quick, gallant reply.[6]

Train ws incredibly popular with audiences throughout the State. "He came! He saw! He conquered!" shouted the *Lawrence State journal*. "Lawrence has had a sensation. He talks with his eyes, his hands, his legs, as well as his mouth!"[7]

Train was at the peak of his powers as a tremendously effective and entertaining public speaker. He was well known as a person who could speak unprepared on any subject and for being able to make up jingles on the spur of the moment. These abilities and his lavender kid gloves were his trademarks. His speeches were full of his claims about what he would do if he were President. In fact, he ran an independent campaign for the Presidency in 1864 and again in 1872.

Nor was he ever lost for words – an important ability when dealing with hecklers. At Leavenworth someone in the crowd referred to

Train's reputation as a Copperhead and shouted: "[N]o damned traitor ought to be allowed to speak in Kansas". Train did not hesitate to launch a counter attack: "I propose three groans," he cried, "for anyone who would swear in the presence of ladies!" He raised his arms and conducted the audience to perfection as they gave the heckler three groans.[8]

Although they lost the vote on election day, Susan B. Anthony was over the moon with joy. It was a heroic failure, since nearly a third of the white male voters supported their platform. There was no doubt in her mind that the cause's efforts would be successful in the future. Anthony and Stanton gave Train full credit as a major factor in persuading the Democrats to support women's suffrage.

Two days after the election, Anthony wrote to summarise the results for her friend Olympia Brown, the Universalist minister who had worked on the Kansas campaign earlier that summer:

"Leavenworth Nov. 7th 1867

Dear Olympia,

Never was so grand a success — never was defeat so glorious a victory — woman though probably lost — runs vastly ahead of negro — Miami Co. goes against 500 — Atchison 500 — Wyandotte 500 — Shawnee 500 — & all others heard from on the line of Rail Road not far from even — but lost — Leavenworth City & County alone for us thus far — the one & only point Geo. Francis Train's work had time to organize & act — But don't despair — we shall win the day breaks — the eastern sky is red. Mr Train consents to lecture for our treasury's benefit — all the way down to Boston & back to Philadelphia — commencing the 20th in't... If only Geo. F. Train could have lighted the fires you had prepared all over the state — we should have carried it overwhelmingly — But depend upon it — there is a wise destiny in our delay — it is not defeat — So let us hope & work to the brighter day..."[9]

However, there was an important difference between Anthony and Train's campaigns. He categorically opposed enfranchising black men, on a principle of educated suffrage (black women's suffrage was altogether too difficult an issue).

"Woman first, and negro last, is my programme; yet I am willing that intelligence should be the test, although some men have more

brains in their hands than others in their heads. (Laughter.)
Emmert's Resolution, introduced into your Legislature last year, dis-
enfranchising, after July 4, 1870, all of age who can not read the
American Constitution, the State Constitution, and the Bible, in the
language in which he was educated, (applause) expresses my views."[10]

Many years later, Stanton and Anthony still believed that Train had
played a crucial role in the campaign.

"At this auspicious moment George Francis Train appeared in the
State… He appealed most effectively to the chivalry of the intel-
ligent Irishmen, and the prejudices of the ignorant; conjuring them
not to take the word 'white' out of their constitution unless they did
the word 'male' also; not to lift the negroes above the heads of their
own mothers, wives, sisters, and daughters. The result was a
respectable democratic vote in favor of woman suffrage."[11]

Elizabeth Cady Stanton also recalled:

"Mr. Train was then in his prime — a large, fine-looking man, a
gentleman in dress and manner, neither smoking, chewing, drink-
ing, nor gormandizing. He was an effective speaker and actor, as
one of his speeches, which he illustrated, imitating the poor wife at
the washtub and the drunken husband reeling in, fully showed. He
gave his audience charcoal sketches of everyday life rather than
argument. He always pleased popular audiences, and even the most
fastidious were amused with his caricatures."[12]

A Kansas suffragist, Helen Ekin Starrett, stated that in 1867 Train:

"…was at the height of his prosperity and popularity, and in
appearance, manners and conversation, was a perfect, though some-
what unique specimen of a courtly, elegant gentleman. He was full
of enthusiasm and confident he would be the next President. He
drew immense and enthusiastic audiences everywhere, and was a
special favorite with the laboring classes on account of the reforms
he promised to bring about when he should be President. Well do I
remember one poor woman, a frantic advocate of woman suffrage,
who button-holed everybody who spoke a word against Train to beg
them to desist; assuring them 'that he was the special instrument of
Providence to gain for us the Irish vote'."[13]

Train also helped set up a dedicated newspaper for the cause. When Anthony explained that they had no newspaper owing to a lack of money, Train promised to give her the money. She dismissed his words as pure talk, until later that evening when Train suddenly announced during his lecture that she was going to start a women's suffrage paper.

> "Its name is to be The Revolution; its motto, 'Men, their rights, and nothing more; women, their rights, and nothing less'. This paper is to be a weekly, price $2 per year; its editors, Elizabeth Cady Stanton and Parker Pillsbury; its proprietor, Susan B. Anthony. Let everybody subscribe for it!"[14]

She was shocked, to say the least, since that was the first she had heard of it, but Train kept his word. The newspaper came into existence and ran from 1868 to 1870, under the title and motto that he had proposed.

The fundraising tour that Train had promised to undertake across the country for the cause began in the middle of November in Omaha. In St Louis Train declared:

> "I am an egotist, and as I, before talking about women, shall talk about myself, suppose we explain what egotism is. It is not properly understood. I think that humility is a swindle — rank cowardice. I believe in egotism, and for this reason: Men can't get above their level in this world. There are certain natural laws that keep us in our positions. Put your hand in the fire and you get burned. It is a natural law. Step off this hall, defy the law of gravitation, and you go down. Assume your position, I say, and be a man or practice humility and be a coward. Strike out for mankind. Water don't run up hill. The big logs will get over the smaller ones in the mill pond, the big rocks over the small ones on the macadamized highway. Assume your position, I say. Put your potatoes in a spring cart over a rough road, and the small potatoes will go to the bottom. Therefore, I say, I am trying to elevate man by making an egotist out of him. Moral courage is not purchasable. Physical courage you can purchase for thirteen dollars, a month in the army... I have made the introductory remarks just to break the ice. I want you to know me, and I want to know you. For it is hard work for these ladies to commence breaking the ice until they get votes, and then they will break ice over the country."[15]

It was another typically hectic undertaking, which Train relished as a platform to express his opinions and views. For example, during three successive lectures in Buffalo, New York, at the end of November, amongst other things, he campaigned for a national capital in the centre of the country, support for greenback currency and the necessity of having a temperance President.

When the tour finally ended in Steinway Hall in New York City on December 14, Stanton told Train that she felt as if she were "fastened to the tail of a comet whisking ten thousand miles a minute through the air".[16] Despite this, they wasted no time in getting out the first issue of the *Revolution*. It appeared on January 4, 1868 with Train's hallmarks all over it:

> "In Religion — Nature, not Dogma... In Politics — Educated Suffrage, irrespective of Color or Sex; Equal Pay to Women for Equal Work; Dignity of Labor with Reduction of its Hours; Abolition of all standing Armies and all party Despotisms... a new Commercial and Financial Policy... Gold, like our Cotton and Corn for sale. Greenbacks for money. Foreign Manufacturers Prohibited. Open doors to Artisans and Immigrants... Wall Street emancipated from Bank of England, or American Cash for American Bills... More organized Labor."

Stanton and Anthony's relationship with Train attracted many negative comments from elements of the women's rights movement and abolitionists because of Train's opposition to black suffrage. They often had to defend themselves from this hostility. The following response to a Quaker abolitionist, Edwin Studwell, shows Stanton's typical reply to such criticism:

> "We are speaking for Woman. Mr. Train is doing the same... He lays his talents & wealth at our feet, giving us a triumphal journey through the states, papers reporting three & four columns. Now you must suppose we lack common sense to drop the only influential man in the nation who is ready to stand by our guns. No! No! I love the cause of woman too well to reject such a power."[17]

Even though Train moved onto new projects after helping get the paper out, the animosity over his participation in the cause did not die away. Stanton and Anthony printed an attack from William Lloyd Garrison in the *Revolution*.

"January 4th [1868]

Dear Miss Anthony:

In all friendliness, and with the highest regard for the Woman's Rights movement, I cannot refrain from expressing my regret and astonishment that you and Mrs. Stanton should have taken such leave of good sense, and departed so far from true self-respect, as to be travelling companions and associate lecturers with that crack-brained harlequin and semi-lunatic, George Francis Train!... The colored people and their advocates have not a more abusive assailant than this same Train; especially when he has an Irish audience before him, to whom he delights to ring the changes upon the 'nigger', 'nigger', 'nigger', ad nauseam. He is as destitute of principle as he is of sense, and is fast gravitating toward a lunatic asylum. He may be of use in drawing an audience; but so would a kangaroo, a gorilla, or a hippopotamus.

It seems you are looking to the Democratic party, and not to the Republican, to give success politically to your movement! I should as soon think of looking to the Great Adversary to espouse the cause of righteousness. The Democratic party is the 'anti-nigger' party, and composed of all that is vile and brutal in the land with very little that is decent and commendable."[18]

In an attempt to head off this kind of criticism, an earlier edition had included an argument of the suffragettes' point of view.

"Since turning our faces eastward from Kansas we have been asked many times why we affiliated with the Democrats there, and why Mr. Train was on our platform. Mr. Train... believes in the enfranchisement of woman, not as a sentimental theory, a mere Utopia for smooth speech and golden age, but a practical idea, to be pushed and realized to-day. Mr. Train is a business man, builds houses, hotels, railroads, cities and accomplishes whatever he undertakes... Though many of the leading minds of this country have advocated woman's enfranchisement for the last twenty years, it has been more as an intellectual theory than a fact of life, hence none of our many friends were ready to help in the practical work of the last few months, neither in Kansas or the Constitutional Convention of

New York. So far from giving us a helping hand, Republicans and Abolitionists, by their false philosophy — that the safety of the nation demands ignorance rather than education at the polls — have paralized [sic] the women themselves." [19]

The editorial went on to relate that when the great Republican abolitionist Charles Sumner presented a women's suffrage petition to Congress he had added the comment that he considered it "most inopportune". [20] Such was the poor level of support by the Republican party for women's suffrage that they preferred to leave aside women's rights until after non-whites were enfranchised.

Stanton also wrote personal letters, such as the one to Thomas Wentworth Higginson, a Boston abolitionist:

"All these men have pushed us aside for years saying 'this is the Negro's hour' now when we turn from them & find help in other quarters, turn up the whites of their eyes! & cry out the Cause. Now let me ask.

Suppose George Francis Train had devoted his time & money for three months to the Negro as he has to the woman [–] would not the abolitionists on all sides be ready to eulogise & accept him, of course they would. Do they ignore everyone who is false to woman? By no means. Why ask us to ignore everyone who is false to the Negro, though Mr T. is not, when black men on the stump & in their conventions repudiate woman. No! my dear friend we are right in our present position. We demand suffrage for all the citizens of the republic in the Reconstruction. I would not talk of Negroes or women, but citizens." [21]

Train sailed for Europe on January 8 with Thomas C. Durant on Union Pacific business. By extraordinary bad luck, he was arrested by the British police when the ship arrived in Ireland on January 17, 1868, for allegedly carrying pro-Fenian literature. On February 26, afraid that he was becoming a liability to the cause, Train wrote to Susan B. Anthony from prison: "I shall join W.L.G. [William Lloyd Garrison] and shall say drop Train...". [22] To their credit, Stanton and Anthony stood by him and continued publishing his letters, sent from prison in Ireland. By way of showing his appreciation for their support, Train wrote an epigram for them:

"EPIGRAM ON EQUAL RIGHTS AND EQUAL PAY.

Dedicated to Susan B. Anthony and Elizabeth Cady Stanton

Woman, as Empress or as Queen,
Can rule an Empire well I ween,
But habit, custom, ancient rote,
In Republic rules she cannot vote,
So Adam did his Eve betray,
No Equal Rights nor Equal Pay.

As Doll, Plaything, Mistress, Wife,
As slave to man throughout her life,
As Teacher, Servant, Drudge and Cook,
'She reigns Supreme' with 'Sovereign' look.
And weeps and works till she is grey
Sans Equal Rights or Equal Pay.

Should Sons, Husbands, Fathers, Brothers,
Enslave Daughters, Wives, Sisters, Mothers,
In what is woman beneath the man?
The Saragossa maid, the French Joan,
The Amazons of Paraguay
Got Equal Rights and Equal Pay.

In what capacity is she inferior,
Painter, Poet, Lady Superior!
Woman in the Christian Revolution,
The wrongs of ages gave solution.
The Saviour where she went to pray
Gave Equal Rights and Equal Pay

With Lunatics, Paupers, Idiots, Slaves,
Women are classed by fools and knaves
Ignoring beauty, virtue, brains.
To keep one half the world in chains,
Why not let woman have her way,
And Equal Rights and Equal Pay.

When women more 'strong-minded' than weak,
In Congress, College, and Pulpit speak,

'Hen-pecked' husbands and 'Cock-pecked' wife,
Perchance may lead a happier life.
And restelism will have its day,
And Equal Rights and Equal Pay.

When mating Mistress and Paramour,
The Sale and Barter of rich and poor,
For diamonds, horses, dresses, carriage,
Infanticide will pass away
With Equal Rights and Equal Pay.

Women are purer – better than men,
Let them use their voice and pen,
To Educate, Suffrage, and Elevate
The Church, the Forum and the State,
And usher in that glorious day,
Of Equal Rights and Equal Pay.

Harlots, Jails, Cards, and Drink,
Will vanish when woman begin to think,
God's noble mission in the Revolution,
Is not Starvation nor Prostitution.
How much longer will he delay,
Equal Rights and Equal Pay.

Ring out your emancipation cheers,
The Bonds of many thousand years,
Will break in spite of manhood's crimes.
Bigots are changing with the times
Ring out ye Belles! And chime the lay
Of Equal Rights and Equal Pay.

GEO. FRANCIS TRAIN
Civis Americanus sum.
Four Courts' Marshalsea, October 1868." [23]

The controversy over Train's involvement in the movement never died away and further highlighted the divisions in the suffragette movement. When he finally came back from Ireland early in 1869, Train decided not to write for the *Revolution*, preferring to direct his energies towards other areas instead, but he still gave financial support to the paper. Susan B. Anthony wrote to him on New Year's day 1870, summing up his much-appreciated efforts for the cause.

"Dear Mr. Train,

As I am looking over documents this New Year's day accumulated during my frequent and long absences from my office – I find this Order on the N.Y. World you so generously sent me. I return it to you – not that I don't want the $2,650.00 – but that you, having returned to the City, may yourself collect the bill and have the added pleasure of handing me the Greenbacks.

As I look back over the two years since we met in Kansas – since I saw you take those immense audiences of Irishmen all opposed to woman's voting – and time after time make every man of them vote aye before you left – since the 9,070 votes of Kansas – since the tour of meetings all the way from Omaha to Boston and back to New York – since the starting of The Revolution *– since your ten months in a British Bastile – since your twelve months lectures almost every night – I was wondering if for once you have ever let an audience go until you had made them* vote for woman suffrage?

For every word you have spoken – for every vote you have taken – for every dollar you have given – and more than all for the increase of respect for and faith in myself with which you have inspired me – my soul blesses you, as does the Good Father and all his Angels –

With not one, but many a happy New Year,

Gratefully Yours,
Susan B. Anthony" [24]

---

[1] George Francis Train, *The Great Epigram Campaign of Kansas; Championship of Women; The Revolution* (Prescott & Hume, Leavenworth, Kansas, 1867), p. 5.

[2] *Ibid.*, pp. 5–6.

3   *Ibid.*, p. 6.

4   Ida Husted Harper, *Life and Work of Susan B. Anthony* (Hollenbeck, Indianapolis, 1898), Vol. I, pp. 288–290.

5   George Francis Train, *The Great Epigram Campaign of Kansas; Championship of Women; The Revolution* (Prescott & Hume, Leavenworth, Kansas, 1867).

6   Buffalo *Express*, December 2, 1867, quoted in Patricia G. Holland, "George Francis Train and the Woman Suffrage Movement, 1867-70" in *Books at Iowa* (University of Iowa, April 1987), No. 46.

7   Quoted in Willis Thornton, *The Nine Lives of Citizen Train* (Greenberg, New York, 1948), p. 178.

8   *Ibid.*

9   Susan Anthony to Olympia Brown, Olympia Brown Papers, Schlesinger Library, Radcliffe College.

10 Quoted from a debate in Ottawa, Kansas – although the source is not cited, it was presumably a newspaper account – and reproduced in Elizabeth Cady Stanton, Susan B. Anthony, Matilda Joslyn Gage, *History of Woman Suffrage, Vol. II, 1861–1876* (Fowler & Wells, New York, 1882), p. 245.

11 Elizabeth Cady Stanton, Susan B. Anthony, Matilda Joslyn Gage, *ibid.*, p. 243.

12 Elizabeth Cady Stanton, *Eighty Years and More: Reminiscences 1815–1897* (T. Fisher Unwin, London, 1898), p. 256.

13 Elizabeth Cady Stanton, Susan B. Anthony, Matilda Joslyn Gage, above, n. 10, pp. 254–255.

14 Ida Husted Harper, *The Life and Work of Susan B. Anthony* (Hollenbeck, Indianapolis, 1898), Vol. I, p. 290.

15 St. Louis *Democrat*, November 21, 1867, quoted in Patricia G. Holland, above, n. 6.

16 Elizabeth Cady Stanton to Elizabeth Smith Miller, December 28, 1867, in Theodore Stanton and Harriet Stanton Blatch, eds, *Elizabeth Cady Stanton As Revealed in Her Letters, Diary and Reminiscences* (Harper & Bros., New York, 1922), Vol. 2, p. 118.

17 Quoted in Patricia G. Holland, above, n. 6.

18 *Revolution*, January 29, 1868; W. Merril and L. Ruchames, eds, *Letters of William Lloyd Garrison* (Belknap Press, Massachusetts, 1981), Vol. 6, p. 29.

19 *Revolution*, January 15, 1868, quoted in Patricia G. Holland, above, n. 6.

20 *Ibid.*

21 *Ibid.*

22 Quoted in the *Revolution*, March 19, 1868, and Patricia G. Holland, above, n. 6.

23 George Francis Train, *George Francis Train in a British Jail. England bombarded with Bastile Epigrams* (New York, 1868).

24 Susan B. Anthony to George Francis Train, Manton Marble Papers, Manuscript Division, Library of Congress, quoted in Patricia G. Holland, above, n. 6.

SIXTEEN

"No matter what rubbish he writes, in with every word of it"

On January 8, 1868 Train and Durant set sail aboard the steamer *Scotia* bound for Europe. They were on Union Pacific business; in fact, on a mission to sell the railway's bonds in Europe. They were an unlikely pair, but worked well together. Train was erratic and compulsive, and complemented Durant, who was patient and calculating. It's evident from their correspondence that they worked closely and that they liked and respected each other. Durant often stayed in Train's Madison Avenue town house when meetings and conferences were held there in the early stages of the railroad project.

Early the previous year a Fenian uprising in the southern Irish province of Munster had occurred. Though it had been easily suppressed by decisive action, it had made the authorities more alert to any real or preconceived threat to stability. Train's reputation as a supporter of the Fenian Brotherhood had preceded him, and his old achievements as an opponent of England were still remembered. As he was going ashore from the *Scotia,* he was arrested and charged for possessing "certain documents for the furtherance of Fenianism".[1]

Train insisted that he was on business for the Crédit Foncier, his real estate promotion, and that he intended only to look into the status of certain street railway matters in Cork and Dublin, begun several years before, but interrupted in the interim by the Civil War. He spent the night in the police barracks at Cobh and then was removed to the County Gaol, Cork. News of his arrest soon found its way into newspapers worldwide, further adding to his notoriety. The Cork *Examiner* described Train as:

> "...a man of about thirty-four or thirty-five years of age – though really we believe considerably older [he was 38] – of prepossessing appearance, with a striking well-cut face, and all that vivacity of manner, quick apprehension, and piquant style of conversation, which distinguish the better class of Americans."[2]

His predicament quickly became a *cause célèbre*, even attracting support from his erstwhile enemy the London *Times*, which commented on the flimsiness of the charge. Clippings of the surrounding newspaper frenzy were collected and published in a volume called *An American Eagle in a British Cage*. Years later Train gave a somewhat embellished and exaggerated account of his misadventure in an after dinner speech to the Irish Revolutionary Brotherhood:

> "Yes! I was arrested in Cork, January '68, by sixteen Irish Constabulary, under Lord Mayo's order! Another case of 16 to 1. (Laughter.) 'Are you a Fenian?' said head constable! 'What is that,' I said. 'Get out of the way; who are you anyway, dressed as Flunkeys? (Laughter.) I am an American citizen!' and I pushed him back, so he nearly fell into the sea! (Laughter.) Arrested for having Susan B. Anthony's Woman Suffrage Revolution in my pocket! (Laughter.) I asked him to let me cable word to Washington, 'Citizen Secretary Seward! These Damn Scamps have arrested another American citizen. Don't trouble yourself. I will fix 'em. G.F.T.' (Cheers, laughter and applause.) They refused to cable. 'Damn,' I said continental damn spelt without (H) en! They were putting me on cattle train! 'Hello!' I said, 'You have First Class Convict!' With monocle to eye... he said Her Majesty did not allow police first class fare! I called superintendent, and chartered train to Cork, with armed guard, both sides, first time they ever had first class ride! (Continued laughter.) It took Seward and Lord Mayo four days' cabling to get me out. (Cheers!) American London legation wired me to come out of Ireland to London! I said I could not get Ireland out of me and spoke in Alhurman to universal audience! (Cheers!) Fifty patriot Priests were present. I went to Rotunda, Dublin! Mounted police called out! I said, 'Keep your cavalry out of sight, and I will surrender after speech!' They did, and I went to Four Courts as guest of the Queen! (Loud laughter!)"[3]

Despite his good-natured retelling of the incident years later, at the time Train was furious about his arrest and immediately sought the assistance of the U.S. Consul, E. G. Eastman. To his credit, Eastman did everything in his power to secure Train's release. The following day Train put his case in writing, vigorously protesting his innocence.

"POLICE BARRACKS,

Cove, Jan. 18, 1868.

PROTEST.

As American Citizens, under our Naturalization Laws of
1802, are not acknowledged to be American citizens by
British Law, *I beg to state that I am a native-born American citizen; that while on my way, on important business, to Paris, I landed, with Thomas C. Durant, the Vice-President of the Union Pacific
Railroad, from the Scotia, at Queenstown, to take the special mail
express,* via *Dublin to Liverpool and London; that I was arrested on
the tugboat, and passed the night on the floor of the police barracks; that I spoke no word, wrote no letter, made no observations
to any one, had no intention of interfering with the laws; therefore
I hereby protest in the name of the American People* — as the
American Government are powerless to protect their citizens — *against this outrage, the offence being words spoken in
America or on the high seas, and of having Irish American newspapers in my trunk, together with other late papers and copies of
my speeches made five or six years ago in London.* I deny the right
at all times of the Government of Great Britain arresting or
detaining American citizens for words spoken in America,
*and hereby hold the British government responsible for this unwar-
rantable delay. My only object in Passing through Ireland was to
ascertain the position of my concession for street railways in Cork
and Dublin.*

*Against these acts of arrest and detention I hereby solemnly and
publicly protest.*

GEORGE FRANCIS TRAIN.

Witness:
E. G. EASTMAN, U.S. Consul."[4]

On a point of principle, many of Train's fellow Americans were outraged at the incarceration of a citizen of the United States. Charles A.
Dana, who had recently bought the New York *Sun,* made the case his

first crusade. Other sections of the American press went so far as to suggest that the incident was worth going to war over! Common sense prevailed, given the weakness of the charges against Train, and the U.S. Consul's pressure persuaded the authorities to release him.

On his release from Cork jail on January 21, Train swore a second protest, asserting that his visit to Ireland was for financial, not political, reasons:

> *"The undersigned hereby declares, deposes and states that he left New York, on the 8th inst., in the steamer Scotia; that he arrived at Queenstown about eight o'clock on the evening of the seventeenth (17th) with the intention of proceeding by the special mail express to London that night; that on arrival at the pier he was arrested in the tender, and lodged in the police barracks that night, and removed in the morning to the County Jail, Cork,* where he was incarcerated in a felon's cell *until Tuesday, the twenty-first inst. —now, therefore, as his mission to Europe was in no way political, but purely on important financial business to England and the Continent, connected with the* Credit Foncier of America, *of which he is the president and financial manager, this detention, imprisonment, and publicity of his arrest has been of serious consequence to his credit and financial reputation,* some important negotiations having already been placed in other hands. *In consequence of this serious pecuniary loss and damage to his character as the chief executive of a great financial institution that comprises amongst its shareholders the President, Vice President and Directors of the Union Pacific Railroad, and the leading shareholders of the Credit Mobilier of America — that owns the contract for building said railroad. He therefore demands compensation from the British Government to the extent of One Hundred Thousand Pounds sterling.*
>
> *George Francis Train.*
>
> *Sworn and subscribed to before me, Consul of the United States, this 21st day of January, 1868.*
>
> *E. G. Eastman, U.S. Consul."* [5]

Train was outraged at his treatment but he behaved impeccably in jail.

Even after his release the harrassment continued. The police went as far as to search his rooms at Queenstown but found nothing but an armload of papers and speeches. When he moved to the Imperial Hotel in Cork city, they repeated the exercise and took confiscated papers from his carpetbag, including a copy of *The Fenian Volunteer,* which carried an article praising him.

Train was smart enough not to land himself in more hot water by resisting the officers, realising that apart from protesting at the inconvenience there was little he could do except to question the legality of the authorities' actions. Even the *Times* was in agreement with him on that point. Throughout the whole debacle Train kept in high spirits. Sometimes he even entertained other inmates with his amusing impressions of various jailers.

On the face of it Train's proposed action against the government for false arrest and defamation of character certainly seems to have had some grounds, though he never carried out his threat to sue. Instead, he assigned all rights to this claim for one hundred thousand pounds "to John Savage, C.E.F.B., or any of his successors, for the sole use of the Fenian Brotherhood, to be devoted exclusively to the Independence of Ireland, and the establishing of an Irish Republic". [6]

It is a measure of Train's courage (or foolhardiness) that he stayed in Ireland instead of hightailing it home, despite knowing the level of the authorities' animosity towards him. In spite of his earlier protests of innocence, Train's arrest stirred up his hatred of the British authorities and he set about lecturing on the case for Irish independence. He seems to have been quite successful, too, if the account of one lecture in Youghal published in the Cork *Examiner* is any thing to go by:

> "It is almost unnecessary to say that Mr. Train's reputation, enormously exaggerated as it is in country towns, is quite sufficient to procure him anywhere in this locality a full audience, and nobody needs to be told that the gathering of last night was no exception to the rule." [7]

That night his lecture subject was "The road to success"; in other words, a typical rant on Irish independence and the injustice of the British. Train stated his long-held belief that a peaceful solution to the problem of Irish independence was the way forward.

> "They call me a Fenian, but I am more than that I am head and shoulders above the Fenians (cheers). No treason in that (cheers).

*My motto — agitate — no breaking of the law — no robbing of gun
shops — no shooting policemen. Leave that to the assassins of other
lands. Don't lower the dignity of the Irish people."*[8]

But, typically, his idea of a solution was grandiose. He claimed that
America was willing to buy Ireland for 150,000,000 dollars in gold.
Train read aloud extracts from his correspondence with Major-General
Sir Thomas Larcom, Under-Secretary for Ireland, in which he stated his
credentials for being the man to make this deal.

*"[W]ith one million of Irish votes to back me, besides being the
Chief of the Council of Eagles — the largest secret order in America
— I possess more power than any one hundred men out of office in
America. Anything I agree to do I will guarantee to be carried out
to the letter. Since my arrival I have been thrown in contact with
all classes — the Irish Constabulary — the jail — the officials — the
subordinates and have mixed with the people, and am satisfied that
the abolishing of the Church Question — the change in the Land
Laws — the application of the English Reform Bill in Ireland, will
only prove expedients that may relieve the patient without removing the disease...*

*Accept my proposition, and the most difficult question of this
or any other now is solved amicably. Civilization is barbarism when
its result is war, and a man of peace myself, I make the offer in good
faith. One hundred and fifty millions in gold, ten per cent margin
of which will be paid on signing the preliminary paper, the balance on making out the deeds. Let your title search be accurate, so
that you can show your authority to sell. I shall forward this
Correspondence to-day to the Hon. William A. Seward, Secretary of
State to the United States, to be laid before the president and cabinet. — Sincerely,*

*George Francis Train,
Independent Ambassador,
On behalf of the People of America."*[9]

Rounding off his lecture, Train read a number of poems which had been
presented to him on arrival, and concluded by announcing another lecture the following evening, which was warmly received by an applaud-
ing crowd. Some young ladies of the town presented Train with "a handsome green sash, trimmed with shamrocks worked in silver".[10]

Train's arrival in Sligo was viewed with mixed feelings. The plight of a fellow American on trial as a Fenian there, "Colonel" Nagle, attracted Train's attention and he even attempted to take advantage of an obscure legal clause allowing a certain number of foreigners to be elected to the jury in such cases. However, his application was refused. The *Times* felt that his presence would incite civil unrest (which never happened). On the other hand, some young Sligo men called to his hotel room and presented him with a shillelagh. In gratitude for their kindness Train performed a satirical parody of Nagle's trial which the Cork *Herald* thought funny enough to warrant two columns. After his tour of the country Train set his sights on conquering Dublin. A short time later the following advertisement for a series of three lectures appeared in the Dublin press:

"Subject:
Westward the Course of Empire Takes its Way!
The landing of the English Pilgrims on Plymouth Rock, and what they did afterwards:
Why England is not the Mother Land of America!
Why America is an Entire Block instead of a Chip, as stated in the stock mutual admiration, Anglo-Saxon Trash!
Evening Lectures – Doors open at 7½ o'Clock.
Mid-day Lectures – Doors open at 2½
Admission – Reserved and numbered Chairs, 4s; Unreserved Seats, 3s; Balcony, 2s; Promenade, 1s" [11]

An audience of some six hundred people assembled to hear him speak on the first evening. Eventually it was announced that Train had been arrested on his way to the hall over a supposed debt owed by the defunct London Tramways. Though the arrest was stated to have nothing to do with Train's politics, this was far from the truth, as Sir Thomas Larcom's papers in the National Library of Ireland show. Larcom, Under Secretary for Ireland, and his boss the Earl of Mayo, who was Chief Secretary, had long kept a close eye on Train's various activities. These two like-minded men governed Ireland with a conciliatory approach combined with a firm repression of sedition and crime. Together they engineered Train's arrest in an effort to shut him up. Initially they had tolerated him as an amusement but finally acted when he became a nuisance. [12]

During the following nine months of imprisonment, his longest stay behind bars, Train made no attempt to extricate himself from jail, leaving the onus on those who had arrested him. He sent a steady flow of articles to the London six-penny weekly *The Cosmopolitan*. Its owner was a fellow American, Colonel Hiram B. Fuller, who had become acquainted with Train when Fuller's New York newspaper, the *Evening Mirror*, had paid tribute to Train on his return from Australia in 1856. Colonel Fuller offered to air Train's grievances and allowed him to write as much as he liked on any subject not connected with his arrest. Train was delighted and enthusiastically set about producing copy. However, the Colonel's offer was more mercenary than philanthropic. Writing from his base in Paris (where he was in exile for financial reasons), Fuller shrewdly issued the following instructions to the *Cosmopolitan*: "No matter what rubbish he writes, in with every word of it. His name is prominently before the public just now and they'll read anything he chooses to write."[13] One *Cosmopolitan* staffer became spellbound by Train and thought he was "of striking appearance, and, despite his gaseous qualities, [he] talked with an eloquence which fascinated and impressed me".[14]

Train also spent time composing anti-British epigrammatic jingles. Many of these were later published in book form under the title *George Francis Train in a British Jail. England bombarded with Bastile Epigrams, by Civis Americanus Sum*. With the menace to society safely behind bars in the Four Courts' Marshalsea Prison in Dublin, the British press printed various unfounded charges that Train was a fraudster and rogue.

On March 26 a cable from Wilhelmina Train arrived from New York simply asking: "What sum required to Eastman, American Consul's credit, for you to return Twenty-ninth. WILLIE DAVIS TRAIN."

The following day her husband replied: "No money wanted. Arrest is political. Insolvency beats these devils. Come over. GEO. FRANCIS TRAIN."

She, somewhat understandably, responded: "I prefer paying [the rail company] Ebbw Vale Co. *twice,* and you return Twenty-ninth. WILLIE DAVIS TRAIN."[15]

Train had no intention of paying his way out of trouble and was quite happy to sit tight in jail until his captors saw fit to release him. As his imprisonment dragged on, Train kept himself occupied. He was allowed the daily papers and was able to keep in touch with outside events through correspondence. He even gave what he described as a "private banquet" to a "Committee of National Schoolmasters in his Bastile Cell". In response to their toast "Civis Americanus Sum, who has taught the young idea of Ireland when, where, and how to shoot", Train recited an "eloquent Epigramatic digest of Education, Morals, Commerce and Religion, embodying the Past, Present and Future History of the Great American Republic".[16] It was called *Epigram on Civis Americanus Sum*.

The prison authorities must have quickly tired of their unusual prisoner. Train often called in the prison's Governor and recited his works to him. In spite of his various anti-British tracts, Train was offended when his correspondence with John D. Fitzgerald, a Justice of the Queen's Bench, remained one-way.

> *"Four Courts' Marshalsea, Aug. 7, 1868.*
>
> *Sir, — The Cork papers report you as having called me in your charge to the jury, in the case of Dillon vs. Tucker (in which I was neither plaintiff, defendant, witness, or juror)* an unscrupulous adventurer. *May I ask you, sir, if you did make use of that expression in connection with my name? Sincerely,*
>
> Geo. Francis Train."[17]

A while later he wrote:

> "Sir, — *Never having mistaken you for a gentleman, I did not expect a prompt reply, and having experienced the absurdity of an American citizen seeking redress in a British court (*in an enslaved country where dress circle Corydons [i.e. *informers: named after John Joseph Corydon*] use a corrupt parliament to elevate themselves to the bench which they disgrace*), I shall not serve a writ upon you for infamous slander, nor, should I meet you in the street, shall I take notice of your impudent remarks by slapping you in the face, or kicking you in your* honorable parts, *if you have any. Sincerely,*
>
> Geo. Francis Train."[18]

One day a message arrived from James Brooks of the New York *Express* informing Train that there was a very good chance that the Democrats would nominate him to the second place on a presidential ticket headed by Salmon P. Chase. Typically, Train was not interesting in accepting second place in anything. He replied that he was only interested in first place and that, since Chase was his friend, Chase could take second place. Train's bravado cannot be taken too seriously since all the evidence suggests that there was no serious attempt by the Democratic Party to nominate Train for either position, though at one stage there was some talk of using him to appeal to the Irish vote by getting him to run for Congress. While this proposal came to nothing, such was Train's standing in the public eye that some papers actually believed he was running. Train wrote later that "it was in jail in Dublin that a feeling of confidence that I might one day be President of the United States first came into definite form – a jail is a good place to meditate and plan in, if only one can be patient in such a place".[19]

Train was at last released from the Marshalsea on December 15, 1868, after almost ten long months of being held without actually being convicted of anything. The *Times* announced victory for the government, reporting that Train had finally paid his debts as well as costs for the amount he had been arrested for, having being spurred into action by the news that his wife was ill in America and was now leaving immediately for New York. Train emphatically denied all of this and there seems to be no way of confirming the story either way. In any event, he was free to go, owing to either his own efforts or the authorities' wish to rid themselves of a nuisance.

A group of people gathered at the railway station to wish him well as he was leaving Dublin, and Train made a speech assuring them that he had not compromised his principles or paid anything. He used the occasion to predict Irish independence and warned that an enormous revolution was coming to Europe, as well as a war which Britain would be forced into after Austria and France. Before he left the cheering crowd, he made them swear to fight for Irish independence. Similarly, before he boarded his ship home at Queenstown, he spoke to another crowd and persuaded them to give "three groans for England".[20]

As a parting shot, he issued a final epigram to the *Times* and other who had called him mad.

"EPIGRAM ON LUNATICS.
Train is mad – *London Times*

Those the Devils hate they first make bad,
Those the Gods love they first make mad.
Hell's Satanic sneers are changed to gladness,
When there is method in the madness.

Demosthenes was mad, and Cicero,
When saving Athens from a foreign foe;
Leonidas, the brave, was mad, alas,
At meeting Xerxes at the Spartan pass.
Pericles was mad, when dwelling on
His genius in the Parthenon.

Columbus was mad as the Spanish Queen,
To cross the ocean before the age of steam.
Gallelio [sic] was mad about the Earth and Sun,
Almost as mad as Washington.
Franklin was mad when he drew, at sight,
The lightning from Heaven with a kite;
Morse was mad when he did aspire
To make it talk along an iron wire.
Field was mad and so unstable
To dream about an Ocean Cable;
Watts was mad, what could he mean,
To draw from a kettle the power of steam.
Stephenson was mad to send the mail
By locomotive o'er an Iron Rail;
Fulton was mad when with his river boat,
He proved that steam a world could float.
Maury was mad when all the world was railing
About his Ocean Circle sailing;
And Newton was the maddest of them all,
To found a system on an apple's fall!

Those the Devils hate they first make bad,
Those the Gods love they first make mad,
Hell's Satanic sneers are changed to gladness,
When there is method in the madness!

The *Times* was mad when insulting our Flag
With leaders of Mason and Slidell Brag,
But sane when buying the Pirate Loan,
And cheering America's dying groan!
Perry was mad for days and hours,
'We've met the enemy and they are ours!'

Bosquet showed he too was insane,
I'm in the Malakoff, and there shall remain.
Lawrence was mad when on dying lip,
He shouted, '*Don't give up the ship*'.
Nelson was mad about his star,
Till after Nile and Trafalgar.
Wellington was mad when in retreat,
He made his victory more complete.
Napoleon was mad in Ham for treason,
The Throne of France restored his reason.
The Seymours were sane for many a generation,
Till Horatio accepted an *English* nomination.
For fear the *Times* shall call me sane,
I'll hold my grip on England's jugular vein,
And not forget these days in Bastile spent,
To prove my madness when President,
Let 'Sic Semper Tyrannis' be the Fenian cry,
Delenda Est Brittania! Do or die!

Those the Devils hate they first make bad,
Those the Gods love they first make mad,
Hell's Satanic sneers are changed to gladness,
When there is method in the madness!

GEORGE FRANCIS TRAIN
Four Courts' Marshalsea,
November, 1868." [21]

---

[1] George Francis Train, *An American Eagle in a British Cage; or, Four Days in a Felon's Cell. By a Prisoner of State* (Cork, 1868), p. 34.

[2] *Ibid.*, p. 32.

[3] Quoted in Willis Thornton, *The Nine Lives of Citizen Train* (Greenberg, New York, 1948), pp. 181–182.

4   George Francis Train, *George Francis Train in a British Jail. England bombarded with Bastile Epigrams* (New York, 1868), p. 3.

5   *Ibid.*

6   *Ibid.*

7   Cork *Examiner*, February 7, 1868.

8   *Ibid.*

9   *Ibid.*

10   *Ibid.*

11   Unattributed newspaper clipping from the Larcom Papers, National Library of Ireland.

12   Various letters from the Larcom Papers, National Library of Ireland.

13   Clive Turnbull, *Bonanza* (Hawthorn Press, Melbourne, 1946), p. 43.

14   W.W. Dixon, *The Spice of Life* (G. Bell & Sons Ltd, London, 1911), p. 60.

15   George Francis Train, above, n. 4, p. 11.

16   *Ibid.*, p. 13.

17   *Ibid.*, p. 10.

18   *Ibid.*

19   Quoted in Willis Thornton, above, n. 3, pp. 188–189.

20   *Ibid.*, p. 190.

21   George Francis Train, above, n. 4, pp. 23–24.

SEVENTEEN

Around the World in Eighty Days

Soon after his return to America, Train set out on a whirlwind campaign for the presidency of the United States. In 1869 he raced from one lecture hall to another, feverishly addressing the masses across the country.

Once, when in a hurry to get from Reno to Virginia City, Nevada, Train hitched a ride in a two-horse Wells, Fargo and Company buckboard, which covered the twenty-two-mile distance in just over an hour, racing the Pacific Express company pony rider. The buckboard's driver, William P. Bennett, later recounted the madcap episode in his book *The First Baby in Camp.*[1]

Bennett described Train as a man "whose name and fame have been spread over two continents and whose strange eccentricity has made him a character sought after in all sections of our country, [and who] as a lecturer, could draw the biggest house of any man upon the boards and as a sensationalist he had no equal."[2]

But Train met his match that day, August 24, 1869. After a fast and furious race across the countryside holding on for dear life, Train was delighted to see the massive reception waiting for him in Virginia City. It seemed as if the entire population was there waiting to cheer him on arrival. As Bennett recalled, Train believed "that this was a grand, spontaneous, popular ovation to himself, personally, and most graciously and gracefully did he bow and lift his hat to the admiring multitude on every side; all that he could see lacking was a brass band playing 'Hail to the Chief'."[3]

It was only when the buckboard came to a stop that Train began to wonder why nobody seemed to recognise him or rush forward to shake hands. Then he realised that the crowd was cheering Bennett. The daily race between the Wells Fargo and Pacific Express riders was a major event in the city and each participant had his own fanatical supporters.

It was one of the few occasions when George Francis Train was lost for words.

The transcontinental railway was finally finished that year, just as Train had predicted. The race between the Union Pacific and the Central Pacific was ended when the two railroads met at Promontory Point. After years of overcoming enormous difficulties, the magnificent project's end was marked by an anticlimactic Golden Spike ceremony. On May 10, 1869 Governor Leland Stanford delivered "a brief, uninspired speech", then tried to drive in the Golden Spike. He "swung and missed, striking only the rail (but) it made no difference. The telegraph operator closed the circuit and the wire went out, 'DONE!'".[4]

It was a momentous achievement with far-reaching implications. As one contemporary commentator claimed:

"Thus, in the consummation of this mightiest work of utility ever undertaken by man, a journey around the world became a tour both easy and brief. The city of San Francisco could be reached from New York in less than seven days running time. Arrived there, the finest ocean steamers in the world, each one of some four or five thousand tons, awaited the traveler, to take him, in twenty-one days, or less, to Yokohama, and thence, in six days more, to any part of China. From Hong Kong to Calcutta required some fourteen days by several lines of steamers touching at Singapore, Ceylon, Madras, or ports off the coast of Burmah. From Calcutta, a railroad runs far up into the north of India, on the borders of Cashmere and Afghanistan, and running through northern India, Benares, Allahabad, etc. Another road intersects at Allahabad, more than six hundred miles above Calcutta, running some six hundred miles to Bombay, where it connects with the overland route to and from Egypt, in twelve or thirteen days by steamer and rail from Bombay to Cairo. From Cairo, almost any port in Europe on the Mediterranean could be reached in from three to five days, and home again in twelve days more, making the actual traveling time around the world only seventy-eight days."[5]

Besides opening up the American West, the railway had a significant importance for the country. As one historian, Stephen Ambrose, quite rightly says:

"Together, the transcontinental railroad and the telegraph made modern America possible. Things that could not be imagined before the Civil War now became common. A nationwide stock market, for

example. A continent-wide economy in which people, agricultural products, coal and minerals moved wherever someone wanted to send them and did so cheaply and quickly. A continent-wide culture in which mail and popular magazines and books that used to cost dollars per ounce and had taken forever to get from the East to the West Coast, now cost pennies and got there in a few days."[6]

Train was notably absent from the dignitaries, despite all his efforts to see the railroad to fruition. It is doubtful if he cared very much. He made no great mention of this snub in his autobiography, perhaps because at the time he was already involved in other matters.

By now Train's sole occupation was lecturing to the masses, which must have been a very profitable pastime, considering the huge crowds who paid to hear him talk. Even his critics had to admit that, though he sometimes made little sense, he always put on a good show.

"In all seriousness Mr. Train is a born orator. His logic may be defective, his study of political economy imperfect, his perception of the ludicrous singularly acute on certain sides and totally obtuse in others, his aesthetic sensibilities may lack refinement and his self-appreciation may be both excessive and pitiably delusive. But, we repeat, he is a born orator. He sways men. He makes them scream with laughter and thunder with applause. He is never at a loss for a word, for a metaphor, for a whimsical analogy. He watches and feels his audience with a tact that seems the tact of instinct rather than of experience, rouses them when they flag, kindles them to enthusiasm with a phrase or a gesture, never for an instant loses his command over them, talks, without stopping half a minute, for two long hours and leaves his audience unfatigued, in riotous spirits, delighted, rubbish or not, with what they have heard, to pour into the streets full of enthusiasm. Now, it is all very well to say that one who can do this is a mountebank and a charlatan. Perhaps he is?"[7]

On January 3, 1870 The New York *Herald* carried a fascinating account of one of Train's New York meetings:

"Train blew his whistle and started on the track of the preachers and politicians last night promptly at eight o'clock. The 'Church of the Bad Dickey,' heretofore known as Tammany Hall, was his depot. A larger 'congregation' than that of the previous Sunday filled

every inch of the hall. The 'reverend gentleman', as he delights to call himself, pirouetted out on the stage amid the usual display of enthusiasm. On his first appearance as a minister of the gospel of buncombe Mr. Train had a table draped with a flag and bouquets of flowers; last night he had two tables, two flags, and a most extensive collection of floral offerings. To this circumstance may be attributed the fact that the sermon was longer, wilder, more unintelligible, abusive and ridiculous than the previous one. It is fearful to contemplate what the result would have been had the management allowed him three flags.

It was understood by the congregation that the preacher would devote himself to a windy defense of Brigham Young, but he said nothing about the Mormons and little about anything else. It was a counterpart of the yarn related by the imbecile, 'full of sound and fury, signifying nothing'. The whole discourse was disjointed, extravagant, and absurd. Whenever he got on a good subject a ridiculous idea was sure to chase it out of his head and off he went on a tangent in pursuit of nothing. Finance, the Bible, the Presidency, church preaching, buncombe and blather were mixed up and hashed together in Mr. Train's inimitable style... Train opened on the Press in general, and worked himself into a towering passion over the fact that his speeches were not fully reported. Then he started to China, nearly got lost in a cyclone, rushed through Java, leaped over several continents, abused Grant, slashed at Colfax, defended Richardson, growled at the Democrats, sneered at the Republicans, yelled at the Church, cheered for himself, howled, leaped, sniffed a bouquet, spoke an epigram, howled again and retired, happy in the consciousness of having performed a public duty."[8]

It's easy to see why Train's flamboyant style drew crowds, and why he began to think of himself as having a hold on the people. He obviously intended to keep himself in the limelight over the next two years until the next presidential election. One such way to do this was, of course, to do something spectacular. Realising that the completion of the Union Pacific Railroad meant that the circumference of the globe had once again "shrunk", he naturally enough wanted to be the first man to utilise this man-made advantage and make the fastest ever trip around the world.

Train went west on the Union Pacific, pausing at Omaha on June 25 long enough to meet a group of Boston Board of Trade members and their wives, who were passengers on the first coast-to-coast train from Boston to San Francisco and back inside six weeks. They were fascinated to hear his predictions for Columbus, Nebraska, which Train proposed to make the country's capital when he became President, and his more practical plans for his trip around the world.

In San Francisco Train gave a banquet for a group of the city's most prominent financiers and politicians and used the occasion to condemn pro-Southern activities in California during the Civil War. While responding to a toast to "The Union", Train conveniently forgot that he had actively avoided soldiering and foolishly said that had he been the Union General in command in California at the time, he would have hanged certain individuals – some of whom were present. It was a bit rich for a man who had been called a "damned Copperhead" himself and who had criticised Lincoln over his handling of the war to judge others. His speech caused a sensation in the next day's papers and, whether this was his intention or not, the surrounding publicity landed him a lucrative lecture tour along the Pacific Coast. He claimed that these twenty-eight lectures netted him ten thousand dollars in gold: "I did not spare my critics, but flayed them alive."

"My lectures made me the most conspicuous man on the Pacific Coast, and I received despatches of congratulations, or invitations to deliver lectures and speeches, almost every hour of the day. I accepted a five-hundred-dollar check to go to Portland, Oregon, to make the Fourth-of-July oration, and the Gussie Tellefair was sent to meet me and take me up the Columbia in state. The oration was delivered to a big audience of Oregonians, trappers and mountaineers, some of them wearing the quaintest garb I had ever seen."

Train also visited the Dalles, where he saw the Indians spearing salmon in the Columbia River in preparation for the winter:

"I went to the place where the braves were spearing the fish and asked one of them to let me try my hand at the fish-spear. Having accustomed myself a little to throwing the harpoon, I found that I could manage the Indian's weapon quite skilfully, and succeeded in landing 200 salmon in two hours. Of course the fish were running in swarms, but this two hours' work would have brought me

$1,000 if I could have taken the catch to New York.

I was the first white man, I believe, that had taken salmon out of the Columbia, and it then occurred to me, if the Indians could lay up a supply of fish for the winter, why could not white men do the same thing? I thereupon suggested the canning of salmon, which has since been developed into so large an industry and has made the Quinnat salmon the king-fish of the world, putting Columbia salmon into almost every household of civilization."

Train's speech in Portland was such a success that he was asked to make another one in Seattle, which was only "a struggling village" at the time. While there he accompanied a delegation from the Northern Pacific Railway which was looking for a good spot to build a terminal for the proposed railway. He claimed to have suggested the site where Tacoma now stands and that the delegation adopted his choice there and then. This was not entirely impossible, for these casual off-the-cuff ideas were Train's speciality – as evidenced by his suggestion that salmon should be canned – and he had always had a strong paternal feeling for Tacoma.

He left Seattle and went to Victoria, in British Columbia, Canada. He arrived to find the town "in the wildest commotion". Troops were waiting on the docks and, from the moment he landed, Train noticed that everyone was watching him closely. Eventually one of the officials came up and asked: "Why, are you alone?"

"Of course," Train replied. "Did you expect me to bring an army with me?" He said it jokingly and only realised how close to the truth he had come when the official took him aside and said: "Read this despatch." Train complied and opened it. It read: "Train is on the Hunt."

"I saw what it meant," he wrote, "and how the good people had been deceived." He continued:

"The Hunt was the vessel I came on, and the telegraph operator at Seattle, knowing that I had been with the Fenians and had been stirring up a good deal of trouble in California, thought he would have some fun with the Canadians. The people of Victoria were on the lookout for me to arrive with a gang of Fenians!

I did not smile, but determined to carry the joke a little further. Walking into the telegraph office, I filed the following cablegram for Dublin, Ireland. 'Down England, up Ireland.' The jest cost me $40 in tolls, but I enjoyed it that much."

By now preparations for Train's trip around the world were nearly completed. Train carefully calculated that he could make the trip inside eighty days, "even with the inevitable losses due to bad connections at different ports". Train's private secretary and cousin George Pickering Bemis, was to accompany him, as were Train's two sons, George and Elsey. Willie Train had other ideas about this. She was determined that one globetrotting eccentric in the family was enough and, unknown to her husband, she gave the boys ten "golden eagles" each not to go. He only found out about this in 1902 – for years he wrongly attributed his sons' change of mind to his daughter Sue's influence.

With everything finally in place, Train and Bemis said their good-byes and set out for San Francisco. From there they intended to sail for Japan and continue onwards around the world in eighty days. Their time in San Francisco proved quite eventful. The evening before they sailed, Train spoke at Maguire's Opera House in defence of Chinese immigrants to America. The issue was a controversial one and there were some elements present that were bitterly opposed to the country's newest arrivals. Train was unafraid of threats of violence and gave his speech as agreed. He had hardly begun when he was pelted with a barrage of eggs. Undeterred, he continued unusually calmly, intending with this effort to persuade the crowd that his viewpoint was the more rational.

According to another witness, someone fired a shot at Train from the gallery during this speech. Whatever actually happened, all agreed that he showed considerable courage in defending the Chinese in such a hostile atmosphere.

On the following day, August 1, 1870, Train set sail for Yokohama, on Donald McKay's *Great Republic*, the largest extreme clipper ever built, determined to circle the globe faster than any had ever travelled. He would set a new 'round the world record that would bring him fame and glory.

The travellers reached Yokohama in good time, and went straight to Japan's capital, Tokyo. Seeing the public baths crowded with people of all ages and sexes without segregation of any kind, Train decided to try them out. "I went to one of the public baths to experience a decidedly new sensation," he wrote, "...and no one, except, perhaps, myself, felt any degree of embarrassment or false modesty." The fact that a foreigner was bathing in the public baths caused a sensation also among the Japanese. Some time before, some Englishmen had gone into one of the public baths and "made themselves very offensive". Train did not expand on this. It is interesting to note that soon after this experience the sexes were forbidden from bathing together.

Observing that the Japanese put tea in small convenient paper packages, Train suggested to a fellow passenger from the *Great Republic*, Susan B. King, who was looking for a way to invest $30,000, that this might catch on in America. Train says that he wrote letters to persuade old acquaintances of his in Canton to help her organise the venture. Apparently she appreciated the potential of Train's proposal and did indeed ship tea to New York in pound and half-pound packages. The idea caught on rapidly since previously tea was sold in large tins and customers had to scoop out and weigh the amount they wanted. Train seems to have had a vast store of ideas.

In his autobiography Train claimed to have invented numerous things – claims that have to taken with a pinch of salt, though Train certainly was a progressive individual at heart and was delighted to find better and more efficient ways of doing things. One of the secrets of his success was speed. He was always interested in finding faster ways of transport, for instance, like persuading his uncle to build bigger and faster clipper ships. He bemoaned:

> "...the want of suggestiveness and resource in men in general. They will continue doing the same thing in the same old way generation after generation, without taking thought for improving methods in the interest of economy, of time, and of money. I have, from time to time, suggested a large number of little improvements, mechanical or other devices, for which I have never taken out patents or received a cent of profit in any way. I shall bring together here a few of these suggestions, made at different times and in different countries.
>
> I used to go to the old cider-mill at Piper's, about a half mile from our farm. We went in an ox-cart, filled with apples. When we got to the cider-mill, all we had to do was to pull out a peg, and the apples would roll out into the hopper of the mill
>
> When I came to New York years afterward I was astonished to notice that there were a half-dozen men around every coal-cart, unloading the coal. I thought of the ox-cart, the peg, and the hopper, which I had used thirty years before. I suggested the use of a device for letting the coal run from the cart into the cellar, but could not get any one to listen to the proposition. Now, years after

my suggestion, all of these carts in New York and other large cities of America have small scoops running from the cart to the coal-hole, and a single man unloads the cart by winding a windlass and lifting the front end of the wagon. In London they still keep up the old, clumsy, and expensive method of unloading with sacks. The English are in some things where we were a century ago.

Once in London I was astonished to see a man, after writing something with a lead-pencil, search through his pockets for a piece of india-rubber with which to erase an error. He had lost it and could only smudge the paper by marking out what he had written. I said to him: 'Why don't you attach the rubber to the pencil? Then you couldn't lose it.' He jumped at my suggestion, took out a patent for the rubber attachment to pencils, and made money.

When Rowland Hill, the great English postal reformer, introduced penny-postage into England, he found it necessary to employ many girls to clip off the stamps from great sheets. I took a sheet of paper to him and showed him how easy it would be by perforation to tear off the stamps as needed. He adopted my idea; and now a single machine does the whole work.

I noticed one day in England a lot of 'flunkeys' rushing up to the carriages of titled ladies and busying themselves adjusting steps, which were separate from the carriage, and had been taken along with great inconvenience. I said to myself, why not have the steps attached? and I spoke about the idea to others. It was taken up, and carried out. Now every carriage has steps attached as a part of the structure.

In '50, I was with James McHenry in Liverpool, and in trying to pour some ink from a bottle into the ink-well, the bottle was upset, and the ink spilled all over the desk. This was because too much ink came from the mouth. 'Give the bottle a nose, like a milk pitcher,' I said; 'then you can pour the ink into the well easily.' Holden, of Liverpool, took up the idea, and patented it, and made a fortune out of it."

Whether any of these claims are true and not simply tall tales meant to entertain is another matter. If they are genuine stories, the question that must be asked is why Train never sought to develop any of them for his own benefit. It might be supposed that he was really interested in only the grandest schemes.

Train and Bemis raced on westwards towards the Asian continent hoping to catch the fastest way home. Quickly passing through Hong Kong, they sped to what was then called French Cochin-China and arrived in Saigon just in time to sail on a ship of the Messagerie Imperiale line called the *Donai* bound for Marseilles. So far everything had gone according to plan and, as Train related, "the remainder of the voyage was uneventful, except just before we left Singapore". At that point they learned that Napoleon III had been utterly defeated at Sedan and had been forced to abdicate and go into ignominious exile. The Second Empire that Train had admired so much was no more and France was now in chaos. They arrived in Marseilles on October 20, at a critical point in the city's history. Train later recalled:

> *"It was the hour when the Commune, or, as it was styled there by many, the 'Red Republic', was born. I was on a tour of the world, the voyage in which I eclipsed all former feats of travel, and circled the globe in eighty days. This served Jules Verne, two years later, as the groundwork for his famous romance Around the World in Eighty Days...*
>
> *The French Empire had fallen and the Republic had risen within the period of my swift flight; and now one of the darkest and most desperate enterprises known in history was afoot — the attempt to transform France and the world into a system of 'communes', erected upon the ruins of all national governments."*

Political turmoil ensued after the fall of the Empire and the two combatants fought each other to gain control of the country. One faction was the Third Republic, represented by Thiers and Gambetta. The other side combined socialist elements such as the International Workingmen's Association, a motley array of Frenchmen, exiles, and foreigners like Train popularly known as the "Communards". Open fighting had not yet broken out, but there was a lot of friction between each side and civil war looked inevitable.

Arriving in the city Train checked in at the Grand Hotel du Louvre et de la Paix, where he took the entire front suite of apartments. Rumours of political plots abounded throughout the city and Train soon found himself caught up in it all. To his absolute astonishment, a delegation called on him within an hour after registering at the hotel, representing the Internationale in its local form, the Ligue du Midi:

> *"Imagine my astonishment when I was received there by a delegation,*

and, for the third time, hailed as 'liberator'. The empty title of liberator — so easily conferred by the excitable Latin races — had become rather a joke with me. The Australian revolutionists who wanted to make me President of their paper republic, were in earnest, and would have done something notable, had they ever got the opportunity, with sufficient men behind them; but the Italians I had not felt much confidence in, nor had I any desire to work for their cause.

The acclaim with which the people in the streets of Marseilles received me, at first jarred upon my sensibilities and seemed an echo merely of the little affair in Rome. However, I was soon to be convinced of the deep sincerity of these revolutionists, and was destined to take an active and honest part in their cause. It is remarkable how a slight incident may turn the whole current of one's life. It had been my intention to proceed as rapidly as possible to Berlin, and take a look at the victorious Prussian army; but here I was at the very moment of my arrival on French soil, involved in the problems and struggles of the French people, as precipitated by the Prussian army, having for their object the undoing of much of the work of the German conquest."

He thought they had mistaken him for someone else and asked the leaders if they had not done so. "No," they said, "we have heard of you and want you to join the revolution." It seemed that they had kept track of his rapid progress around the world. They had known when he was at Port Said and had prepared to meet him as soon as he landed in Marseilles.

"Six thousand people are waiting for you now in the opera-house," they told him.

"Waiting for me?" he repeated incredulously. "How long have they been waiting, and what are they waiting for?"

"They have been assembled for an hour; and they want you to address them in behalf of the revolution."

The political persuasion of the audience probably did not make a difference to him. An opportunity to speak to six thousand people was too good an opportunity to pass up, especially for someone who loved the limelight as much as Train.

"Well," Train said, making a decision immediately, "I can not keep these good people waiting. I will go with you." Later he reasoned:

"I had decided to trust to the inspiration of the moment, when I

should stand face to face with that volatile French audience.

From the moment I entered the opera-house, packed with excited people from the stage to the topmost boxes, I was possessed by the French revolutionary spirit. The fire and enthusiasm of the people swept me from my feet. I was thenceforth a 'Communist', a member of their 'Red Republic'."

Train was rushed through the crowd, down the aisle, and up onto the stage. About 250 people were before him, the more important members of the movement, he supposed, were standing up, cheering at the top of their voices. As he got up on the stage, the crowd started chanting: "Vive la République!" "Vive la Commune!"

"Many were shouting out my name with a French accent and a nasal 'n'," he fondly remembered. "It was irresistible. I stepped to the front of the stage and tried to speak, but for several minutes could not utter a word that could be heard a foot away, the din of the shouting and cheering was so overwhelming." When the shouting died down Train explained that he was merely stopping off in Marseilles while on a trip around the world. But since they had asked him to help, he would be glad to do what he could for their movement, as a small token of payment of the "enormous debt of gratitude" owed by his country to France for Lafayette, Rochambeau and de Grasse.

Next Train gave a crowd-pleasing rendition of the "The Marseillaise", which thrilled the crowd no end. Caught up in the moment, he urged that France should not yield an inch of French soil to the Prussians. Bemis recalled that Train "stirred up those Frenchmen as they had never been stirred before" and was "cheered to the echo". [9]

Train was certainly in his element. He wasted no time in inciting an invasion of Germany, rousing the crowds with just the patriotic war cry that the occasion demanded:

"En avant! Aux Armes! A Berlin! Viva la Republique [We go! To arms! To Berlin! Long live the Republic of France]" [10]

By now Train estimated that the six thousand-strong crowd inside had been joined by another twenty thousand people outside. He said that the entire gathering escorted him back to the hotel, noisily singing "The Marseillaise".

Bemis reported that Train spoke to the crowds seven times a day, for twenty-three days, from the hotel balcony, always winding up with the same magnificently insane declaration: "To Berlin! I will lead you and we will surround and besiege the German capital as the Prussians have the French capital – la Belle Paris!"[11]

Although Train was probably quite confident of his own military abilities, despite never having been in action, the Ligue du Midi were smart enough to realise that they needed a tried and tested military genius. They wanted Gustave Paul Cluseret and asked Train to help recruit him. Cluseret was almost as colourful a character as Train. Early in his career he had won the Legion of Honour for his role in suppressing the June uprising of 1848. He fought in Algeria, Crimea and had been a Garibaldi volunteer in 1860. In 1861 he had travelled to America to fight for the Union. Briefly he had served as an aide to General McClellan before McClellan sized him up as a scoundrel and gave him the boot. But he seems to have fought well in the war: by the time he resigned in 1863 he had been promoted to Brigadier General in the U.S. Volunteers. Cluseret's involvement in French politics later resulted in his exile in Geneva. He had also participated in the 1866 Fenian insurrection in Ireland.

How ironic that the soldier who had helped defeat the 1848 uprising should now turn out to be such a revolutionary himself. The "Red Days of June", as the revolution was called by desperate and starving working-class Parisians, was led by a group of extremists whose only objective was to destroy the government. In now-familiar fashion, they had rioted, destroyed property, looted and erected barricades on the streets of the French capital. In three blood-soaked days, soldiers – Cluseret included – had mercilessly crushed the ill-prepared civilians. Thousands were killed.

Now on his return to France, Cluseret had become a dyed-in-the-wool revolutionary and member of the International Workingmen's Association. He was in Switzerland, where he had fled after Gambetta's forces had driven him out of Lyons, when he received a message inviting him to join the Commune in Marseilles. To their surprise he replied that he would need a force of two thousand armed men to reach it. "This settled Cluseret, as far as I was concerned," was Train's caustic comment.

Only a few days later, a card was brought to Train at the hotel from someone called "M. Tirez". It invited Train to visit the gentleman in room 113 of the same hotel. Intrigued by the card, Train satisfied his curiosity by duly calling upon the stranger. The occupant was "a splendid-looking fellow with a great military mustache".

"Are you M. Tirez?" Train enquired.

"I am General Cluseret."

"I thought you wanted two thousand armed men?"

"You can probably give me more than that number," Cluseret said, with a smile. "You seem to be in command of everything and everybody here."

"We shall see," responded Train.

It emerged that Cluseret had hung about Train's eighty-dollar a day suite for several days before even Bemis knew who he was. That evening Train took him to a mass meeting at the Cirque – a huge amphitheatre that held at least ten thousand people – and presented him to the crowd in a short speech by saying he wanted to give them a surprise: "You want a military leader. I have brought you one. Here is your leader – General Gustave Paul Cluseret."

According to Train, the crowd went wild at this unexpected arrival. Train also introduced Cluseret to the crowd in a speech from his hotel balcony, telling them that the city was now in Cluseret's charge. With Cluseret now in command, they organised military headquarters and prepared to take possession of the city. The next day Cluseret led a crowd to take possession of the Hotel de Ville and the fortifications which were the headquarters of the National Guard. They achieved their aim peacefully, despite a show of strength at the National Guard Headquarters. Train seems to have saved the day.

> "I observed the officer in charge of the guns at the entrance about to give an order, which I knew meant a volley that would sweep us into the next world. I sprang forward and seized the officer by the arm. 'Come to see me at the hotel,' I whispered in his ear. The order to fire was not given, and we filed into the fortification and took possession in the name of the Commune – the 'Red Republic'."

The next day M. Gent, Marseilles representative of the Third Republic, and some one hundred and fifty of the Guarde Mobile appeared at the hotel to arrest Cluseret. Desperate action was called for. Train told the officers that the General was not there, but they insisted on the need to search Train's rooms for themselves. Train told them:

> "...that they would not be permitted to cross the threshold alive. I was armed with a revolver, and three of my own secretaries were armed in the same way. I said to the chief officer at the door that there were four men inside and we would shoot any one who tried to enter; we thought we could kill at least two dozen of them. The

Guarde held a short council outside, and I soon heard their mili-
tary step resounding down the hall. They had given up the search
for Cluseret."

The next morning Train looked out of his window and saw an army marching down the street. He thought it was the Commune's army and he impulsively rushed out to the balcony and began to shout "Vive la République!" and "Vive la Commune!" An ominous silence from the troops puzzled him; he realised his mistake when he spotted M. Gent in a carriage with the troops.

Suddenly Train heard a shot and saw Gent dive to the carriage floor. "Some one had tried to kill him, but missed, and the préfet did not care to be conspicuous again," Train dryly noted. The troops stopped in front of the hotel and Train saw the angry looks the officers gave the red flag of the Commune, which flew beside the American and French flags in front of Train's suite.

Train heard orders being given, then saw five men step forward from the ranks, form a firing squad, kneel and take aim at him. His response was laughably suicidal. "I knew it was their purpose to shoot me," he said.

> *"I do not know why, but I felt that if the thing had to be, I should*
> *die in the most dramatic manner possible. There were two other*
> *flags on the balcony, the colors of France and America. I seized both*
> *of these, and wrapped them quickly about my body. Then I stepped*
> *forward, and knelt at the front of the balcony, in the same military*
> *posture as the soldiers below me. I then shouted to the officers in*
> *French:*
>
> *'Fire, fire, you miserable cowards! Fire upon the flags of France*
> *and America wrapped around the body of an American citizen — if*
> *you have the courage!'."*

An order was given, which Train didn't hear, but the soldiers lowered their rifles, got to their feet, and rejoined the ranks. Another order was shouted along the line, and the troops marched on down the street and out of sight.

The attempted assassination of M. Gent had an unexpected effect on public opinion in Marseilles. It turned the people against the Commune. Seeing which way the wind was blowing, Train advised Cluseret to leave for Paris at once. He even bought the General a gold-laced uniform so he would look the part. Bemis described another incident, which Train never mentioned. At this stage M. Gent's people routinely sent notes to the hotel suite demanding that Train leave the country. Train paid no attention to the demands but, as Bemis says, was prudent enough to take some precautions against arrest:

> "In our rooms we had ten small one-shot revolvers, all I could buy in the city. Train buckled on his belt in which he shoved a big revolver, and, placing one of the little ones between each finger on either hand, he threw open the door and confronted the hotel clerk.
>
> 'Sir,' he said, 'Go back and tell those who sent you, and take part of it yourself, that the first man who attempts to molest me will be shot. There will be as many dead bodies piled up here in the corridor as there are shots in these revolvers. Also tell those who sent you that I will kill the next man who brings me a message. Go!'" [12]

Even Train could see that he had backed the wrong horse once again. All the signs suggested that the Marseilles Commune would not survive and it was clear that it was time for him to get out. Leaving Bemis to pack up in Marseilles and follow on, Train and Cluseret made a simultaneous getaway by rail. Cluseret went to Paris while Train headed for Lyons. Cluseret became the Delegate for War of the Paris Commune, but proved to be terribly inept. As a result the Commune arrested him, charged him with treason and sentenced him to execution. But Cluseret's luck held even at that bleak moment. Ironically, his life was saved when the third Republic forces finally stormed Paris.

Train left Marseilles with Cremieux, one of the leaders of the Ligue du Midi. On their arrival in Lyons, both the amateur and the professional revolutionists were arrested – evidently, spies had tracked them to the city. Remembering that he had Cluseret's address on a piece of paper in his pocket, Train quickly swallowed it before he could be stopped. The officer in command of the solders rushed to stop Train, but was too late.

"That was the address of General Cluseret!" shouted the officer.

"Of course," Train responded matter of factly. "And it has gone to a rendezvous with my breakfast!"

The prisoners were taken to the Bastille, in Lyons, to await their fates. Realising that any attempt at interrogating the pair would prove fruitless, their captors placed them together in a cell. Hoping that the prisoners would let something slip if they thought they were alone, a spy was placed next door to eavesdrop on every word through a crack in the dividing wall. Fortunately, Train accidentally discovered the ploy. When they had been put in the cell, dog-tired, he had slumped against the wall in question and rested his head against it. He was surprised to hear the sound of someone breathing near him, until he spotted a crack in the wall. Only then did he realise that someone had an ear up against the crack, listening to their every word, hoping that they might incriminate themselves. Train was left to rot there for thirteen days. He says he was poisoned and lost thirty pounds during his incarceration there, but it is more likely that he was being paranoid and merely fell ill in such unsuitable surroundings.

In the meantime Bemis had been desperately looking for Train. He had arrived in Lyons on a later train and had spent a frantic week searching for his cousin. Willie Train had even cabled the American legation in Paris to enquire about reports that her husband had been shot in Marseilles. Train said later that Bemis had gone to the city's Guarde Mobile for help, as it was sympathetic to the communist cause. He recalled that they in turn had gone to the city's prefect and demanded Train's release.

Bemis, on the other hand, recalled that he only tracked down Train's whereabouts when a scrap of paper was given to him with the message "Am in St. Joseph Prison and secretly incarcerated" scribbled on it. At once he directed all his efforts towards securing Train's release. The omni-competent Bemis – a tough Civil War veteran who had worked for his cousin for years, getting him out of scrapes just like this one now – swung into action. He cabled the *Times,* Charles A. Dana of the New York *Sun* (an old supporter of Train's), and even President Grant, who probably had no great love for Train. When he was refused permission to visit Train in the prison, Bemis shrewdly appealed to an old friend of Train's, the famous novelist Alexander Dumas. Through Dumas' influence, Bemis's persistence paid off and he was finally allowed to see Train. Bemis reported that he then wired Gambetta at his headquarters in Tours, hoping to put Train's case before him personally, but Train contradicted his cousin and claimed that Gambetta sent for him. It is quite likely that Bemis is the more reliable (and less haughty) source. Whatever the truth, Train was escorted to Tours in a private train car by two secret service agents.

Leon Gambetta was a very busy man when Train arrived to see him to state his case. Though he had opposed the steps that led to the outbreak of the Franco-German War in July 1870, once it had begun

Gambetta had urged the quickest possible victory over the Germans. After the disastrous defeat at Sedan, and the capture of Napoleon III in September, Gambetta played a central role in the new republic and in forming a provisional government of national defence. The provisional government's most immediate problem was the defence of Paris, which was besieged by the Germans. While most government members stayed in the city, Gambetta had made a spectacular escape in a balloon, floating to safety over the German lines, only two weeks before Train's arrival at Marseilles. Establishing himself at Tours, he began his almost impossible task of raising and training a new army to defend France against the Germans. He could have done without the distraction of a foreign troublemaker.

"I found everything in confusion," Train wrote. "The prefecture was filled with men who had been waiting for the Dictator's pleasure. In the first anterooms I saw men who had been waiting for three weeks... they took me for some grand personage, and I heard whispers that I must be the ambassador from Spain or the Papal Nuncio."

When Train was ushered in for his interview with Gambetta, the statesman, seated behind a desk in the large and well-furnished room, seemed to pay no attention to him. Only later did Train find out that Gambetta had a glass eye and could in fact see Train clearly at that angle. Train stood there until he got tired of waiting to attract Gambetta's attention, forwardly volunteering:

"When a distinguished stranger calls to see you, M. Gambetta, I think you might offer him a chair."

Gambetta took the hint, smiled, and motioned Train to a chair.

"M. Gambetta, you are the head of France and I intend to be President of the United States. You can assist me, and I can assist you... Send me to America and I can help you get munitions of war, and win over the sympathy and assistance of the Americans."

> "I knew, of course, that he was going to send me out of France in any event, and I wanted to discount his plan.
>
> The Dictator smiled again, and said: 'You sent Cluseret to Paris, and bought him a uniform for 300 francs.'
>
> 'You are only fairly well informed, M. Gambetta. I paid 350 francs for the uniform.'
>
> 'Cluseret is a scoundrel,' he said.
>
> 'The Communards call you that,' I replied."

It was clear to Gambetta that Train was no menace to the Republic, so he simply ordered Train to leave the country and turned back to more pressing problems at hand. Once again, a private train car and two distinguished-looking secret service men were ready to ensure that Train left the country – in style, leading Bemis to wryly comment: "It is doubtful if any other man was ever so politely put out of a country as was George Francis Train."[13]

They were taken to the coast and watched until they left France on a ship bound for Southampton. Train wrote to Gambetta from London, probably trying to drum up some business. When Gambetta sent no response, they finally departed for the United States from Liverpool aboard the *Abyssinia* on the final leg of their journey around the world.

They arrived in New York eighty days after they had set out, excluding the time they had wasted in France. Despite not actually travelling around the world in eighty days in the strictest sense of the phrase, there can be little doubt that his unique journey and extraordinary life acted as an inspiration to Jules Verne. Two years later Verne published his famous novel *Around the World in Eighty Days,* and Train was immortalised as the fictional character that he had always threatened to become: Phileas Fogg.

---

[1] William P. Bennett, *The First Baby in Camp* (Rancher Pub. Co., Salt Lake City, 1893), pp. 9–13.

[2] *Ibid.,* p. 9.

[3] *Ibid.,* p. 12.

[4] Stephen Ambrose, *Nothing Like It in the World* (Simon & Schuster, New York, 2000), pp. 365–366.

[5] R.M. Devens, *Our First Century* (Hugh Heron, Chicago, 1878), p. 914.

[6] Stephen Ambrose, above, n. 4, p. 370.

[7] Quoted in A.C. Edmunds, *Pen Sketches of Nebraskans* (R. & J. Wilbur, Omaha, 1871), p. 6.

[8] Quoted in Willis Thornton, *The Nine Lives of Citizen Train* (Greenberg, New York, 1948), pp. 195–197.

[9] *Ibid.,* p. 204.

[10] John Wesley Nichols, *The Man of Destiny* (New York, 1872), p. 11.

[11] Quoted in Willis Thornton, above, n. 8, p. 204.

[12] *Ibid.,* p. 207.

[13] *Ibid.,* p. 210.

EIGHTEEN

Stranger than Fiction

Although the inspiration for *Around the World in Eighty Days* may be open to speculation, one thing is certain: it was the novel that finally made Jules Verne's reputation and fortune.

Verne was born into a prosperous family in Nantes, France. In his youth he once ran away to become a cabin boy on a merchant ship, but he was discovered before it was too late and returned to his parents. A deeply rooted fascination with the sea and exploration probably dated from this time and seems to have stayed with him, heavily influencing his writing. His early years are thought to have been happy and unremarkable, apart from a schoolboy's unrequited love for his cousin.

In 1847 his parents decided to send him to Paris to follow in his father's footsteps and become a lawyer. He dutifully completed his law studies, but Verne's heart was not in it. His real passion was writing and he devoted his life to this all-consuming interest, abandoning a career in law. For the next decade or so he lived a hand-to-mouth existence composing plays and poetry. In order to make some much needed extra money, he also wrote numerous historical and scientific short articles for a popular French magazine. His plays were moderately successful, probably due to the patronage of his friend and mentor Alexandre Dumas.

In 1857 Verne married. With a new wife and two stepdaughters to support, Verne needed a stable job, so he became a stockbroker by day and wrote at night. In 1862 all his efforts finally paid off when his first published book, *Five Weeks in a Balloon*, was an instant success. It was also the beginning of a fruitful partnership between Verne and his publisher Pierre-Jules Hetzel that lasted for over forty years. Under Hetzel's guidance Verne's works adopted a formula that was a sure-fire recipe for success. They became fast-paced adventures infused with dashes of scientific knowledge and an optimistic view of the future. In Hetzel's own words, the publishing partnership intended "to sum up all the geographical, geological, physical and astronomical knowledge amassed by modern science, and to rewrite the history of the world".[1] These slick, extremely intelligent works earned Verne his reputation as the father of science fiction.

Verne was an incredibly prolific writer, producing well over sixty novels during his lifetime. His most famous ones are *Five weeks in a Balloon*, *Journey to the Centre of the Earth*, *From the Earth to the Moon*, *Twenty Thousand Leagues under the Sea*, its sequel *The Mysterious Island* and, of course, his most successful work *Around the World in Eighty Days*. Early English translations of Verne's works were often crude and hurried affairs, designed to cash in on Verne's commercial popularity. They usually omitted most of the books' scientific worth and emphasised the sensational aspects of the original texts. Unfortunately, because of these translations, English-speaking critics dismissed Verne's works as children's tales. Verne's reputation suffered a long time from such poor versions of his novels. It is only in more recent times that his works have been translated as he intended, allowing modern-day readers to get the full flavour of his writing. The efforts of William Butcher and others have gone some way in rescuing Verne's reputation in the English-speaking world and ensuring the acknowledgment of his status as a highly literary and prophetic writer whose predictions have often become reality. The best translation of *Around the World in Eighty Days* is William Butcher's classic and highly informative edition published by Oxford World's Classics.

Around the World in Eighty Days is a race against time to save face and fortune; a thrilling, humorous adventure, and a classic of travel in a bygone age. The novel opens with a wonderful description of its hero, Phileas Fogg: practically nothing is known about him, except that he is the most laconic and orderly of men. His house in Saville Row is run like clockwork and his life is calculated to the last second.

One day he hires a new servant called Passepartout and then heads straight for the Reform Club. Passepartout is delighted with his new position, as he only wants to lead a quiet life, and all the indications tell him that this post will be just what he was looking for. Little does he know what surprises he is in for. That same day Fogg bets half his fortune with his fellow club members that he can circumnavigate the world in eighty days. He immediately sets off with Passepartout to perform the feat.

Detective Fix of Scotland Yard is immediately suspicious. He finds it too much of a coincidence to believe that Fogg should want to leave the country in such a hurry at the same time that the British police are searching for a notorious bank robber. As all the circumstantial evidence indicates that Fogg is the thief, Fix follows him around the world in an attempt to bring Fogg to justice. Thus the stage is set for one of the most memorable and popular adventure stories of all time.

As several writers point out, *Around the World in Eighty Days* is riddled with inaccuracies. "He mixes up East and West, left and right, and there are many chronological and geographical slips," John Sutherland noted in his essay on the novel.[2] Other textual mistakes appeared. Verne's lack of familiarity with the conventions of Victorian Britain was blindingly obvious. His main sources of information were an unpublished book of his own that he wrote in 1860, *Journey to England and Scotland,* and Francis Wey's 1854 book *Anglais chez eux: Esquisses de moeurs et de voyage.* He relied heavily on these for information on British society. Overall Verne was very sloppy in the small details, but since the reader is whisked so fast through the story, without a dull moment to stop and notice the inconsistencies, it does not really matter.

The traditional story of the origins of *Around the World in Eighty Days* tells that Verne was inspired by an advertisement issued by Thomas Cook's travel agency. In June 1872 Thomas Cook did in fact publish a brochure announcing that he intended to organise the first tourist trip around the world, and even went so far as to suggest it would take 102 days to complete. The reality was quite different, however. Cook's global tourists left on September 20, 1872 and eventually returned seven months later. In letters to the *Daily Mail* and the *Times* running from November 1872 through to May 1873 Cook described the epic journey to captive readers. These letters proved so popular with the public that they were published in 1873 as *Letters from the Sea and from Foreign Lands, Descriptive of a Tour Round the World.*

Although Verne never explicitly detailed the extent of his inspiration, there are several similarities between the real and fictional accounts, though Cook travelled via Ceylon. In the first letter alone there are references to the rebuilding of Chicago after the great fire, the Sioux Indians' activities, crossing the Rocky Mountains by the recently completed Union Pacific Railway, time zone changes, and the gaining of a day in the Pacific. Despite these similarities, it has been argued that the trip happened too late to influence Verne, especially when one considers that Cook's true account and Verne's fictional tale ended up being serialised simultaneously for about a month in the *Times* and *Le Temps,* respectively, in late 1872.

On the other hand, Verne himself repeatedly stuck to the story when questioned on several different occasions. Once Verne did say that inspiration came about "one day in a Paris café" when he by chance spotted a tourism advertisement in the columns of a newspaper.[3] The novel itself seems to suggest that its origin lies in a newspaper article, but it is far from clear whether this advertisement was on hoarding, brochure, or newspaper form. On other occasions Verne contradicted himself, saying that he had had the idea for the novel many years before he had fully developed it.

Even the notion of circling the globe in eighty days was commonplace. Jules Verne certainly did not have a monopoly on the idea or the name. On October 3, 1869, the periodical magazine *Le Tour du monde* contained a short article called "Around the World in Eighty Days". It referred to the idea and the fact that 140 miles of railway were not yet completed between Alahabad and Bombay. In its bibliography it cited an earlier source, the *Nouvelles Annales des Voyages, de la Geographie, de l'Histoire et de l'Archeologie.* It was published in August of that year and it had included an article entitled "Around the World in Eighty Days". Verne was quite familiar with the *Nouvelles Annales* and had even quoted them in *Five Weeks in a Balloon*.

A subtle but significant difference between these proposed trips and Verne's fiction is that they started and finished in Paris and travelled westwards. But their choice of title and reference to the incomplete Trans-Indian railway, added to the fact that Verne was familiar with *Le Tour du monde* and the *Nouvelles Annales*, is highly telling and strongly indicates their use as source material. Interestingly enough, the *Nouvelles Annales* were only repeating facts previously published in the July 30 edition of a Dutch magazine, *De Hollandsche Illustratie,* which broke down a journey around the world in eighty days into readily achievable stages, showing how practical it actually was. Starting from Amsterdam, it allowed one day to reach Paris, after which the travellers would head westwards around the globe. The article also refers to 180 miles of track missing between Alahabad and Bombay.

Commenting on the imminent opening of the Suez Canal on November 17, the November 12 issue of *Le Tour du monde* finally got around to suggesting its own itinerary for an eighty-day jaunt round the world:

"Paris to Port Said, head of the Suez Canal, railway
and steamer.....................................6 days
Port Said to Bombay, steamer........................14

Numerous newspapers and periodicals referred to the feasibility of trips around the world in eighty days or more and Jules Verne would certainly have been well aware of this. The reason for this new-found interest in trips around the globe was stimulated by the completion of three important advances in global transportation. In 1869 the Suez Canal and American Transcontinental railway were completed. The following year the last section of the trans-Indian Peninsular Railway was also finished. Taken together, these innovations cut thousands of miles off journeys and helped to shorten travel times.

In 1872 alone the following books appeared: *Around the World by Steam, via Pacific Railway,* by the Union Pacific Railroad Company; *Around the World in A Hundred and Twenty Days,* by Edmond Planchut; and an American called, coincidentally, William Perry Fogg went around the globe in 1869–72, describing his tour in a series of letters to the *Cleveland Leader,* published as *Round the World: Letters from Japan, China, India and Egypt* (1872).

The origins of the character of Phileas Fogg are less clear. He almost certainly distilled the essence of the novel's hero from Wey's 1854 book. He described the British as "timid, a little touchy… indifferent to feminine beauty". They "present the appearance of a pronounced coldness… the Englishman, who does not wish to appear subordinate to events, never runs… When he walks, he counts each step."[5]

Verne was almost certainly influenced by George Francis Train's extraordinary life. After all, Train had actually gone around the world in eighty days in 1870 (excluding his brief stay in a French prison). There is a definite connection between the two, as both were friends of Alexander Dumas. Undoubtedly Verne would have heard of Train and his various adventures, even without Dumas, but there is no record that these men ever met, and Verne never acknowledged Train as a source. Train later expressed his indignation at this omission. "Remember Jules

Verne's *Around the World in Eighty Days?* He stole my thunder. I'm Phileas Fogg." [6]

He was right to complain. Even at a most superficial level there are a number of similarities between Train's life and Fogg's adventures. Both were calm in the face of storms and typhoons and thought nothing of hiring private forms of transportation to complete their journeys more quickly. Fogg had Passepartout, his irrepressible French servant, while Train had George Pickering Bemis for his long-suffering private secretary, whose duties often involved extracting Train from various scrapes. Train ended up in prison during his trip around the world, as did Fogg. Train was once falsely accused of stealing ($2,000,000 of gold in Australia), as was Fogg (£55,000).

Most tellingly, Verne saw fit to include in his book an incident when the wooden innards of a ship are burned to provide fuel for its engines. This once happened to Train in the 1850s, though he was trying to escape Chinese pirates intent on robbing and murdering him at the time. Unfortunately, we will never know the true extent of Verne's sources, since his archive of files has long since been dispersed.

The novel was initially published in serial form in a Parisian newspaper, *Le Temps*. It was an overnight success and nearly tripled the newspaper's circulation while instalments of Verne's suspenseful novel were published. Ever since *Five Weeks in a Balloon* Verne had cheerfully interwoven fact and fiction into a seamless narrative in his novels. He was now such an expert at it that the closing date of the story, December 22, 1872, was also the closing date of the serialisation. Some of Verne's biographers report that, as *Around the World in Eighty Days* came out, several British and American newspapers published extracts from it. Some readers were allegedly so convinced that it was actually a true story that bets were placed on the outcome. The novel was published in book form in January 1873 and became Verne's greatest best-selling work.

It was an ideal candidate for dramatisation. Even before the serialisation had ended in *Le Temps*, Verne had teamed up with the dramatist Edouard Cadol to adapt the novel for the stage. Unfortunately, Cadol was unable to find a producer and the play remained in limbo until January 1874. The directors of the Porte Saint-Martin Theatre suggested to Verne that a talented playwright called D'Ennery try his hand at adapting it. He was more successful and soon had a new plot devised for production. The play opened on November 7, 1874 and was an immediate critical and financial success. It ran for 415 nights, first at the

Porte Saint-Martin Theatre and then at the Chitelet, and then continued on and off until the Second World War.

A columnist in *Le Figaro* wrote that: "*Around the World* has put all Paris in a holiday mood, and when the theatre opens its doors, the Boulevard Saint-Martin presents a curious and joyful spectacle." He also reported that the box-office takings were another reason for joy. "Yesterday it was 8,037 francs, and in a fortnight, it had amounted to 254,019 francs."[7] These kind of takings continued for two years. A transparent globe was set up in the theatre's entrance; the progress of Fogg and company was marked on it at every interval. The play's success attracted widespread attention. Verne was caricatured in a magazine as an acrobat juggling the earth on his feet before an enraptured crowd; and in *L'Eclipse* turning the globe on a handle like a chicken on a spit. It was even suggested by one wit that Mr Fogg's real feat was not his spectacular circumnavigation of the world, but the making of Verne's fortune.

In adapting the novel D'Ennery had utilised every opportunity for surprising stage effects, such as snakes for a cave scene in Malaya and, the greatest triumph of all, a real elephant. As the one in the Paris zoo had been eaten during the siege of 1870–71, this was the first chance that many Parisians had been offered for some time to see such an exotic sight. They were delighted with the play.

During the rehearsals, Verne had been burdened with doubts. After all, Dumas had failed in the theatre. He asked his old friend Felix Duquesnel what he thought: "Between ourselves, a success?"

"No," answered Duquesnel, "a fortune."[8] He was right. A fortune it was, for Verne, D'Ennery and the producers, and even for Edouard Cadol. In January 1874 Cadol sent a letter to *Le Figaro* stating that the novel was partly his work. Verne protested to Hetzel that Cadol had "made absolutely no contribution to the book".[9] However, Cadol did establish copyright on the play and, as a result, received royalties on it thereafter.

According to William Butcher, the play differs significantly from the book. It is less polished and, most notably, the plot contains two shipwrecks and several new characters, including Nakahira, the Queen of the Charmers, a servant called Margaret who marries Passepartout, and Aouda's sister, Nemea, who marries an American blackballed by the Reform Club called Archibald Corsican. The play also displays environmental credentials with an impassioned speech by a Pawnee Chief protesting at the rape of the Indian lands by the Palefaces.

In his review of October 18, 1874, the poet Mallarmi called the drama a "fairy-delight... One really must see the Snake Grotto, the explosion and sinking of the steamer, and the ambush of the train by the Pawnee Indians".[10]

Verne later complained that he received "much less than his fair share of proceeds from the highly successful play" and claimed to have sold the novel for "a tenth of its value".[11] He was quite correct in this assumption. As it turned out, over their forty-year collaboration Hetzel made five times as much money as Verne.

Following Towle and d'Anver's English translation of the book, literally hundreds of publicity seekers have tried to imitate or improve on Fogg's performance. Verne even satirised these efforts in *Claudius Bombanac*, which tells the story of Baron Weisschnitzerdörfer's efforts to go around the world in thirty-nine days. He misses numerous trains and ships, and ends up limping home in 187 days! The most recent, rather more high profile, follower was the actor Michael Palin, whose very successful 1989 television series and wonderful accompanying book did for him what the novel and play had done for Verne. Although already a successful writer, performer and comedian, the success of his excellent programmes and book catapulted Palin to an even higher level of fame and fortune, and resulted in him being sought after as a presenter of other globe-trotting travel shows.

There have also been several film versions of Verne's novel. The first was a German silent film made in 1919, but the most famous and successful one was the 1956 Oscar-winner featuring David Niven and a whole array of stars. The last decade or more has seen a kind of revival of film versions: most notably, Pierce Brosnan starred as Phileas Fogg in a wonderful 1989 television mini-series. More recently, two versions of *Around the World in Eighty Days* are rumoured to be in the development hell that is pre-production.

There is no simple answer to the question of why the circumnavigation of the world has held such a place in people's imaginations, inspiring them to go out and try it for themselves. In the introduction to his book, Palin rationalised it as follows:

> "The compulsive urge to travel is a recognised psychical condition.
> It has its own word, dromomania, and I'm glad to say I suffer from
> it. The ambition of every dromomaniac is a circumnavigation of the
> planet, but it's a less fashionable journey now than in Jules Verne's
> day. Part of the reason is that you can do it by air in 36 hours (a

technological feat that Verne would have greatly appreciated). But air travel shrink-wraps the world, leaving it small, odourless, tidy and usually out of sight. There are container vessels which will take you round in 63 days, but you will see only water on 58 of those. The reason why Phileas Fogg's 80-day journey retains its appeal is that it is still the minimum time needed to go round the world and notice it. To see it, smell it and touch it at the same time."[12]

Was Train a dromomaniac? In his case there seems to be no simple answer. Certainly ego and the never-ending lust for publicity, as well as the desire to achieve a lasting fame, all fuelled his spectacular worldwide adventures. Whatever the extent of Train's influence on Jules Verne when he wrote his novel, one thing beyond debate is that George Francis Train's life is proof of the saying that sometimes the truth is stranger than fiction.

[1] Jules Verne, *Around the World in Eighty Days* (Trans. Jacqueline Rogers, Penguin Books, 1994), p. 1.

[2] John Sutherland, *Who Betrays Elizabeth Bennet?* (Oxford University Press, 1999), p. 212.

[3] The translator's notes on principal sources in Jules Verne, *Around the World in Eighty Days* (Trans. William Butcher, Oxford University Press, 1995), Appendix A, p. 204.

[4] Jules Verne, *ibid.*, pp. 204–205.

[5] Quoted in the translator's explanatory notes in Jules Verne, *ibid.*, p. 216.

[6] Don C. Seitz, *Uncommon Americans* (The Bobbs-Merrill Company, Indianapolis, 1925), p. 178.

[7] Peter Costello, *Jules Verne* (Hodder & Stoughton, London, 1978), p. 123.

[8] *Ibid.*, p. 124.

[9] The translator's notes on the play in Jules Verne, above, n. 3, Appendix B, p. 207.

[10] *Ibid.*

[11] *Ibid.*

[12] Michael Palin, *Around the World in 80 Days* (BBC Books, London, 1989), p. 9.

NINETEEN

Candidate for President of the U.S.A.

Train once wrote: "I have passed a great many days in jail. A jail is a good place to meditate and to plan in, if only one can be patient in such a place. Much of my work was thought out and wrought out while living in the fifteen jails of which I have been a tenant."

After all, it was in a jail in Dublin that he first became confident that he would one day become President of the United States. In between planning his presidential campaign, Train also found the time to plan his dream house. For a number of years the Trains had rented pleasant but unassuming houses in Newport. With a view to building a house more fitting for a person of his stature, Train bought a two-and-a-half-acre site overlooking the sea.

The plans were made before he was imprisoned in Dublin. His wife built Train Villa, or began work on it, while he was still in the Marshalsea prison. It was a pleasant, comfortable-looking frame house with octagonal towers and with a spacious hedged lawn all around it. There was a separate building for billiards and bowling. A fine cottage was also built for Colonel Davis, his father-in-law. Train guessed that it cost him a hundred thousand dollars, though he was never sure. One thing is certain: it was the height of luxury.

> "We lived there in manorial style, entertaining so lavishly and freely that the Villa became a free guest-house for all Newport. I also recollect that my living cost me more than $2,000 a week. Now I manage to live on $3 a week in the Mills Hotel, or Palace, as I call it. Here I am more contented than I was at Newport. I seem to be saving $1,997 a week. We turned out, in Newport, six carriages when we went driving; but this was a display that I always set my heart against. It seemed to be mere wastefulness."

Train's casual attitude to money is typical of him. He wrote: "I was called rich and had never, at any time, given a thought to the mere details of money. What I wanted I got. In those days that was the substance of my economic system in personal matters." It was pure luck that the Villa was in Willie Train's name, with her father Colonel Davis acting as trustee, when Train was declared a bankrupt a few years later.

The Villa was once turned into a jail, though this time Train was not the captive. In the famous Crédit Mobilier case of 1872–73, a unnamed man, who was Train's guest at the time, was arrested. As the Crédit Mobilier men, then in Newport, could not or would not pay the man's million-dollar bail as demanded, an arrangement was made with the sheriff whereby the Villa temporarily became a jail, where Train's guest was confined.

Of course, it was not his first chance of becoming a President. Back in Australia the revolutionaries had once offered him the Presidency of the Five Star Republic, but he had wisely turned them down without any regrets. Since then he had been sporadically involved with various political campaigns but had never actually delved into mainstream politics. He had even refused a chance to run for Congress.

> "In '65, the Fenians, after I had espoused the general cause of the Irish, as of the oppressed of every country, asked me to attend their first convention, which was to be held in Philadelphia. They wished me to address them. This I did, but I took no active part in the work of the convention or of the faction. I had already attended the Democratic Convention in Louisville in '64, when I held a proxy from Nebraska, and had hoped to have General Dix nominated for President and Admiral Farragut for Vice-President, but I was not permitted to take my seat. [His accreditation was rejected]."

Instead, Train began his own one-man campaign for the Presidency. Summing up his brief and insubstantial political career years later, he recalled that he sat out the 1868 presidential election in jail. "But the seed of ambition had been sown," he reminisced, "even before this, and it germinated in the old Irish prison."

> "As soon as I got out of that jail, I began my campaign for President of the United States, and in '69 started on a program that involved 1,000 addresses to 1,000 conventions. It seemed to me that, with the effect I had always had upon people in my speeches and in personal contact, and with the record of great achievements in behalf

*of the progress of the world, especially with regard to the develop-
ment of this country, I should succeed. I supposed that a man with
my record, and without a stain on my reputation or blemish in my
character, would be received as a popular candidate."*

There was only one thing that could hold Train back and that was lack
of funds. As a result of his long stay in various Irish prisons, his business
affairs were in a mess. Train had long earned a living by brokering deals
and his various incarcerations had seriously compromised his ability to
do this. The surrounding publicity probably did not do him any favours,
either. His fortune was based on the income generated by his assorted
deals and not as a result of any financial investments or commercial
interests.

Necessity is the mother of invention, they say, so Train quickly
adapted to his changed circumstances and innovated. He did something
quite unique: he charged people admission to hear him campaign for
the presidency at rallies throughout the country. By all accounts it was a
highly lucrative novelty. People flocked to hear Train, and they usually
got their money's worth. But, he was probably too eccentric for people
to take seriously. Train usually began his campaign speeches by saying:

*"I am that wonderful, eccentric, independent, extraordinary genius
and political reformer of America, who is sweeping off all the
politicians before him like a hurricane, your modest, diffident,
unassuming friend, the future President of America – George
Francis Train."* [1]

As it turned out, the American public did not share this opinion, though
Train was breathtakingly confident of victory and said as much:

*"I had not the slightest doubt that I should be elected; and, with
this sublime self-confidence, threw myself into the campaign with
an energy and fire that never before, perhaps, characterized a
Presidential candidate. I went into the campaign as into a battle.
I forced fighting at every point along the line, fiercely assailing
Grant and his 'nepotism', on the one hand, and Greeley, and the
spirit of compromise and barter that I felt his nomination represented, on the other."*

In 1869 Train had made twenty-eight speeches in California and eighty
on the pacific coast. He also made a trip over the Union Pacific Railway

on the first train over the line and campaigned throughout the country. The following year he made a concerted effort to set his campaign on a higher note. Relentlessly campaigning throughout the year, he spoke on all the issues of the day. Towards the end of the year he interrupted his campaign by going "Around the World in Eighty Days". This consumed his time from August to December. Seeing the way Train worked, it is most likely that the journey was a calculated effort to achieve a publicity coup. Train probably saw it as a way to gain significant news coverage out of proportion to his meagre resources. He was always an inspired self-publicist.

Throughout the spring and summer of 1871 he made speech after speech at meetings which he liked to call "Presidential Conventions". He planned to raise his public profile to a fever pitch, which would ultimately force either the Democratic or Liberal Republican convention to nominate him. Failing that, he was certain he could mount a successful independent campaign that would result in a landslide victory to place him in the White House.

By the end of the year (though it was interrupted by another trip to Europe in July) he claimed to have addressed more than eight hundred meetings and to have spoken to something like two million people. During three years of active campaigning Train claimed to have earned around ninety thousand dollars in admission charges. If he did indeed rake in this amount, one wonders where it all went, especially considering that Bemis, Train's long-suffering secretary, was only paid sporadically throughout this time.

Will Carleton, the author of *Over the Hill to the Poorhouse*, was at that time a young, ambitious poet and journalist fresh out of college. He painted a pen portrait of Train at this time. Carleton sought out Train in the latter's hotel during one of his lecture tours and remembered the visit vividly after Train's death, when he wrote his recollections for *Harper's Weekly*. Train never even bothered to get up off the bed on which he was resting when Carleton entered his hotel room. He took a quick look at the book of Carleton's poems with which the eager youth presented him. In response to Carleton's plea for career advice, Train answered:

> "I'll tell you what I want you to do, and what'll be better than anything you've got in here (indicating the book). I want you to write a good, long WAIL; one that will reach from the Atlantic to the Pacific Ocean. Do you understand? A great big long wail —

lamenting the terrible fact, which of course you have already
learned, that everything in this world is dead wrong. Of course you
know that you are talking to the next president.

I am also the greatest man in the world. I can give Buddha,
Confucius, Moses, Mohammed, and all the rest of them, fifty on the
string, and then discount them."[2]

Many years later Carleton encountered Train again. Train instantly recognised him and hailed him: "I have followed you ever since you called on me in my little room in one of the worst hotels I have as yet found on the face of the earth. Have you written the Wail yet?"[3]

With talk like this, it was no wonder people began to believe that Train was quite mad. For some time Train had been prophesying Chicago's destruction. In numerous lectures he mapped out his logic on a blackboard, foretelling the destruction of the "doomed city of sin". He believed it would be flooded.[4] One newspaper, remembering his involvement in various disreputable fringe causes such as women's suffrage, Fenianism, Italian independence, Communism, Australian Republicanism, and assorted campaigns, brazenly called him a lunatic and implied that Train might actually have had something to do with the burning of Chicago in the Great Fire. The sole grounds for this accusation lay in the fact that Train had told a Chicago audience on October 7, 1871 that: "A terrible calamity is impending over the city of Chicago! More I cannot say; more I dare not utter." By an eerie coincidence, the Great Chicago Fire started the next day – nobody knows how – and swept through the largely timber-built city, leaving ninety thousand homeless and three hundred dead. It could have been worse, since heavy rainfall extinguished the inferno after a twenty-seven hour rampage.

This blatantly ridiculous charge, along with others damaging but perhaps less far-fetched, provoked a response from Train. On New Year's day 1872 he sent letters to some of these offending papers, threatening a fifty thousand-dollar defamation action unless they published an immediate retraction of both charges. The letters ended in a manner that must have had some wonder whether there might have been some truth in the accusation of lunacy after all:

"Any newspaper copying the aforesaid libel... can make no defense
against a verdict in his [Train's] favor. Any judge or jury attempt-
ing it in this corrupt age might possibly be assisted in forming a

correct opinion through the wild, but stern justice of the Internationale."[5]

It was like waving a red flag to a bull. His talk of imminent action against the offending newspapers only made matters worse. Ever since his return from France, Train had sung the Internationale's praises. Earlier in the year, several papers had noted a sudden appearance of anti-British articles in the New York *Herald*. The Cleveland *Leader* even suggested that Train had become its editor. There was no truth in this particular rumour, though the *Herald* was always a good friend to Train and often published his views. This in itself was bound to attract attention.

"News from London on the Alabama arbitration has thrown Train into violent hysterics," said the *Leader*, "and he immediately sends up his flag, runs out his guns, and raises the war whoop. The *Herald* is filled with paragraphs setting forth what English and Irish members of the Internationale would do to quiet Britain."[6]

As the nominating conventions neared, Train switched his one-man campaign into a higher gear, in the hopes of being adopted as a candidate by some party. Wherever he went he drew crowds and caused a sensation. Even the newspapers, which did not take him too seriously, had to recognise his talents. Don Piatt, editor of the Washington *Capital*, wrote the following incisive analysis of Train:

> *"The majority of people incline to think that Train is but one remove from a madman; he may be in a political point of view, but if he would cease howling for the Presidency, and go on the stage, there would be no actor to compare with him... on the platform people laugh at him; on the stage they would worship him...*
>
> *He has a most startling versatility – passing from the broadly humorous to the most touchingly pathetic with the rapidity of lightning in a fierce storm. His wit is so quick and vivid that its brilliancy blinds the lightning, and the blackness which succeeds is needed to restore the sight.*
>
> *His manner on the platform, like his language, is not unexceptionable. His gesticulation is somewhat muscular. He slaps his thighs until the noise resounds the length and breadth of the hall. He drags himself almost on all fours from corner to corner; then knuckles himself, so to speak, back to the reading desk, which he falls upon as if he would shiver it in pieces and then eat them. He double shuffles and stamps on the floor 'till the dust obscures him;*

he beats his breast, clenches his fist, clutches his hair, plays ball with the furniture, out howls the roaring elements, steams with perspiration, foams at the mouth, paces up and down 'till he looks like a lion in a cage lashing his tail. And yet he is not happy; no, he wants to be President...

And such a mimic is he, that when he placed a chair in the center of the platform, and kept trotting around it to show how certain old fogies revolve in the same everlasting orbit, he actually resembled a dog trying to make time against his disappearing tail. Imitative art can go no farther."[7]

Train's campaign literature was typically bombastic. John Wesley Nichols, the self-styled "Presidential Photographer to the Next President of America" wrote a pamphlet called "The People's Candidate for President, 1872". Train's flamboyant prose ran right through it.

"The Coming President. The Man of Destiny. First Campaign Gun. Victory, 1872; Six million votes, Nov. 12, for the Child of Fate. Train and the People Against Grant and the Thieves! Associated with Mr. Train in the Credit Foncier of America are 100 of the wealthiest men in the country, which is the nucleus of the White House Pool to form the People's Ring that elects the President in 1872.

Is it possible to elect a President who does not drink, smoke, chew, swear, gamble, lie, cheat, steal, who never held public office, never played the demagogue, who has always been right on great national questions, and who believes he is an instrument in the hands of some mysterious power, to emancipate the people from the slavery of Party and the Fanaticism of ages, and who challenges anyone to find a blemish on his reputation..."[8]

Train and Nichols were quite out of their depth. Believing that Don Piatt's description of Train's public speaking skills was something that would attract support, they included his incisive analysis in their campaign literature.

To the disillusioned American electorate the 1872 presidential campaign was an opportunity to show their dissatisfaction with President Grant, who had turned out to be a failure in office. He had even managed to alienate a large section of his own party. These disaffected elements succeeded in organising an anti-Grant or Liberal

Republican movement, as it was called. For many voters the key issues of the election were reconstruction of the Confederate states, corruption in Grant's government, and the need to issue paper money. Many debtors felt this latter measure would benefit them.

The Liberal Republicans met in Cincinnati on May 1, 1872. Many expected Charles Francis Adams, a distinguished diplomat, to be nominated. On the second day of the convention Train made one of the bizarre speeches for which he was now famous. He predicted that America must either "follow him into Utopia over night or go bust". He rounded of his outburst with a war cry of: "All aboard! Get aboard the express train of George Francis Train!" On this cue Train's followers snake-danced down the aisles, their elbows moving in sync like the pistons. As the "train" continued, they "chanted slogans in the rhythm of the steam-exhaust puffing of an engine".[9]

Despite five ballots, Adams's nomination failed to be ratified. Horace Greeley and B. Gratz Brown were nominated on the sixth ballot. The Republican convention met at Philadelphia on June 5–6 and re-nominated Grant. The Democrat meeting in Baltimore on July 9–10 accepted Greeley and Brown on the first ballot. Many Democrats considered this a sell-out. The Republicans ridiculed Greeley and the Democrats. Only a short time before Greeley had been a life-long opponent of the Democrats. Now he was running on their ticket with the Liberal Republicans in the hopes of beating Grant.

The Democrats that were put out by Greeley's nomination split from the main party and became known as the Straight Democrats. They held another convention in Louisville on September 3, 1872. Train arrived in Louisville as a greenback delegate[10] from California, Nebraska, and Wyoming. Despite his credentials, Train was again excluded from this convention. In response, he went out and hired the Louisville Opera House, where he staged his "1028th Presidential Convention" and announced his intention to run as an independent candidate.

Train felt confident that his years of campaigning would pay off and more than make up for his lack of party support. He even went as far as to make plans for a victory dinner at his Newport villa. He refused to retire from the race and back Greeley, or join forces with another candidate, Victoria Woodhull, when such a suggestion was made to him.

Perhaps secretly Train knew it was a hopeless fight. Though he maintained to the end of his life that he fully expected to be elected, he had sailed to Europe again in September and returned in October –

hardly the best way to wage a presidential campaign. True to form, he plunged into the fray against Grant and the Democratic "sellout". He was full of claims of what he would do when elected as "The Coming Man"; for example, he would import millions of immigrants to speed the West's settlement. Under his leadership, Train declared America would become the world's leading economic power.

On November 2, only three days before the election, Train was making a speech from the steps of the Wall Street banking firm when someone in the crowd thrust a newspaper into his hand. Thinking it had something to do with him, Train paused and glanced at it. The report told of the arrest of Victoria Woodhull and her sister, Tennessee Claflin, for publishing libellous material. The Equal Rights Party had nominated Victoria Woodhull for the Presidency in May, so she was in fact an opponent of Train's. Despite this and the fact that Train had no great liking for the two sisters, he gallantly raced to their defence.

---

[1] Don C. Seitz, *Uncommon Americans* (The Bobbs-Merrill Company, Indianapolis, 1925), p. 170.

[2] Quoted in Willis Thornton, *The Nine Lives of Citizen Train* (Greenberg, New York, 1948), pp. 217–218.

[3] *Ibid.*, p. 218.

[4] From the Nebraska City *News*, October 28, 1871, quoted in John Wesley Nichols, ed., *The People's Candidate for President* (New York, 1872).

[5] Quoted in Willis Thornton, pp. 218–221. Karl Marx and Friedrich Engels set out the principles of communism in London in 1848. In 1864 they founded the International Workingmen's Association to further the communist cause against capitalism. It is sometimes known as the First International or, as Train called it, the Internationale.

[6] Quoted in Willis Thornton, above, n. 2, p. 221.

[7] *Ibid.*, pp. 221–222.

[8] *Ibid.*, p. 223.

[9] *Ibid.*, pp. 224–225.

[10] This political party wanted the government to adopt a new monetary policy, namely to issue paper money not backed by gold reserves. They believed that this move would help the nation to prosper.

Victoria Claflin Woodhull was considered the most outrageous and eccentric women in America. She kept all her lovers under the same roof, promoted spiritualism, suffrage, more flexible divorce laws and free love. She was an extraordinary, beautiful woman, who shocked America for more than a decade, as she conducted a personal crusade against convention. For outspokenness she was dubbed "Mrs Satan".

It was not any of these widely advertised qualities that persuaded Train to take up her cause but the fact that he believed that an injustice had been done. When Train read that the two sisters had been jailed for publishing an account of a scandal involving a famous clergyman, he was incensed to see that they had been charged with "obscenity". Train immediately observed that "this may be libel, but it is not obscenity".

The sisters came from a poor background, which they conveniently glossed over in favour of a more picturesque one. They rose without trace by relentlessly self-promoting their clairvoyant and miraculous healing powers. They were enormously successful, especially with the men. It probably did them no harm that they were two stunningly beautiful sirens.

A turning point came when Cornelius Vanderbilt, the richest man in America, sought them out. He was a rapidly ailing man who had lost patience with orthodox medicine. Victoria became a good friend and Tennie became his mistress. Sometimes Vanderbilt asked Victoria for advice about the stock market from the spirit world. He quickly realised that his own intuition was far better than any that her spirits could offer and ended up giving her stock market tips. The sisters opened a brokerage office in 1870, the first to be run by women in the history of Wall Street. It was front-page news and business boomed.

A few months later Victoria Woodhull was once again front-page news when she announced her intention to run for the Presidency. Just as Train had done over the past few years, she promoted her campaign by lecturing across the country. She even launched a newspaper called

Woodhull & Claflin's Weekly that she used to attack her critics. Her opinions were extremely controversial. She supported free love, abortion, birth control, legalised prostitution, vegetarianism, magnetic healing and easier divorce laws. Of course the newspaper was incredibly successful, as everyone wanted to see what the scandalous woman was going to say next.

Victoria's personal life made her an easy target. She had obtained a divorce from her first husband, Canning Woodhull, and married Colonel James Blood. Things got complicated when Woodhull, now a drunken morphine addict, turned up on her doorstep. He had nowhere to go, so she took him in. Her mother, who hated Blood, seized the opportunity and brought a suit against Blood, swearing that he had assaulted her. She casually added that her daughter now had two husbands under one roof, if not in the same bed. Public outrage erupted and the press had a field day on the would-be President's love life.

It was lucky the press never got wind of Victoria's other men. One was Stephen Pearl Andrews, an intellectual who knew thirty languages and had even written a book in Chinese. He, too, joined her collection. Then there was Theodore Tilton. His wife had been seduced by one of Victoria's most outspoken critics, Reverend Henry Ward Beecher, then the most famous preacher in America, believed by everyone to be the nearest thing to a living saint. In fact, between sermons on morality, Beecher had been making love to every pretty female he could lay his hands on. Victoria used this knowledge to her advantage and attempted to blackmail him into supporting her publicly. Reportedly Beecher burst into tears, and begged for her mercy and to be let off the hook. But Victoria was made of sterner stuff and stuck to her guns. When Beecher broke his promise and refused to introduce her at a meeting in Steinway Hall, Victoria went on stage and angrily declared: "My judges preach against free love openly, and practice it secretly."[1]

The good Reverend should have known better than to cross Victoria, and she made sure that he paid for his hypocrisy. She decided to expose Beecher's adulterous affair at a meeting of the National Association of Spiritualists when she addressed their convention, as their president, in the autumn of 1872. When the press ignored her accusations, Victoria and Tennie brought out a special edition of *Woodhull & Claflin's Weekly* revealing the whole sensational truth. The Beecher-Tilton scandal, as it came to be known, caused a sensation. Anthony Comstock – a former travelling salesman and zealous, self-appointed guardian of the nation's morals – had the sisters arrested and thrown into jail for circulating "an obscene and indecent publication". The sisters spent six months behind bars before a technical point gained them a verdict of "Not Guilty". While the details of the scandal were reported in most of the major papers, the sisters were the only ones Comstock went after, because he detested their outspokenness.

Train hurried from Wall Street to Ludlow Street jail, where he found the two sisters in a cell about eight feet by four feet. He assured them that the language used in the papers was "grand, and the truths were eternal". [2]

Train was incensed over the women's treatment. With a piece of charcoal, he wrote epigrams condemning their predicament on the whitewashed walls of their cell. Train assured them that he would never desert them, and he kept his word.

Train hardly noticed as the presidential election came and went. Grant won easily with 3,597,132 of the popular votes and most of the electoral votes. Greeley did surprisingly well, polling 2,834,125 popular votes, which showed how unpopular the Grant administration actually was. If Train got any votes at all, it is not recorded. [3] He was too busy acting in the imprisoned sisters' defence. He started a newspaper, which he called The Train Ligue, and reprinted the material the sisters had been jailed for. When nothing happened, he included erotic extracts from the Bible under sensational headlines. "Every verse I used," he said, "was worse than anything published by these women." This edition was an immediate bestseller. The public eagerly bought the paper on account of these notorious extracts from the Bible. In a few days the price of the paper rocketed from five cents to two dollars a copy. It must have been hot stuff.

At last Comstock took the bait and sought to prosecute Train. Federal authorities sensibly refused to handle the case, but the state legal authorities obliged. [4] Police were soon dispatched to apprehend the moral terrorists. John Wesley Nichols was arrested first. The Train Ligue had been published in his Broadway photographic studio, and he was arrested while overseeing the distribution of a new edition to retailers. Nichols sent a message of warning to Train, but detectives, who must have delighted at their luck when Train practically fell into their laps, followed his messenger. The New York Times reported:

> "He made no resistance... but was exceedingly violent and blasphe-
> mous in his language on the way to the station-house, declaring
> that his paper was obscene, and its object was the refutation and

suppression of the Bible... Train bears his incarceration quietly, and
says that he is too much accustomed to 'Bastile' life to mind this."[5]

Train was sent to the "Tombs" to await trial and sentencing, if any. Although its proper name was "The Halls of Justice", everybody called it the Tombs since an ancient mausoleum in Egypt had inspired its design. It was built on a marshy site and soon after its construction it started to sink and crack. Needless to say, it was a damp hellhole. Its grim, Egyptian-influenced exterior and interior were foreboding. Prisoners were kept in four tiers of cells whose only source of heating was a large stove in the centre of the ground level corridor. Despite all of this, the Tombs had a certain charm.[6]

Train provided great copy for the press, dressed in his fashionable five-hundred-dollar sealskin overcoat, with a flower in its buttonhole. He gave numerous interviews and repeatedly told reporters: "I'll raise hell in this Egyptian sepulchre!" Then he did just that. He wrote endless letters, and received streams of interviewers and guests. He wrote epigrams everywhere in his cell. He refused bail, declared himself guilty of the charges against him, asserted that the liberty of the press was at stake and that no less than two thousand newspapers would fall if the action against his publication succeeded. He insisted that "the mob of the Commune" would tear down the Tombs within thirty days.[7] Amongst other things, he sent this poem to the New York *Sun* as a protest against the freezing conditions in the Tombs (his attorney, Clark Bell, noted that it was nine degrees below zero outside at the time):

> "No gas! No light! No fire!
> Oh, God, how cold is my cell,
> If I had my desire
> I choose a room in Hell!
>
> How well we keep our fast
> Oh, holy saints, how cold!
> The Ring could stop this wintry blast
> With some of their stolen gold.
>
> Money paid for Bibles and priests
> In prayers, tracts, churches and God
> Would keep human beings at least
> From freezing while this side the sod!

Foreign jails have chapels for prayer
And beds and food are clean
Exercise two hours in open air
And your cell is warmed by steam.

The prison inspector ought to be shot
Or be forced to share our graveyard lot
What right have they to stifle our breath?
And why are they paid to freeze us to death?" [8]

Thankfully, Train's public protest forced the authorities to act and conditions were improved.

On December 19 Train was formally charged; it was claimed that he "with force and arms, unlawfully, wilfully, feloniously and maliciously did have in his possession, with intent to sell the same, a certain obscene and indecent paper, entitled *The Train Ligue*." [9] The indictment stated that the paper's contents were too indecent to be read out for the record.

Train was locked up in Cell 56 of "Murderers' Row". At that time twenty-two men charged with murder were incarcerated there. Across the corridor was Edward S. Stokes, charged with the murder of James Fisk, Jr. The men in the cells flanking Train's later rose to become prominent men in the city's administration. Another fellow inmate was a man Train called "the famous Sharkey", who was in worse trouble than any of the others. Fortunately for Sharkey, he made a daring escape owing to the "pluck and ingenuity" of his lover, Maggie Jordan. Realising that they were about the same size, she changed clothes with him in the cell. Next morning the warden was horrified to find a woman instead of Sharkey. That was the last Train ever heard of the escapee.

Train organised his fellow inmates into a society. They responded in kind by electing him president. Perhaps it was some consolation to Train that at last his peers had elected him their leader, albeit of Murderers' Row. His preliminary hearing was held on December 23. The New York *Sun* reported that Train "did not walk in with moody air and cautious tread, like an ordinary prisoner. He rushed in like a modern Achilles, his face lit up, his eyes bright and resolute, and his whole bearng indicative of soul-set determination". [10] Although Train had to compete for newspaper space with the selection of jurors for a scandalous murder case, he still received a large amount of coverage, especially in the New York *Times*, which reported impartially:

"The subject of entering a plea had barely been mentioned to the Court by the Assistant District-Attorney, when Train broke forth with the exclamation, 'I am guilty!'

THE CLERK: *Do you plead guilty to the indictment?*

TRAIN: *I am guilty of publishing an obscene paper composed of Bible quotations.*

The Assistant District-Attorney here moved that the prisoner be remanded for sentence on some future day.

TRAIN: *I wish to hear the indictment against me read in full.*

THE CLERK: *under directions of the Court, then read the indictment.*

TRAIN: *I published the paper; I am the sole proprietor and editor, and Mr. Nichols who was arrested with me, has nothing to do with it; he is simply a newsboy, and I alone am responsible. The statement in the indictment that I gave Comstock a copy of the paper is a lie.*

THE CLERK: *Then you plead Not Guilty?*

TRAIN (very excitedly): *No, sir! I am guilty!*

JUDGE BOARDMAN: *Enter a plea of not guilty; remove the prisoner.*

A plea of not guilty was thereupon entered in both cases by the clerk, Mr. Sparks, and both prisoners were removed from the court in custody of the officers, amid considerable merriment on the part of members of the Bar and the audience. In the wake of Train followed a number of well-known Spiritualists and Free-Lovers. The whole conduct of Train, as well as that of some of those present and sympathizing with him, tended to impress those who witnessed it with a disbelief in their sanity."[11]

In one interview for the New York *Sun*, good-naturedly as ever, Train outlined his plans for America when he became its Dictator. Among his first acts, Train declared, would be to hang the country's murderers, thieves, leading politicians, then a few editors here and there, before working his way through Congress.

By now Train's presidential campaign calling cards had "President, 1872" scored out with a line and replaced with a hand-written "Dictator, 1873". He wrote articles for any newspaper that would print them, signing himself: "Geo. Francis Train. The Coming Dictator".

When John A. Lant, editor of the Toledo *Sun*, was arrested for reprinting some of the material from *The Train Ligue*, it only made Train more determined to make an issue of the obscenity charges against himself. He saw it as a test case, and believed that the charges would never stand up in court.

The authorities were equally determined, but to *avoid* trying Train on the obscenity charge, and tried to get shut of Train any way they could.

> *"I was offered a hundred avenues of escape from jail, every conceivably one, except the honest and straightforward one of a fair trial by jury. Men offered to bail me out; twice I was taken out on proceedings instituted by women; but I would not avail myself of this way to freedom. Several times I was left alone in the courthouse or in hallways, or other places, where access to the street was easy, entirely without guards, in the vain hope that I would walk off with my liberty. I was discharged by the courts; and I was offered freedom if I would sign certain papers that were brought to me, but I invariably refused to look at them. In all cases I merely turned back and took my place in the cell, and waited for justice."*

Train even claimed that one night he dined alone at Delmonico's. "My chief purpose in jail was not to get out, but to be tried on the charge of obscenity. I had been arrested for that offense, and determined that I would be either acquitted or convicted." The Court's attitude was summed up and shared by the *Times,* which referred to "this dreadful person" who for months "obstructed business, distracted judges, and made a travesty of justice, uttering his vapourings and trumpetings."[12]

Early the following spring Train was examined by a Dr Nealis, who found him perfectly sane. On March 17 and again on March 26 he was examined by Drs Hammond and Thaddeus, who formed a joint opinion that he was a monomaniac, that is, a person who is obsessed by one or more subjects; of unsound mind, but not insane.

By late March Train had been three months in the Tombs without any trial at all. The newspapers went to town when it finally came, and named the proceedings the "Train Matinées". The hearing was before Chief Justice Daly. Train's attorney, Clark Bell, acquitted himself well in defence of the charge of insanity. While he conceded that his client expected to become Dictator and asserted that Horace Greeley was poisoned, Bell added that these beliefs were hardly the product of an insane imagination. After all, Train had accomplished a great deal in his career. Bell listed the prosecution's remaining evidence supporting their charge: that Train had formed the Crédit Foncier, the Crédit Mobilier, the Commune in France, the Internationale; and that Train had "deliria de grandeur". Bell went on to review Train's life to show that he had actually done these things, and there was no evidence of any delusion on Train's part.

Bell pointed out that Train's arrest for obscenity was due to his support of Victoria Woodhull's public accusation that Henry Ward Beecher had committed adultery. Train might, he argued, have had "ultra hostile" views, but they did not constitute insanity. People who had known Train in his heyday, men such as George Bemis, the banker Augustus Kountze, and others, came forward and testified that Train was essentially no different than when they had known him as a successful businessman. Bell went on with his essentially accurate description of his client:

"He is a born revolutionist — a magazine with the fire constantly at the fuse — a Vesuvius constantly erupting. He has a front box in the balcony, and admires, in a mirror, the pyrotechnical display of his own volcanic eruptions...

Mr. Train is not the first politician who was very much surprised at the election returns, but he was not insane because he was misled and deceived by all this movement, parade and applause, which he mistook for honest, hearty and candid support."[13]

At the end of Bell's long speech, the jury retired and within a few minutes returned with the verdict: "We find Mr. George Francis Train to be perfectly sane, and responsible for his acts."

The moment of truth for Train finally arrived in 1873 when he was brought to court again before Judge Davis in the Court of Oyer and Terminer. Clark Bell and William F. Howe defended Train. Howe took the stance that, obviously, there could be nothing obscene in the publication of extracts from the Bible and, secondly, even if there was, that Train was insane at the time of the publication. The judge quickly responded that he would instruct the jury to acquit Train if the defence took this position. Bell asked that a simple verdict of "not guilty" be given, but the judge insisted on a verdict of not guilty on the grounds of insanity. This was the verdict rendered.

Train was furious at the turn of events. Instantly he stood up and said: "I protest against this whole proceeding. I have been four months in jail; and I have had no trial for the offence with which I am charged." The judge took no notice of this. Train continued, shouting so that all could hear him: "Your honour, I move your impeachment in the name of the people!"

Needless to say, the judge did not take this outburst well. Train's impassioned speech caused a sensation in the courthouse. "Sit down!" roared the judge. He was heard to say that he intended to send Train to the state asylum at Utica. However, Train was taken back to the Tombs. Now he was a changed man – a lunatic by judicial decree. However dubiously it was declared, this label would now forever taint him.

On May 27 habeas corpus proceedings were instituted before judge Fancher. Train was freed three days later. The moment he got out of the Tombs, he went downtown, "had a bath, got a good meal, put on better clothes, and bought passage for England". From there he travelled on to join his family in Bad Homburg, Germany, since his sons were studying in Frankfurt.

Train would only be jailed once more, in 1889 over a trifling debt for which he had stood guarantee.

"Was it fitting that Boston, where I had lived and worked; where I had devised the building of the greatest ships the world had known up to that time; where I had projected and organized the clipper-ship service to California, and opened a new era in the carrying trade of the world, and where I had organized the Union Pacific Railway to develop the entire West and draw continents nearer together, should put me in jail for a petty debt that I did not owe, as in some sort an evidence of its gratitude?

My prison experience has been more varied than that of the most confirmed and hardened criminal; and yet I have never committed a crime, cheated a human being, or told a lie. I have been imprisoned in almost every sort of jail that man has devised. I have been in police stations, in Marshalseas in England and in Ireland, in common jails in Boston, in the Bastille of Lyons, in the Prefecture at Tours as the prisoner of Gambetta, Dictator of France, and in the famous old Tombs of New York. I have used prisons well. They have been as schools to me, where I have reflected, and learned more about myself – and a man's own self is the best object of any one's study. I have, also, made jails the source of fruitful ideas, and from them have launched many of my most startling and useful projects and innovations. And so they have not been jails to me, any more than they were to Lovelace:

'Stone walls do not a prison make,
Nor iron bars a cage;
Minds innocent and quiet take
That for a hermitage.'"

---

1   Margaret Nicholas, *World's Greatest Cranks and Crackpots* (Hamlyn, London, 1995), pp. 71–77.

2   Heywood Broun and Margaret Leech, *Anthony Comstock* (Wishart & Co., London, 1928), p. 117.

3   Dr Edmund Sullivan, "George Francis Train: Knight of the Rueful Countenance" in *The Rail Splitter* (April 1999), Vol. 4, No. 4.

4   Heywood Broun and Margaret Leech, above, n. 2, p. 118.

5   New York *Times*, December 21, 1872, quoted in Willis Thornton, *The Nine Lives of Citizen Train* (Greenberg, New York, 1948), p. 233.

6   http://www.correctionhistory.org

7   Heywood Broun and Margaret Leech, above, n. 2, p. 119.

8   Quoted in Willis Thornton, above, n. 5, pp. 241–242.

9   Clark Bell, *Speech... upon the Inquiry as to the Sanity or Insanity of George Francis Train* (Russell Bros., New York, 1873), p. 1.

10 New York *Sun*, December 23, 1872, quoted in Heywood Broun and Margaret Leech, above, n. 2, p. 119.

11 New York *Times*, December 24, 1872, quoted in Willis Thornton, above, n. 5, p. 235.

12 Quoted in Heywood Broun and Margaret Leech, above, n. 2, p. 120.

13 Clark Bell, above, n. 9, p. 23.

For the next few months the Trains tried to pick up the pieces of their lives. For a while it seemed that they might be left in peace. Then the *Times* and Reuters press agency published some articles in Europe emanating from America that declared Train was in an asylum. He was furious and demanded an apology for the offensive articles. It's not recorded if he got it. After a six-month stay in Germany, the Trains returned to America towards the end of 1873.

The America they returned to was a very different country than the one they had left to seek peace in Europe. A series of scandals had left America in uproar over the magnitude of political corruption and unethical business practices. The extent of one of the greatest financial and political scandals of the nineteenth century finally became public knowledge that year. It became known as the "Crédit Mobilier scandal", as it revolved around the same institution that Train had helped set up. Luckily for Train, he was not implicated in any way since he had been squeezed out by the other shareholders long before. It had been turned into a construction company, to which the dominant Union Pacific stockholders had awarded extremely lucrative contracts, thereby lining their pockets with huge amounts of money, to the detriment of the entire railway. The construction costs reported by Crédit Mobilier were hugely inflated. It charged more than $94 million for construction that actually cost only $44 million.

One of the dominant shareholders, Congressman Oakes Ames, tried to block a congressional investigation into their activities by distributing Crédit Mobilier stock among his colleagues in the House of Representatives. Congressmen were allowed to make long-term purchases of the stock by using the interest and dividends to pay for the stock itself. No risk was involved, and the profits were high; a reported $33 million profit was made by those who accepted these bribes. Only a few refused.

During the 1872 presidential election a list of those congressmen owning Crédit Mobilier stock was published by the New York *Sun*, along with letters written by Oakes Ames describing his dealings. The taint of this scandal permeated the government. Crédit Mobilier's operations were halted and the Union Pacific Railroad, stripped of all its assets except the roadbed and machinery in order to repay the government loans, was left debt-ridden. Among those implicated in the scandal were Vice-President Schuyler Colfax, Representative James A. Garfield, House Speaker James G. Blaine, and Henry Wilson, the Republican candidate for vice-president.[1]

Although not all charges were proven and the full investigation was finally dropped, many political careers were ruined as a result of these disclosures. A number of judges were impeached or forced to resign, and Oakes Ames was finally censured by Congress in February 1873; he died a few months later. This scandal brought to the public's attention the extent of widespread political corruption and unethical business practices and, as a result, new concern was shown for reform in both areas.

Added to this scandal was the exposure of the so-called "Tweed Ring". Politicians in New York were shown to have systematically diverted massive amounts of taxpayers' money into their pockets.[2] Train later claimed to have been one of the first to attack the Tweed Ring, as early as 1871, before the New York *Times* and Thomas Nast campaigns. By a curious twist of fate, when the ringleader "Boss" Tweed was arrested late in 1873, he was held in the same cell in the Tombs in which Train had scribbled his epigrams on the walls.

Cynicism abounded in the country in such an uneasy political climate. American subversive elements flourished. Clandestine plots to establish a Commune along French lines were mentioned in the press. Eccentrics also prospered. Taking his cue from the court verdict, Train became a professional eccentric, calling himself "the Great American Crank".

He assigned his assets to his wife and went his own way. For years he lived in an attic room under the mansard roof of the Hotel Continental at Broadway and Nineteenth Street, New York. In 1896 his Friend D.O. Mills opened his Mills Hotel No.1 in Bleecker Street. Train moved there and claimed to live on three dollars a week until his death. It is strange to think that among all of Train's voluminous writings are only the briefest of references to his wife and family. Nothing untoward should be read into this, as it is clear that he loved them deeply.

Instinctively, he never publicly spoke about his family. It is clear that Train was never meant to have a quiet life, and his career must have put great strain on them. Throughout the years he not only provided for them, but ensured that they had the best of everything. In his heyday, he prudently put aside large sums of money in trust for his wife and children, so that they would always be well looked after. He saw that his children, in stark contrast to his own upbringing, had the best education money could provide.

It is hard to calculate what Willie must have endured. Apart from a life punctuated by arrests, political agitation, and numerous other diversions, Train had made his presence felt at home. A prime example of his eccentricity is the contract he made with his three children, binding them to keep certain rules drawn up by Train for their benefit. It was so unique, if that is the most apt description, that a lifestyle magazine, the *Herald of Health,* published it.

> "*George Francis Train as Father, Physician and Preacher*
> *His Contract With His Children,*
> *As bends the twig, so inclines the tree*
> *A Child His Own Doctor*
> *Temperance Inculcated, Diet Recommended, Cleanliness*
> *Enforced…".*[3]

Even the *Herald*, which was not widely known for shying away from new fads, had the good sense to add this cautionary caveat: "While there are two or three points in the article slightly at variance with our practice and preaching, it is both interesting and valuable, and will provoke healthy thought."[4]

"LAWS OF HEALTH

> The Chinese only pay their doctors when they are well.
> *George Francis Train covenants and agrees with his beloved children, to pay the following amounts to each, for each and every month the said children refrain from breaking any of the following laws of health:*
> *[It is not to make you love money, except for the good you can do with it, that I make this agreement, but simply as a reward of merit.]*

> *1. Every morning take a bath (first wetting your head and chest)*

RIGHT: The decorated cover of the 1874 edition of Jules Verne's *Around the World in eighty days*.
Courtesy of the Mary Evans Picture Library.

BELOW: Jules Verne, whose celebrated book *Around the World in eighty days* was inspired by Train's exploits.
Courtesy of the Hulton Getty Picture Collection.

A rare photograph of the Trains' son, "Junior", from a sitting in Vevey, France, in 1871.

Collection of Dr. Edmund B. Sullivan.

A photograph of Mrs Wilhelmina Train from a sitting with the same photographer in Vevey, France, in 1871.

Collection of Dr. Edmund B. Sullivan.

George Francis Train.
*From the Laurence Hutton Collection, courtesy of
Princeton University Library. Photograph by Brady's
National Photographic Portrait Galleries, Broadway and
10th St., New York / 627 Pennsylvania Avenue,
Washington, D.C.*

George Francis Train wrote to Ulysses S. Grant in April 1870 informing the President that he was about to be replaced in that office. Train tried to fulfil this promise by campaigning in 1872 – needless to say, Grant won re-election. He drew a small typhoon beneath his signature, presumably in reference to one of his nicknames.

The text reads:

"A Canadian Army is invading Red River Country through American Territory (Canal Sault St. Marie). In name of Ten Million Fenians I protest against this National outrage, while American Citizens are being tortured in British Bastiles and Alabama claims unpaid. Our Flag is already sufficiently dishonored by the inactivity of your Administration, without Submitting to this new disgrace.

Geo. Francis Train
Your Successor as Chief Magistrate of America*"*

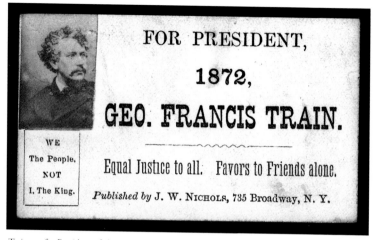

FOR PRESIDENT,

1872,

GEO. FRANCIS TRAIN.

WE
The People,
NOT
I, The King.

Equal Justice to all. Favors to Friends alone.

Published by J. W. NICHOLS, 735 Broadway, N. Y.

Train ran for President of the United States in 1864 and again in 1872. This card from the second
campaign featured his photograph and slogan: "Equal Justice to all. Favors to Friends alone."
Collection of Dr. Edmund B. Sullivan.

A campaign carte promoting the 1872 candidacy of George Francis Train for President.
Collection of Dr. Edmund B. Sullivan.

A small campaign card, printed front and back and distributed in 1872, details the issues of concern for the Train platform and his positions on issues of the day.
The Rail Splitter Archives.

ABOVE: A typical, good-humoured Train autograph, written in the style of a promissory note during the celebration of the centennial of the United States in 1876: "Good for one thousand dollars at the next Centennial..."
Collection of Jonathan H. Mann.

RIGHT: Cartoon *carte de visite* depicting Train on his way back to Ireland. Such cards were actively collected in the mid-to-late nineteenth century. This is a photograph of an engraving by Thomas Nast, the famous American political satirist. GFT was sometimes called "Express Train", hence this caricature.
The Rail Splitter Archives.

LEFT: GFT in his Mill Hotel room, dictating his memoirs, circa 1900.
Collection of Dr. Edmund B. Sullivan / The Rail Splitter Archives

RIGHT: George Francis Train, October 1903.
Courtesy of the University at Albany, SUNY.

LEFT: Train in his last years was as dapper as ever.
Courtesy of Brown Brothers.

RIGHT: Dr Carleton Simon (pictured circa 1950),
who shared Train's belief in the "science" of
phrenology. Simon arranged his friend's funeral
and later assisted at an autopsy of Train's brain.
Courtesy of the University at Albany, SUNY.

The last photograph of George Francis Train.
This unique, previously unpublished portrait is a cabinet card by Schinkel of New York City.
Jonathan Hugh Mann Collection.

with water degrees from seventy to seventy-five, not over five minutes; running around the room with a linen sheet over you, instead of rubbing with rough towels... Five Cents.

2. Every morning brush your teeth, using cold water, instead of... compounds which ruin the teeth... Five Cents.

3. Play in the open air, exercise by walking, riding, driving, swimming... Five Cents.

4. Wear no silk, cotton, woolen, or flannel under-clothes next the skin — being non-conductors they close the pores; linen, being a conductor, should always be used... Five Cents.

5. Wear no corsets, tight dresses, tight waistbands, suspenders, or tight shoes, and never use powder or rouge or eat slate pencils... Five Cents.

6. Drink no water at meals... Five Cents.

7. No meat for breakfast; but one glass of new milk, with bread (one day old), boiled rice or farina, and ripe domestic fruits. (Remember that fruit is gold in the morning, silver at noon, and lead at night.)... After supper eat nothing, drink nothing... Five Cents.

8. Eat nothing between the several meals... Five Cents.

9. Always eat slowly and be regular at meals. Cut your food finely... Five Cents.

10. Drink no kind of wine, spirits, beer, cider, bitters, or other fermented liquors... Five Cents.

11. Use no cigars, tobacco or snuff... Five Cents.

12. Drink no coffee, tea, chocolate, cocoa, or any other warm slops... Five Cents.

13. Take no sugar... Five Cents.

14. Take no pepper... Five Cents.

15. Take no mustard, catsup, or oils... Five Cents.

16. No candy of any kind... Five Cents.

17. No nuts of any kind... Five Cents.

18. No cheese... Five Cents.

19. Very little butter and very little salt... Five Cents.

20. No ice cream or other confectionery... Five Cents.

21. No cakes, pies, or pastry... Five Cents.

22. No pickles, olives or peppers... Five Cents.

23. No lobster, oysters, crabs, salmon, or any kind of fish... Five Cents.

24. Drink no soda, congress or mineral waters of any kind; they are poisonous... Five Cents.

25. Take no salt-water baths... Five Cents.

26. Sleep always with your windows open, and do not be afraid of catching cold... Five Cents.

27. Never sleep during the day time, or read while lying down; especially never read at night while in bed... Five Cents.

28. Don't stand over the register or too near the fire... Five Cents.

29. Take no medicines, nor drink Bourbon, even if the doctor advises it. Medicine and intoxicating liquor are poison... Five Cents. When twelve years old one more important law will be added."[5]

While some of these laws were quite farsighted for their time, the Spartan regime did not allow for many of life's simple pleasures. It would be interesting to know how long the children stuck to it, if they ever did.

Train also issued "The Child's Pocket Etiquette in Ten Commandments [Obey these and you shall have five dollars every Fourth of July, which you may give to the poor.]". They are the usual advice to children, except the tenth, which again showed the kindliness and well-meaning that underscored Train's eccentricity:

> *"Treat all with respect, especially the poor. Be careful to injure no one's feelings by unkind remarks. Never tell tales, make faces, call names, ridicule the lame, mimic the unfortunate, or be cruel to insects, birds, or animals."[6]*

Train closed these warnings to his children with what he called "The New Religion":

> *"Also, my child, commit this short sermon to memory, and teach it to your little friends at school, and you shall receive ten dollars every Christmas:*

Don't drink. Don't smoke. Don't chew. Don't swear. Don't gamble. Don't lie. Don't steal. Don't deceive. Don't tattle. Be polite. Be generous. Be kind. Be neat.

Study hard. Play hard. Be in earnest. Be self-reliant. Be just and fear not. Read good books. Love your fellow man as well as God. Love your country and obey the laws. Love truth. Love virtue and be happy." [7]

For the remainder of his life he became a vegetarian. Peanuts were a particular favourite. He shared his food with the squirrels and pigeons of Madison Square, where he frequently made one of the benches his headquarters. He began to refuse to shake hands, claiming that such contact robbed him of his "psychic forces". Whenever he met a new acquaintance, Train would shake hands with himself as a means of conserving his energies. For a while he stopped talking with everyone (except children) and wrote messages on a writing pad when he wanted to communicate. Two years before his death he even went as far as to state: "Through psychic telepathy, [I] am doubling [my] age. Seventy-four years young". He believed he would live to be around 150 years.

Shunning the traditional Christian calendar, he invented a new one based on his date of birth. For example, 1876 became P.E. 47, (Psychological Era, forty-seven years after his birth).

It was a period of introspection for him. For some time Train had been drawn toward the Shakers. Though he did not count himself one of them, "our affinities are strong," he wrote, "on diet, exercise, hygiene, sexual continence, abstention from poisonous stimulants, freedom from bigotry, fanaticism, superstition, and in bold advocacy of great truths." [8]

Recalling that Brigham Young, Jr., one of the leaders of the Mormon movement had visited him in the Tombs, Train wrote that Mormonisim was not for him: "I endorse their temperance, frugality, thrift, enterprise, independent thought, etc., yet I am not a Mormon...". [9]

Neither was he a Christian: "I never drink, smoke, swear, lie, cheat, steal, fornicate, never back-bite, make pastoral visits, nor wish I was dead... I do not believe it possible by any act of mine that I could injure my fellow-man – yet I am not a Christian...". [10]

Train went on to debate the positive aspects of Infidels, Pagans, Scientists, and Spiritualists, before acknowledging in each case that he was not one of them. "What I am," he concluded, "all the world will soon know." [11]

He was clearly optimistic about the future and saw great opportunities on the horizon.

"Having eaten no meat, eggs, fish, oysters, poultry, or animal food of any kind for many months, all the ancient argument, antagonism, ferocity of my nature has died out, and yet I am in savage health and terrible mental vigor. ... I am either incubating some gigantic power to develop love and truth in mankind, or I have culminated in the most magnificent fizzle produced for centuries."[12]

He continued to wear in his buttonhole the fresh flower that had always graced it in the days of his prosperity. He often sported a red or scarlet ribbon across his chest, as a symbol of his "Communard" adventure. He preferred to be known as "Citizen" Train, evoking French revolutionary ideals, though he emphasised that he did not belong to any political party or religion, but was merely a citizen of the United States of America.

Hydrotherapy is the use of water in the treatment of disease. For a while Train lived at Miller's Bath Hotel and Home of Health on 28th Street and received care. The owner, Dr E.P. Miller, got to know Train quite well. Instead of Miller looking after Train's health, it turned out the other way around. Dr Miller stated, on the record, that Train had cured him of an old illness.

Miller believed that Train had concluded that the American people were unworthy of his leadership after they had let Train rot in the Tombs instead of securing his freedom and proclaiming him their leader. He also explained Train's obsession with his health:

"His religious belief is that God thinks the most of and will only save those who take the best care of themselves, and consequently his motto is to take care of Train."[13]

Eventually Train lost interest in Dr Miller and his hydrotherapy. The Shakers also lost their attractiveness when Train discovered that their principal means of making a living was cultivating and preparing herbs for the drug industry, since he was an ardent hater of such medicines.

By this time Train made a living by writing and lecturing. He wrote numerous articles for newspapers with some success, as many were friendly towards him. Men such as E.P. Mitchell and Amos J. Cummings of the New York *Sun* held the brilliant, self-constituted crank in high regard. He would write countless numbers of weird and almost illegible postcard notes on current topics, and indeed on any topic that took his fancy, using a double-ended red and blue pencil to striking effect. In time these coloured pencillings became a trademark of his.

He certainly was a prolific source of material and stories for newspapers. A typical example, quite characteristic of his life in Madison Square, is taken from the New York *World* of August 8, 1892:

> "*A tall, lank man walked across Madison Square Park yesterday morning and accosted nearly everybody he met with the query 'Want to buy a mocking bird?' He carried a flat pasteboard box about eight inches square in his hand. Inside fluttered a bird, which apparently did not relish its confinement at all. Small holes punctured in the sides of this improvised cage gave the songster a chance to breathe.*
>
> *George Francis Train was occupying his usual bench. As the vendor approached he asked him to let him view the mocking bird.*
>
> *'How much do you want for him?' inquired the philosopher.*
>
> *'It's worth $1,' said the man, to whom it would appear such a sum was something as large as the side of a house.*
>
> *'Can he fly?' queried the philosopher.*
>
> *The man nodded his head. 'My little boy ketched him in a trap,' he said.*
>
> *'Will the little boy get the dollar?' went on Mr. Train.*
>
> *'His mother will,' answered the man.*
>
> *'Well,' returned George Francis, 'if this bird has been in 75 jails the way I have, he will appreciate getting out,' and fishing one dollar out of his white coat pocket, the sage handed it to the man. Then untying the string he lifted the cover off the box. There was a whirr as the bird flew out like a shot.*
>
> *The vendor, who didn't appear to be a particularly industrious soul, looked at Train with an expression of disgust. 'You're a chump,' he said.*
>
> *'You're another,' returned the Citizen. 'Why don't you go to work instead of peddling your little boy's pets?'*
>
> *The man muttered something and slunk off, as the bird, evidently weary with his cramped wings, sat on a neighboring branch and began to make his toilet, meanwhile thanking his liberator in a chirp or two.*
>
> *'That gives me more real pleasure than a pint of peanuts,' said Mr. Train, and the mocking bird doubtless thought the same.*"[14]

His lectures were sensational and highly successful. As time went on they became more and more eccentric. Because of the free publicity Train received from his time in the Tombs, he found himself in greater demand than ever. He took to the lecture circuit and was able to make a living from a few evenings of work here and there. It is said that the greatest form of flattery is imitation and Train certainly had his imitators. Ike Ives – a sort of eccentric like Train, though on a more modest scale – once brought Train to his home town of Danbury, Connecticut, for some appearances. When Train failed to turn up for one of the scheduled lectures, Ike disguised himself as Train and gave the promised "wild-eyed oration to a full house, declaiming that he/Train considered Danbury 'a dead place, eaten up by fogyism', and that he was coming here to live, to shake the place out of its lethargy".[15] At the end of his performance Ike astonished the crowd by revealing his true identity. It is not recorded what Train made of all this.

Train still had his wits about him and was a match for any critic in the audience. While delivering a lecture in Omaha, the city that Train came to be closely associated with, Pete Ihler, a distiller who had purchased the Cozzens House from the Crédit Foncier through foreclosure, denounced Train as an anarchist. "My fellow-citizens," Train answered, "I have been informed that Pete Ihler has referred to me as an anarchist. In reply allow me to say that there is more anarchy in one barrel of Pete Ihler's whiskey than there is in 100,000 George Francis Trains."[16]

As time went on and Train became less of a crowd-pulling attraction, he resorted to clever marketing as a means of attracting audiences. Advance notices of his lectures were given a makeover to make the public aware of the forthcoming showman. For example, lecture bills for "P.E.–49" (i.e.1878) looked as if a circus was coming to town:

"Geo. Francis Train is in Town!

CITIZEN: Keep this (handbill) as White House Introduction!

G.F.T. On His Way! This is Mr. Train's Last Public Appearance in Boston before the Psychologic Evolution organizes Absolute Dictatorship.

Mr. Train requests that no 'acquaintance,' 'relative,' or 'friend' will shake hands with, touch, or speak to him when he leaves the hall, as he wishes to conserve his magnetism, electricity, and longevity for the use of his little friends in Madison Square, where all children, poor as well as rich, are invited to call upon him; but their

parents and nurses are requested not to draw on his psychology by
remaining with them when at his peanut bench."[17]

Though the papers would often publish accounts of Train's sensational
lectures, this was not good enough for him. He started up his own
paper, *The Dictator*, as a means of getting his views across to the public.
It was apparently a four-page handbill filled with accounts of his lectures and, of course, his life story, with a "boiled-down history of the
World" thrown in for good measure.

As the years passed Train's popularity declined, despite his stunts.
Gradually his lecture rates fell down to one hundred dollars, but he
still gave excellent value. He usually illustrated the lectures using a
huge blackboard. As he dashed around the stage, he reinforced his
points on it in his wild handwriting without interrupting his flow of
words.

If Train's own figures are an accurate indication, he was quite successful. On the P.E.–49 (that is, 1878) handbill he claimed, "1400 people paid Sunday night in Milwaukee! Lectured 19 successive nights in
Newark! 9 Toledo! 6 Detroit! 9 Chicago! 8 Boston!" He even quoted a
"Press Dispatch" as saying: "Train delivered his 16th lecture to 2000
persons in Newark last evening amid great excitement, the audience
repeatedly voting him Dictator."[18]

With his lightening-quick mind and elephant-like memory, Train
spoke without any prepared notes on any subject that the audience
wanted. He specialised in answering any questions asked. This in itself
was no mean feat, since in the course of one lecture there would often
be as many as a hundred. Much to the enlightenment and amusement
of audiences, he pulled off this feat of mental agility with seeming
effortlessness.

Besides making a living from writing and lecturing, Train was able
to indulge in his passion for causes. In 1874 he became a champion of
the working man.[19] Throughout most of the nineteenth century the law
viewed labour unions as illegal "conspirators" against employers and
their interests. As a result, union activists, organisers and leaders were
arrested wholesale and jailed. The local authorities similarly broke up
pickets, boycotts and strikes. Peaceful demonstrations were termed
"riots" and violence was used to break them up. In short, the supporters of any kind of organised protest against poor working conditions
were arrested and jailed or dealt with in a heavy-handed matter. Train
became a strong supporter of their cause. He actively made speeches on
their behalf and even lobbied his old Union Pacific colleague, General

Dix, now governor of New York, to pardon Christian Mayor, a victim of the 1874 Tomkins Square "riots".

Train's petitions for workers' rights were somewhat at odds with his treatment of his own "employees". On August 16, 1876, this legal notice appeared in the *Omaha Bee*:

> *"To George Francis Train, non-resident of Omaha.*
>
> *You are hereby notified that George P. Bemis, on the second day of May, A.D. 1876, commenced a civil action against you by filing his petition in the District Court in and for Douglas County, Nebraska.*
>
> *The object and prayer of which said petition is to recover from you the sum of $47,660.68 and interest thereon from November 15, 1874, due said Bemis from you for his services as your private secretary, and moneys by him expended for you.*
>
> *You are further notified that an order of attachment has been duly issued against you in said action and levied upon the following described real estate...".*[20]

Train's dream of a chain of cities along the route of the Union Pacific was long dead by now. The key to his plan, his holdings in Omaha, had been sold when the cheap loans he had bought them with were foreclosed. Whatever assets remained were now held as security to pay Bemis's unpaid salary. Unfortunately for Bemis, the remainder was calculated later that year to amount to, not millions, but $1,500.

In a later petition Bemis stated that he started working as Train's private secretary in November 1864. He recalled:

> *"The said Train at that time was a man of large influence and was indirectly connected with some of the largest enterprises in the United States, to wit: The Corporations known as the Credit Mobilier of America and the successful construction in the shortest possible time of the Union Pacific Railroad — procured the passage of an act in Nebraska by its Legislature incorporating what is known as the Credit Foncier of America whose pretended object was to buy large tracts of land along the line of the Union Pacific Railroad, as well as being engaged in the construction of street railways in London, as well also as being and becoming an aspirant for the highest office in the gift of the people.*

> *Plaintiff further says, that by reason of his various business con-*
> *nections with these important enterprises and his unbridled ambi-*
> *tion for political preference, he deemed it important and necessary*
> *to employ some competent and true man to act as his confidant and*
> *private secretary in all his business and political relations.*"[21]

Bemis went on to say that Train agreed to pay him $5,000 a year. Although he had faithfully performed his duties, "in many instances jeopardising his own personal safety and life", up to December 10, 1875, Train had paid him a total amount of only $17,974.65, leaving a balance of $47,660.68 due. In other words, while Bemis had acted as his cousin's private secretary for twelve years, he had actually only received four years of pay. He had, however, gained in other ways through Train's influence. He had seen the world serving as a sort of omni-competent and long suffering Passepartout, extracting Train from misadventures along the way, but he had also been appointed the Crédit Foncier's secretary and manager. Besides this, he had a lucrative sideline as a real estate, loan and collection agent in Omaha, owing in part to Train's patronage. By all accounts, he seems to have been very success-ful at this. In time he became one of Omaha's most prominent towns-people and was eventually elected its mayor.

Bemis had nothing against Train personally, and remained on friendly terms with him. He only naturally wanted what was legally due to him, before it was too late to press his claim. In fact, he was too late. There was nothing left to pay Bemis with. The man whose efforts had gone beyond the call of duty in Train's service was never properly reim-bursed financially. Other creditors had beaten Bemis to the courts, not that they had any significant success either. On March 31 Train's financial affairs were examined in minute detail by New York's Marine Court. That day's Omaha *Herald* contained an account of the proceedings:

> *"George Francis Train Fails and Counts Up His Assets and Liabilities. A Funny Showing.*
>
> *In the Marine Court today George Francis Train was examined in regard to his property in consequence of proceedings instituted by creditors.*
>
> *He said he lived at No. 61 Lexington Ave., and he had a wife and three children (not living there); that he was in no business at present, but had obtained large profits by lecturing as a*

Presidential Candidate, and that he has expended large amounts in
charity and in advancing his claims as a candidate.

He said he had no personal property except his clothes and
watch worth about $100 and he had paid about $10 a week for
his board.

Fifteen years ago he settled $100,000 on his wife.

Among his claims of assets he mentioned the following:

Claim against British Government, $1,000,000
Claim against James McHenry — negotiating bonds of the
Atlantic and Great Western Railway, 500,000
Claim against the Home Railroad Co. of Birkenhead County,
England, 1,000,000
Claim for helping to build the Union Pacific Railroad, 300,000
5000 lots in Omaha and Chicago, 10,000,000
Claim for exposing the Beecher-Tilton scandal, 100,000
Claim for false imprisonment by the New York authorities,
1,000,000

His other assets consist of claims against various governments,
and of lots throughout the United States.

In a few days Justice McAdam will appoint a receiver for the
estate of Mr. Train." [22]

Although he had tens of millions of dollars conjured up on paper, the
only tangible assets that George Francis Train could be said to own were
a watch and the clothes he wore. It seems that his various political
enterprises had led to an appalling neglect of his business affairs, dis-
solving any chance he had of making a fortune and silencing his critics
once and for all.

Early in 1877, Train surfaced again. When publisher John A. Lant
was arrested for selling his newspaper, the Toledo *Sun*, containing a
prayer for Henry Ward Beecher written by Train and Ingersoll's
"Oration of the Gods" — similar material to that which had got Train
jailed in the Tombs — Train started another newspaper and donated the
proceeds to Lant's family while he was in jail. Lant, a long-time associate of Train's, was pardoned by President Grant in March and Train shut
down the paper. Later on Lant sold copies of Train's newspaper *The
Dictator* at his lectures, and his children hawked Train's picture up and
down the aisles.

In 1879 Willie Train died. Though they had lived separate lives for some years, there was no animosity between the Trains or thought of divorce. Her husband had simply left to live his life the way he preferred. There did not seem to be another woman. Years before his financial ruin, Train had prudently set up a trust fund for her. This money had allowed Willie to live out the remainder of her days in the quiet obscurity she preferred, far from the limelight. In any case, their separation was amicable, since the children were grown up. Train had seen them raised and well educated in America and Europe, and given a chance to see the world. The two boys, George Francis Jr. (called "Junior") and Elsey McHenry, had been started in careers at Augustus Kountze's bank in Omaha and his only daughter, Sue, was married to Philip Guelager.[23] She was the one who remained closest to him. Occasionally Train visited her at her home in Stamford, Connecticut, but he repeatedly turned down her invitations to stay permanently.

A December issue of the *Canadian Illustrated News* showed that Train still had potential as a lecturer. Phineas T. Barnum, perhaps the greatest showman the world has ever seen, reputedly offered Train fifty thousand dollars for one year's lecturing in America and Great Britain. Quite uncharacteristically, if the story is true, Train turned him down flatly. Perhaps the story is entirely false, since it makes great copy. It is questionable if Train would have ever turned down such a golden opportunity to travel, lecture to the masses and rake in the cash, just like the old days. The *News* wrote:

> "Train's mind may now be a little unbalanced, but he used to talk
> to the public in a very interesting way, and his lectures on the stage
> at one time created a sensation and were pecuniarily successful. We
> believe Train long ago made up what he is pleased to call his mind
> never more to speak to an adult. In pleasant weather he spends his
> days in Madison Park, playing with children in an affectionate but
> very innocent way. He daily carries candies, jumping-ropes and
> toys to the park, and amuses the children to their heart's content
> and his. Train lives at the Ashland House in Fourth Avenue, and
> spends much of his time in reading the newspapers and in scrib-
> bling. He sits in the southernmost corner window with his back to
> the street, and the left lapel of his coat always bears an immense
> bouquet of gorgeous fresh flowers. His hair is iron gray; his com-
> plexion dark brown, from exposure to the sun. His physique is fine-
> ly formed, and he looks the very picture of health. Train takes no

*notice whatever of the passersby, and seems to be very well satisfied
with himself. We believe he has large means."*[24]

In early 1886 labour unions began actively campaigning for an eight-hour day. Serious trouble was anticipated. On May 1 many workers struck for shorter hours. An active group of radicals and anarchists became involved in the campaign. Two days later, a shooting and one death occurred during a riot in Chicago. May 4 brought events to a tragic climax at the city's Haymarket Square, where a protest meeting was held to denounce the events of the previous day. As police were trying to disperse the crowd, a bomb exploded, killing eight officers. Eight men were arrested and tried. One received a sentence of fifteen years of imprisonment, but the rest were sentenced to death. A campaign was started to secure a new trial and then clemency for the condemned men. Train was one of those who supported this campaign and gave a series of lectures on their behalf throughout the country. Four of the men were hanged. The wife of one of these men, August Spies, sent Train a photograph of her husband as a means of showing her appreciation for his efforts.

Another condemned man committed suicide. The remaining two on death row had their sentences commuted from death to life imprisonment. The campaigners' efforts finally paid off in 1893 when Governor John P. Altgeld pardoned the three remaining Haymarket prisoners.

Train's lectures were as sensational as ever, as his lecture poster testified. It was a wonderfully charming example of a showman at work and is full of magnificent exaggeration – anything to draw crowds:

*"Geo. Francis Train, the Orator, Scholar, Statesman and Walking
Encyclopedia of Knowledge will lecture in your city
upon one of the following subjects:*

*'The Downfall of the American Public' 'Ireland and its Cause'
'Monopoly and Monopolists'
'Canada and Canadians'
'Universal Knowledge'
'How to Dispose of the Surplus' and supplement his lecture with
a discussion of the resources of your own city.*

*Geo. Francis Train was a name once familiar in every American
household, and was the synonym of Courage, Energy and Ability.*

He was regarded throughout the civilized world as the representative American. Mr. Train has traveled three times around the world, visiting all the Barbarians, semi-Civilized and Civilized Nations of the Earth, becoming thoroughly familiar with the customs of the people, and mastering their language and dialects. His memory is phenomenal, never forgetting anything that has at any time in his life appealed to any one of the five senses.

A man with the brains of twenty men, the energy of a hundred, and the magnetism of a God. His oratory is grand — majestic. His satire as keen and piercing as the poigniard. His wit and repartee as spontaneous and brilliant as a flash of lightning. He is accused of eccentricity, very cheerfully accepting the term, he defines it as being without a fixed orbit. For fourteen years Mr. Train has made Madison Square, New York City, his headquarters; his companions being crowds of innocent children, who come to him with their confidence and their love, and the little sparrows that flocked about him to take the crumbs from his hand. He would not communicate with adults by word of mouth. This rest so much needed has recuperated his wonderful vitality, and the long pent up forces refuse longer to be imprisoned. Again he has concluded to take to the rostrum, and again he will wield the same charm over his auditors as in years past. His resources are inexhaustible; his magnetism irresistible, and with the sceptre eloquence he reigns supreme." [25]

Train saw the inside of his last jail in late September 1889, while on a lecture tour in Boston. When he had been declared bankrupt in 1876 one of the judgments against him was a note which he had endorsed for John A. Lant, of the Toledo *Sun*. Lant had written to Train in Europe in 1872, asking him to guarantee a small loan to allow him to buy type. Train had done so, since he saw Lant as someone whom he was obliged to help. As the years passed the note had changed hands until it reached Dr Oscar M. Spiller, who bought it on account of Train's personal endorsement.

Spiller had made several fruitless attempts to collect from Lant. Then, in desperation, he approached Train on his Madison Square bench. Unfortunately, he met with a similar response. As a final resort, the Doctor went to court and got a new judgment for the money, which now amounted to $669-07 (including interest). The sheriff and several reporters easily found Train, who was sitting in the cafe of the Tremont

House. Somewhat bemused, Train surrendered peacefully, no doubt reminiscing that it was like old times. After a gentle stroll back at the sheriff's office, Train good-naturedly filled out his jail registration papers thus:

"*Registered No. Cell 10. Mittimus No. 2,000.*
NAME: Geo. Francis Train, more commonly known as 'Champion Crank.'
BIRTHPLACE: 21 High St., Boston.
RESIDENCE: Continental Hotel, New York City, now but generally in some jail!
COLOR: Octoroon. [Train's own joke at his swarthy complexion.]
AGE: Sixty! SEX: Male. HEIGHT: 5 feet 11.
BIRTHPLACE OF FATHER: Boston. He founded Boston Port Society and Father Taylor's Seamen's Bethel!
BIRTHPLACE OF MOTHER: Waltham, Mass. (My room, bed, desk, in homestead 200 years old, still shown strangers!)
MARRIED: Yes! 1851! Wife died 1879!
EDUCATION: Three months. Winter School.
TEMPERATE: Yes. (Never tasted liquor!)
PROPERTY: Own half Omaha when I choose to become sane!
EVER IN REFORM SCHOOL? WHERE? Yes! Three times 'round world, 27 times across Atlantic!
NO. OF CHILDREN UNDER 15: None! (Three living grown up!)
OCCUPATION: Aristocratic loafer!
WHEN COMMITTED: Sept. 24, 1889! (Tremont House, Boston.)
OFFENSE CHARGED: Helping poor printer buy printing press 16 years ago.
NO. OF TIMES COMMITTED: Twice for this one offense! In 14 jails for telling truth!
SENTENCE OR OTHERWISE: So long as blackmailer pays my board.
NON-PAYMENT OF FINE AND COSTS: Have not paid cent for anything, and don't intend to!
WITNESS: Geo. Francis Train, who has Boston? Bay State? Republic? American justice's generating power in steel trap!

Geo. Francis Train
(Fifteenth jail)"[26]

Basking in the limelight, Train gave the newspapers his own version of the episode, adding:

> "It is all a political dodge. This man is connected in some way with the politicians who want to get me out of way because I have let in the light on the Crapo-Brackett arrangement [a banking scandal] and opened the eyes of the voters. I told them in my two lectures how there was not a cent in the savings banks, and we were on the eve of a financial crash, and they got back at me in this way."[27]

The sheriff's office was good enough to allow Train to send a short but incoherent dispatch to the New York *World*. The following day the prisoner was brought from the Charles Street jail to the poor debtor's court before Judge Ely. His performance was reported in the September 24, 1889 edition of the Boston *Daily Globe*.

> "'Can I in law do anything here to satisfy this court?' asked Train. The judge said he could give bail.
>
> MR. TRAIN: *Which I refuse.*
>
> THE JUDGE: *Or take the poor debtor's oath.*
>
> MR. TRAIN: *Which I cannot, as I don't believe in God, and am a lunatic.*
>
> THE JUDGE: *Well, I have only to commit you to jail.*
>
> MR. TRAIN: *Precisely. I am a lunatic, and as I have won that reputation by careful attention to business, I don't want to lose it now. (Great laughter, in which the judge joined.)*
>
> *Mr. Train then commenced to pitch into the Boston newspapers for not having published his lectures. He asked, 'Is this in order?'*
>
> *The judge said, 'Certainly.'*
>
> *'Well,' said Mr. Train, 'I rather like this court. 'Tis kind of genial.' (Laughter.) 'I was six months in jail in New York for quoting a statement which the authorities did not like.'*
>
> THE JUDGE: *It looks as if you would be compelled to stay in jail here forever.*
>
> MR. TRAIN: *It looks that way. Well, everywhere I go I demoralize the prisoners. (Laughter.) The only place I ever met honest men was in jail. All the thieves are outside. If I ever get out I will go to the dime museum as a freak. (Laughter.)*
>
> *The judge then wrote an order for Mr. Train's committal to the*

*Suffolk County Jail, and Train, with a courtly bow to the court and
the reporters, left in the custody of Sheriff Fitzpatrick."*[28]

Everyone except Dr Spiller was entertained. It quickly became apparent to him that Train would never pay his debt: he was quite comfortably ensconced in the jail and happily announced his intention to spend the rest of his life there, if needs be. It was generally felt that he had acted very heavy-handedly with the harmless eccentric. The treatment meted out to Train came in for an inordinate amount of criticism from the public and the Doctor was forced to respond. In a letter to the Boston *Globe*, published on September 25, Dr Spiller explained his not unreasonable point of view. He defensively pointed out that the judgment had stood for years and that he had been unable to collect. Only then did he take the only further option available to him, namely having Train arrested.

The following day the *Globe* editorialized: "Citizen Train says that he has been in 14 jails and that Boston's is the best. We return the compliment by saying that of all the prisoners that Charles Street jail ever contained, George Francis Train is the most interesting." A similar sentiment was expressed on October 5 in a letter, signed simply "C.B.". It protested against the unnecessarily harsh arrest.

*"I regard that as an outrage on such a man as George Francis Train,
a worthy American citizen. In no other city in the country would
Mr. Train, I believe, have been arrested on a similar charge. I believe
the note was a pretext. Malice was what prompted this arrest, as he
gave expression to his honest thoughts, in Boston, the other night.
It recalled the days of Garrison when he was mobbed on State
Street, and were Wendell Phillips alive today he would say that the
arrest of Mr. Train was a blow at the dignity of free speech on this
continent."*[29]

Train was delighted to receive the attention. On his release he moved into the Tremont House and was soon the centre of attention. A fire broke out in the nearby Houghton & Dutton's department store and one of the firemen was overcome by smoke. Train acted quickly, breaking into the hotel bar, which had been closed for the night, and commandeered a bottle of whisky, which he administered to revive the man. Then he made a speech on whisky, of which he said he was a judge, although he did not drink alcohol. He added he had once laid fifteen Englishmen drunk with whisky under his table and remarked that they could drink more of it than any people on earth – when it was free!

He lectured to a large audience at the Boston Music Hall, calling the city a "backwoods town"[30] where a man could be imprisoned on a bogus affidavit. Harvard, he said, had become a school for football players, and poor ones at that, while Massachusetts had produced no great alumni since such politicians and lawyers as Rufus Choate and Daniel Webster. Train rounded off his stay by paying a visit to his home town of Waltham. He gave a huge children's party, playing Santa Claus himself. By all accounts it was a tremendous success.

[1] Charles Phillips and Alan Axelrod, eds, *Encyclopedia of the American West* (Simon & Schuster, New York, 1996), p. 414.

[2] *Encyclopedia Britannica* (15th edition, Chicago, 1994), Vol. 12, p. 78.

[3] An article from *Herald of Health*, courtesy of the Western Reserve Historical Society.

[4] *Ibid.*

[5] *Ibid.* This "one more important law" remains a mystery.

[6] *Ibid.*

[7] *Ibid.*

[8] Quoted in Willis Thornton, *The Nine Lives of Citizen Train* (Greenberg, New York, 1948), p. 263.

[9] *Ibid.*

[10] *Ibid.*

[11] *Ibid.*

[12] *Ibid.*, pp. 263–264.

[13] *Ibid.*, p. 264.

[14] New York *World*, August 8, 1892.

[15] Jan Swafford, *Charles Ives – a Life with Music* (W.W. Norton, New York, 1996), p. 14.

[16] Quoted in Willis Thornton, above, n. 8, p. 267.

[17] *Ibid.*

[18] *Ibid.*, p. 268.

[19] Thomas W. Herringshaw, "George Francis Train" in *Prominent Men and Women of the Day* (A.B. Gehman & Co., Chicago, 1888).

[20] *Omaha Bee*, August 16, 1876.

[21] Quoted in Willis Thornton, above, n. 8, pp. 259–260.

[22] *Ibid.*, pp. 260–261.

[23] Guelager was head of the Gold and Silver Department of the New York City Sub-treasury.

[24] *Canadian Illustrated News*, December 29, 1883.

[25] From a lecture poster in the Carleton Simon papers at Albany University, New York.

[26] Don C. Seitz, *Uncommon Americans* (The Bobbs-Merrill Company, Indianapolis, 1925), pp. 176–177.

[27] Willis Thornton, above, n. 8, p. 272.

[28] *Ibid.*, pp. 272–273.

[29] *Ibid.*, p. 273.

[30] Don C. Seitz, above, n. 26, p. 178.

TWENTY-TWO
Outdoing Phileas Fogg

If there was one certain way to achieve fame and fortune in the latter half of the nineteenth century, even only of a fleeting kind, it was to cut a few days, hours or minutes from the time of the fastest previous journey around the world. It became particularly fashionable after the publication of Jules Verne's *Around the World in Eighty Days*. Such journeys were no mean feats in themselves, even if new railroads and faster ships speeded things up. In Train's day, each journey that cut a few days from the time of global circumnavigation was greeted with cheers, frenzied publicity, and sometimes considerable monetary returns.

"This hustling around the world for the mere sake of hustling had come to be quite a fad, you know," wrote S.W. Wall. "Train back early in '89 had declared that he could compass the circuit in sixty days – that he knew a way just a little out of the beaten path, that would make Phileas Fogg appear really silly."[1]

Train had indeed seen a way that would cut a considerable amount of time off the journey. He had even gone as far to plan another mad dash around the world, accompanied by A. Miner Griswald, editor of *Texas Siftings*, but all his efforts had come to nothing when he was jailed in Boston for a debt he had guaranteed for a friend many years before.

In November that year the New York *World* attempted a sensational newspaper coup by sending one of its reporters, Nellie Bly, on a trip around the world in an attempt to break "Phileas Fogg's record".[2] She was one of the *World's* star reporters, with several scoops to her credit. The *Cosmopolitan* magazine dispatched Elizabeth Bisland on a simultaneous trip in an attempt to make its name in an increasingly cut-throat and sensationalistic market place. Nellie Bly won the race and set a new record of seventy-two days, six hours, and eleven minutes, while Elisabeth Bisland completed the trip in seventy-six days – close, but not close enough. While Nellie Bly returned in triumph and became one of the most famous women of her time, history has not been as kind to Elisabeth Bisland, whose only crime was to come second.[3]

Train was incensed that his efforts had been eclipsed and immediately began planning to restore his honour. Early in 1890 he went to Col. John A. Cockerill of the New York *World* and proposed that it sponsor his journey for a new record. Col. Cockerill, already holding the record by virtue of Nellie Bly's efforts, was not interested. Fortunately, fate intervened on Train's behalf. One morning while sitting at breakfast at Tremont House, a note was handed to him. It was from Mrs R.F. Radebaugh, acknowledging some material of Train's that she had used in her husband's newspaper, the *Tacoma Daily Ledger*. Train took the bill of fare lying before him, and on the back, wrote:

> *"To Citoyenne (Old Friend) Mrs Radebaugh. In acknowledgment of kindly note. O. K. Why not sell Theatre for $1,000 lecture, and I will go round world in sixty days.*
>
> Geo. Francis Train"[4]

After receiving a telegram from Mr Radebaugh, proprietor of the *Ledger*, guaranteeing him 1,500 dollars, Train set off for Tacoma. When he arrived on the morning of March 14, he found that the streets were crowded with people and with an eighty-piece band, headed by military and civic organisations. Officials and prominent citizens were present in carriages, and a barouche carriage with six white horses and a gilded harness waited on the distinguished and eccentric "Citizen" himself: clearly, it had become known that the great journey was to begin and finish in Tacoma. This, it appeared, had been Train's plan from the first. This was the route he had referred to. He had long known that the northern route (by way of Puget Sound) across the Pacific Ocean was between two and three days shorter – by some eight hundred miles – to Yokohama and Hong Kong, than travelling by way of San Francisco.

News spread like wildfire of Train's journey. More than 4,200 dollars were raised in one night alone when Train lectured in Tacoma Theater the following evening. Crazy prices as high as 500 dollars were paid for a box. It was seen as a once-in-a-lifetime event. Audiences packed into the Germania hall on two further nights. Train held them spellbound. "This is but the re-telling of a more than thrice-told tale," he said, standing before these enthusiastic audiences.

> *"I have circled the globe four times. I am the chief, the argonaut of fast travelling. I was the Phileas Fogg of Jules Verne; I made the tour in fact, in eighty days, two years before he made a fictitious hero*

for the performance. But that was twenty years ago. I shall show you how quickly the journey can be made in these days. I shall make as absolute connections as may be.

Entering the port of Yokohama, for instance, I see a ship sailing out of it for Hong Kong. I shall say to the captain: 'Put me aboard that vessel, quick!' And he will do it. And so, from port to port, around the world. The circuit of the globe at the equator is twenty-four thousand miles. But the line of travel is farther north, running down, however, almost to it, then on a parallel for fifty-one hundred miles, then north again toward the point of starting, and is some twenty-one thousand, five hundred miles in length.

Of this, about five thousand miles of travelling is by land, and the balance, between sixteen and seventeen thousand miles, by water. Now, say the distance is travelled over without rest, the water at an average of fourteen knots, which strikes a liberal average between the twelve knots crossing the Pacific, the thirteen or fourteen knots through the Japan and Yellow Seas, the fourteen and seventeen knots of the main lines on the China Sea, Bay of Bengal, Indian Ocean, Red and Mediterranean Seas, the nine and ten knots of the Suez Canal, and the nineteen knots on the Etrurias of the Atlantic.

You see that going round the world westward is a gradient upwards in the development of commerce and the science of transportation. Fourteen knots an hour will cover the distance in about forty-nine days.

Then, say five thousand miles by rail from Brindisi to Queenstown, and from New York to Tacoma, at thirty miles an hour, would cover that part of it in a little less than seven days. That would be short fifty-six days. Thus with four days for coaling and mishaps I will make the journey in sixty days. Besides, I will have a special train from New York across the continent, if need be, that shall travel sixty miles an hour." [5]

The crowd cheered. They were so eager to see and hear the traveller that it was decided to build an immense pavilion during these sixty days of absence, in which they might be accommodated upon his return. That was how it came about that, at seven seconds after six o'clock on the morning of March 18, at the instant a cannon from the bluff overlooking Commencement Bay boomed the signal, George Francis Train stepped from a brass plate that had been set into the sidewalk in front of the Ledger office on C Street and took a seat in a carriage there waiting. Wall recalled:

> "Six o'clock in the morning in March is a very premature hour. It is always dark, and very often it is chilly and foggy, but quite a crowd had overlooked all this, and at the roar of the cannon, the slamming of the carriage door, the crack of the driver's whip, they cheered lustily, and many started on a run, following the carriage down the long drive to the wharf."[6]

In the carriage with Train were R.F. Radebaugh, and a young man, S.W. Wall, one of the *Ledger*'s editors, who was to accompany Train as a sort of travelling secretary but who would also cover the story for the paper. In a carriage, which kept close behind, were the timekeepers of the race, Isaac W. Anderson, W.J. Fife and C.A. Snowden.

The plan was to carry the travellers by the Union Pacific Steamer *Olympian* down Puget Sound to the straits of Juan de Fuca, in time to catch the outgoing Canadian Pacific Steamer *Abyssinia*. Figuratively speaking, Wall said that the epic trip was:

> "a cup of tea in Japan, another in China, a breath of the spices of Ceylon and Araby, a glass of wine in Paris, a momentary struggle with a London fog, and then the boom of cannon on the hills of Tacoma... Sixty-seven days driving behind the world's swiftest engines ceaselessly, sleeplessly; sixty-seven days churning the ocean, rattling over rails; the throbbing of engines and propellers through all the earth, from Tacoma to Tacoma, looking west."[7]

Wall had never met Train before and was apprehensive. Train was similarly unsure of what to expect of Wall. When the ship had got underway they retired to Train's stateroom to confer. The first question Train asked Wall was: "Do you drink and carouse around?"

The young reporter replied that he would do the best he could.

"On the contrary," Train replied, a little coldly, Wall thought. "I do not drink anything intoxicating myself. This is very important business we are going upon, and it will require clear heads and prompt execution."

That was different, Wall answered, as he looked out of the porthole to get a last glance of American soil. He wondered what he had got himself into.

"We must do this thing like princes all the way 'round,"Train continued, "and to carry out the idea – there being two of us – we will have to adopt some plan – come to some understanding."

Wall agreed with Train, realising that he was making perfect sense. Without agreeing the way forward, they were liable to get separated or lost in the switch between ships, trains, and countries, not to mention the language barriers.

"Now suppose you figure as my private secretary. That would simplify the thing."

Wall hesitated, then jokingly asked if the position would require him to interpret much of Train's handwriting – obviously Wall was aware of its famous illegibility. Train took this as a pleasant acceptance and concluded the meeting.

The crossing to Yokohama was a rough one through stormy weather. Though the weather slowed the ship's progress, Train was in high spirits throughout the trip. Day after day he sat on a pile of cushions in the corner of the smoking room reminiscing and telling stories from a seemingly inexhaustible store. He gave recitations, sang songs, played checkers, and wrote his "psychos", as Train called his newspaper articles. As well as all these activities, Train finally found the time to read Jules Verne's novel *Around the World in Eighty Days* for the first time. He jotted down his thoughts on the book as he read it. Wall says that these "criticisms were striking, to say the least". On their arrival in Japan he gave them to the editor of the Japan *Gazette*, who published them in the newspaper. We have Wall's word that it was the "most original, erratic, and striking material that had ever appeared in that Oriental journal".[8]

As the weather worsened, Train seemed to be in better form. Train noted with a touch of contempt that fellow passenger Lafcadio Hearn, the distinguished writer, was so seasick that he never left his stateroom for the entire voyage. Wall once asked Train why he was undertaking the trip. "I go round the world every twenty years, to let it know I am still alive. They think I am dead," he answered.

> "I want to call the attention of the world to the shortest way around it; to give commerce a lesson. I expect to establish a line of big and fast steamers between Puget Sound and Yokohama, and to promote the laying of a cable across the Pacific, completing the telegraphic circuit of the earth."[9]

Train went on to describe his plans in detail. He even went so far as to predict that the completion of the Russian railway from St Petersburg to Vladivostock would reduce the circuit of the globe to thirty days. Finally, he rounded of his speech with a stirring: "I am going 'round the world to teach it this lesson in geography."[10]

As they reached Yokohama, Train got down to business in earnest. "Here we begin work," he told Wall. "You are rarely fortunate. We shall do this thing like kings and princes." Breaking into the inevitable anecdote, he continued:

> *"On a visit to Salt Lake, once... Brigham Young called upon me at the hotel, and said, 'I would call oftener, Mr. Train, but I must not be seen upon the streets. I must not make myself too common with these people.' I have remembered and lived to that idea ever since. For I am to be Dictator. I must not be too common with the people. I have reached a point beyond that of any other man. And here, once again, I must set the prairie on fire. Running forty miles an hour across the American continent, I lit the prairie, at night, and roused the sleeping train to look at a sea of fire. You shall witness the like again. I have the twist upon the whole world. I shall enter the United States, like Monte Cristo rising from the sea: I have found the riches, and the world is mine."[11]*

The moment they landed, Train telegraphed the American legation in Tokyo for passports. It customarily took three days to obtain them, but Train demanded them at once and rushed to Tokyo and got them signed the same day. They raced several hundred miles across Japan to catch a ship bound for Hong Kong, a hectic pace typical of the one they kept up for the entire journey. Of course, they saw little of the countries they raced through. Train lamented that the trip was "a mere question of rushing from vessel to vessel the moment you get into port, or of catching trains, or of chartering boats to bridge gaps, or of haggling with ship-captains or railway managers about getting extra accommodations at very extra prices."

The otherwise monotonous voyage was livened up when the Chief, as Wall came to call Train, delivered a lecture to the other passengers as a means of explaining his outlook on life.

> *"For fourteen years I sat in Madison Square Park and spoke only to children, and them because they are truth. Men went by and whispered: 'Yes, that's George Francis Train; he has suffered some great disappointment.' Bah ! I wouldn't live in the White House, now. It*

is supreme Dictatorship with me, or nothing. I am plaintiff against the whole world. I have been in fifteen jails for expressing my opinion, but I never robbed even a henroost." [12]

After a busy day's sojourn in Hong Kong they set sail on another German steamer, the *Preussen*, bound for Singapore. Train expressed his admiration for the ship with childlike delight:

"The days of the Flying Cloud and Red Jacket have certainly passed. They were giants in those days; and who would have dreamed that men, then in the prime of life, would live to see a vessel in which any of them could be easily stowed in the hold! And the idea of the German government supplying me with such a magnificent yacht in which to travel the world. I lie in the bath in the morning and, in my perfect enjoyment of it all, play the Star Spangled Banner with my toes on the hot and cold water cocks. After that I go and play bear with the children." [13]

The Chief once confided to Wall: " I am living to a great purpose. I shall be Dictator of the Nation. I am as certain of that as that we two are here together." [14] In more contemplative moments Train questioned his future. After a life of achievements there seemed nothing left to do. "What am I to do? That's the question! I have nothing to do! – and I am a cormorant. I must be kept busy! I do not think of committing suicide! but what am I to do?"

"Why not keep moving?" Wall replied. "Keep moving all the time – keep going around the world. What more picturesque figure could there be, than that of the silent man of Madison Square, rising from the bench from which he had not moved for fourteen years, to wander forever all the earth?"

Train agreed with Wall's poetic sentiments. "You have answered my question." [15]

After a delay in Singapore they eventually sailed on to Columbo, Ceylon, then to Aden. There Train hijacked some daytrippers' pleasure boat to take him back to the Preussen when he could not find a faster ship. The frenetic pace of the travellers and the interest of the public was illustrated by many a leg of their journey.

"[I] went through the Suez Canal in sixteen hours, was at Brindisi two and a half days later, and left Brindisi at two p.m. on Thursday, May eighth.

> *Upon arriving at Calais I found there was no boat which I could catch. I telegraphed to Dover for a special boat and was told I could have one for forty pounds. All right. The boat came, but there were many people who desired to come, so they charged the others 17s. 6d. a head and charged me nothing; forty pounds saved. I reached Calais at nine o'clock this morning, telegraphed for special train from Dover to London, left Dover at noon, arrived in London at five p.m., and will leave at twenty minutes past eight."* [16]

It was in London that Train boasted to reporters of his unique journey:

> *"Fifty-two days on the way and will finish my journey around the world in ten days more. Remember the fuss some people made when a young woman went around the world in seventy-two days and some hours? It's enough to make one sick. Nothing. Anybody could do it. Remember Jules Verne's 'Around the World in Eighty Days?' He stole my thunder. I'm Phileas Fogg. But I have beaten Phileas Fogg out of sight. What put the notion into my head? Well, I'm possessed of great psychic force."* [17]

Train was triumphant and especially proud of each bureaucratic impediment he had overcome on the way. Notably, he had got passports signed in Japan inside thirty minutes, compared with the usual wait of three days, by threatening to "see the Mikado or burst the Empire"!

He must have been a remarkable sight with his carpetbag emblazoned: GEORGE FRANCIS TRAIN, ROUND WORLD IN SIXTY DAYS. He usually wore a red fez with a tassel. Sometimes over that he wore a double-decker hat with the same motto that was on his carpetbag written on its broad white rim in large black capitals.

From London the travellers caught a train to Holyhead. There they sailed to Dublin, Ireland, and went on to Cork by another train. On this occasion Train was not arrested. At Queenstown, the site of his arrest all those years ago, they boarded the *Eturia* for America. Arriving in New York, Train was disappointed to find that there was no special train, as previously planned with the trip's sponsor, Radebaugh, to whisk him across the continent in style. After a delay of thirty-six hours he hired a train, packed it with eager newspaper reporters and set out on the final leg of his historic journey. At Portland, Oregon, a mere 150 miles from Tacoma, they were held up again when another special train that Radebaugh had promised failed to materialised. Train reached Tacoma sixty-seven days, thirteen hours, two minutes, and fifty-five seconds after setting out.

Though he had set a new record, he was disappointed by all the time wasted, since he felt that they had lost more than a week at various points around the globe through no fault of his own. Radebaugh's failure to live up to his word and organise special trains and build a special pavilion in Tacoma for the homecoming celebrations also deeply disappointed Train. It was only on arrival in Tacoma that he learned Radebaugh had been dangerously ill for six weeks and in no condition to do anything.

There was ample compensation for these disappointments when Train arrived to a hero's welcome in Tacoma. It was a spectacular occasion. Crowds of people showed up at the train station to welcome the conquering hero. Soldiers were on hand to marshal the crowds and a band played as Train was brought up the street to the starting point. People leaned out of windows, got up on roofs and climbed anywhere they thought would provide the best vantage point. In the following days Train's wondrous accomplishment was celebrated by "a long procession of entertainments… a lecture, and banquets, and dinners, and receptions, until they lost their charm".[18] Train basked in the publicity, certain that at the age of 61 he had confirmed his place in history as the real Phileas Fogg.

Wall wrote a book about the trip called *Round the World with Train – a Typhoon. Being the Confessions of a Private Secretary Concerning a Tour of the World in 67 days*. As well as undertaking to write an account of the trip, Wall was its official photographer. Despite having never used a camera before, he did remarkably well. He read the instructions and followed them as closely as circumstances allowed. Generally these circumstances may have proved unsuitable, but Wall doggedly snapped everything of interest around him in all weathers and hoped for the best. As a precaution he always had one of his two cameras ready to go at all times.

Success was not certain, though. It was only when the films were developed back at home that he found out if he had managed to take any pictures. About three hundred of these blurry photographs made it into the book. Despite Wall's questionable photographic skills, it's a marvellous account, full of character, wonderfully illustrated with the aforementioned photos along with a further two hundred ink drawings by G.H. Blair. Wall's account gives a real insight into the epic undertaking and Train's personality.

Train took a small cottage on the southern outskirts of the city, adjoining a school. There, surrounded by mementoes from foreign lands, he happily entertained the children. He had a playhouse built and fully fitted, along with a platform for dancing and skating and a huge wooden swing. For a while he was happy there. But, as the year went on, the summer holidays came and the children went elsewhere. A feeling of loneliness crept up on Train.

In August he stirred from his solitary station, during the brief battle of the transpacific steamship lines, when the Pacific-mail fast steamship *China* invaded its competitor's territory and came to Puget Sound to operate a sailing to Yokohama and Hong Kong. Train saw this as an ideal opportunity to make another trip around the world in under sixty days and seized the chance. He planned to try and persuade them to postpone the sailing date, so that he could make a close connection with the German steamship *Lloyd* in Hong Kong. Taking no luggage except the suit he wore, and without telling anyone, Train turned the key in the lock of his cottage and nailed a card on the door, on which he had written:

> *"GONE TO TACOMA,*
> *PERHAPS AROUND THE WORLD.*
> *The Greatest Wanderer,*
> *GEO. FRANCIS TRAIN."* [19]

Unfortunately, the steamship's captain would not defer the sailing to another date. It was useless to make another attempt without close connections, so he returned to his cottage, and nailed the card on the inside of the door, as a sign of what he might have done, but for unfavourable circumstances.

Wall had become quite close to Train during their journey earlier in the year and often visited him at his cottage at Fir-Tree Hill. Like so many others who had come into Train's orbit, Wall had came to admire and like Train, fondly calling him the "Chief". He realised that Train was depressed in his lonely exile and often tried to persuade him to return home to the people and life he knew in New York. He was well aware that Train often questioned his life, repeating: "I wonder what it all means?" The last time Wall saw the Chief, he was in one of these increasingly frequent introspective moods. "Can it be," he asked Wall, "that after all my life is in the past?"

"To think of the plans I had, all around the world! I cannot under-

stand what it means, unless it be that I have accomplished all that
there is for me to do. I should have listened to the call of the chil-
dren from Cherry Hill. There seems to be nothing left, for me, but
to return to silence."[20]

Eventually, Train's self-doubt passed. In two years Train was ready to
have another shot at the record. In 1892, at the age of sixty-three, he
made his final circumnavigation of the globe, this time in sixty days.

On this occasion the newly-founded town of Whatcom further up
the northwest Washington coast was to be his starting and finishing
point. Like Tacoma, Whatcom was attempting a publicity coup in an
effort to secure its place on the map by sponsoring another mad dash
for the world record. Who better than George Francis Train to undertake it? Since his previous attempt, faster Pacific steamers had entered
use and the various connections were much improved on their once
haphazard nature. Railroad connections had also greatly improved, so
there would be no chance of a repeat of the disorganisation that had
greeted Train on his last train journey across America.

Train raced from Whatcom to Vancouver and boarded the new
Empress of India, which made Yokohama in eleven days, compared to six-
teen days two years before. Four days later Train reached Shanghai.
After a slight hiccup finding a fast steamer, he landed in Singapore in
time to catch the *Moyune*, the last of the fast tea ships, bound for
Europe. At Port Said he jumped ship and boarded the *Ismaila* for
Brindisi, Italy. With no Carbonari, communist, or any other kind of rev-
olutionary in sight, he rushed across Europe. He caught the *Majestic* at
Liverpool for New York, sailing with a distinguished company that
included the then United States ambassador John Hay, Lady Stewart,
Mrs Paran Stevens, Senator Spooner and D.O. Mills, Train's old friend.
The *Majestic* made New York in good time. This time there was only a
slight delay in catching a train, so he raced across the continent and
reached Whatcom in sixty days.

Oddly enough and despite Wall's encouragement, Train never considered these trips as defining moments in his life. In fact, in his autobiography he was downright modest (for him) of his achievement in this
respect:

> *"To these three trips I attach no more importance, I hope, than is*
> *fairly their due. In each of them, in succession, I had beaten all pre-*
> *vious records of travel; and this was something in the interests of*
> *all persons who travel, as showing what could be done under stress,*

and as a stimulus to greater efforts to reduce the long months and days consumed on voyages from country to country. But they were, as I consider them, merely incidents in a life that has better things to show. One of these voyages, the one in which I 'put a girdle round the earth' in eighty days, has the honor of having given the suggestion for one of the most interesting romances in literature. This, at least, is something."

---

[1] S.W. Wall, *Round the World with Train, A Typhoon* (Round the World Publishing Co., Boston, 1891), p. 6.

[2] "Nellie Bly" in *Macmillan Dictionary of Women's Biography* (Macmillan, London, 1982), p. 422.

[3] Karen S.H. Roggenkamp, "Elizabeth Bisland, the Cosmopolitan, and Sensational Trips Around the World":
http://www.english.upenn.edu/Travel99/Abstract/roggenkamp.html

[4] S.W. Wall, above, n. 1, p. 6.

[5] *Ibid.,* p. 7.

[6] *Ibid.*

[7] *Ibid.,* p. 8.

[8] *Ibid.,* p. 82.

[9] *Ibid.,* p. 27.

[10] *Ibid.,* p. 28.

[11] *Ibid.,* pp. 30–31.

[12] *Ibid.,* p. 118.

[13] *Ibid.,* p. 142.

[14] *Ibid.*

[15] *Ibid.,* pp. 142–143.

[16] Quoted in Don C. Seitz, *Uncommon Americans* (The Bobbs-Merrill Company, Indianapolis, 1925), p. 180.

[17] *Ibid.,* p. 178.

[18] S.W. Wall, above, n. 1, p. 310.

[19] *Ibid.,* p. 311.

[20] *Ibid.,* p. 312.

TWENTY-THREE

The Last Hurrah

In 1893 Chicago celebrated the 400th anniversary of Columbus's discovery of America by holding the World's Columbian Exposition. After beating strong competition from New York, the city had secured Congress's support for the location of the exposition. The Chicagoans were determined that the exposition would help showcase the city to the world. Under the supervision of Daniel H. Burnham, a park that had been little more than a swamp was transformed into a fabulous White City of stylish buildings, statues and fountains.

Despite this grandeur, the Columbian Exposition got off to a poor start. There seemed to be little interest in it. Train left his Madison Square park bench and announced that he was going to "save" the show.[1] He went to Chicago and organised a "Parade and Grand March" to the fairgrounds. When Train led the parade personally with a belle from Dahomey on his arm, it caused a sensation. Train enlisted the help of his cousin George Pickering Bemis, his one-time secretary and Passepartout, to help him drum up more interest for the exposition. Working together, they came up with a series of publicity stunts which actually helped to generate some interest in it.

Around this time the writer Will Carleton happened to bump into Train once again and wrote his recollections of the man who had once asked him to write a "wail":

> *"His egotism was unbounded, but his good-nature unfailing. His wit was as sharp as the point of a driver's whiplash, but he seemed notably lacking in humor. His kindness of heart was unquestionable, but his humanity was never to the fore, if he had any. He was a pessimist, first, last, and all the time; a rebel against the established order of things, an avowed pagan in religious matters, and, in fact, what might be called, in general terms, a professional iconoclast."*[2]

After his efforts concluded in Chicago, Train returned to New York. Besides spending his time on his Madison Square bench entertaining children, Train kept fully informed of current affairs. He read the daily newspapers avidly and wrote articles for them, with some success. He also occasionally lectured, now asking only expenses and half the gross receipts. All in all, he kept rather quiet. Some might even have said he was becoming predictable.

In 1896 Train found a new home that was to his liking. It was the Mills Hotel at 160 Bleecker Street, New York. It was one of three men's hostels built by a businessman and philanthropist friend of his, Darius Ogden Mills. Built as a hostel for poor gentlemen, this block-wide building contained 1,500 tiny rooms at affordable rates. Train relished the fact that he paid only three dollars a week for his six-foot by eight-foot room. It was cheap and comfortable and very well run as it paid its own way. He always referred to it as the Mills Palace due to its wonderful architectural style.

During the 1896 presidential elections Train deserted Madison Square to lend his support to Jacob Coxey's campaign. The two main runners in the race were the Republican McKinley and the Democrat Bryan. Train lambasted them as best he could and lectured and wrote articles on Coxey's behalf. "I have heard orators of all nations and languages," he declared at one such meeting. "I will back Coxey against Parliament, Congress, and all the stump speakers of the world!" The crowd cheered for Coxey.

"Nothing in the whole world but Coxey's Legal Tender ideas, and smashing Hanna and Huntington, McLean, Rothschild, Morgan, and the whole Union Pacific Railway steal could have gotten me away from the dear little tots in Madison Square! (The applause swelled; they all knew of the speaker's park bench surrounded by children. They loved it.)

The Union Pacific is the government's road... I don't want the New York Journal and the World to syndicate the government as Hanna's agent sub rosa! I know this road! I helped to build it! Instead of being valued at $58,000,000, it will be worth $500,000,000 when I remove the mortgages with greenback currency. That will make real prosperity, instead of McKinley's 'airship prosperity' with five millions of tramps on the road.

I demand that the government own these roads, now under receivership, as they are being run in Europe, Asia, Africa and

South America; run them under the Coxey Plan!

The political pirates of both parties are united to steal the Union Pacific Railroad which I built! Rather than see this happen, I shall organize a Commune to free 75,000,000 slaves now in bondage to those two united parties."[3]

McKinley went on to win the election and Train's logical proposal that the government take over the bankrupt railroad, since it was the railroad's main backer, was ignored. It was a disappointing end to what proved to be Train's last active political endeavour.

Train went back to his Madison Square bench to entertain his beloved children. When the weather was fine he preferred to walk rather than use the courtesy pass presented to him by the New York surface car lines in recognition of his services to urban transport. When the weather was too raw and harsh to sit on his park bench he usually stayed indoors in his little room at Mills Palace, which was cluttered with several lifetimes of mementos from his assorted adventures. He often held banquets in the hotel for friends and acquaintances, just as he had done in the old days at the much plusher Fenton's Hotel in London or at the St. Nicholas in New York.

From his earliest years he had lived a healthy life and had not indulged in vices such as alcohol or tobacco. This stood him well in his later years. In 1898 he met Professor Mike Donovan, the famous boxer, who had attracted a high flying following. He even had boxed with President Roosevelt at the White House. Donovan, who was only ten years younger than Train, was delighted to give boxing lessons to the elderly embodiment of clean living.[4] Train became so competent at the sport that a series of boxing bouts between the two gentlemen were planned for the public's benefit. Several of these events were actually staged in New York, much to the delight of the press, who reported that Train landed forty blows on Professor Mike within thirty seconds during one such match. They must have been disappointed when the organised tour fell through. By all accounts George Francis Train, now aged seventy, must have been in perfect shape.

Though the bitter 1898–99 winter kept Train mostly indoors in his room at the Mills, he kept active occupying himself with a new project. January 1899 saw the fruits of his labour, when he published *Train's Penny Magazine*. Its price was humorous: "On News Stands 2c, on Trains 5c." Its manifesto was puzzling:

"The Penny Magazine *is the work of amateurs and enthusiasts:*

cranks, if you please! And these essentials are the requisites of civ-
ilization! If it is an experiment it is because life is such.

Its Platform: We declare that everything is perfect in its present
state! For a thing cannot be different than what it is. Finding
imperfection in nothing, the work of God then is for a higher per-
fection in all things!

Its Hopes: The question of its cost belongs to a day of little
things; its survival, to the law of natural selection."[5]

The first number featured eleven poems by Train, a long essay on "The
Future of History", and another on "The Divine and Human Elements
in Religion". Also included was a reprint of Hugo's oration at the death
of Voltaire, an anti-imperialist article on the Spanish War, an article on
money, and a reprint of a defence of mail-order houses.

Its already eclectic scope was broadened in the second edition, in
February, by a masthead announcing: "The work of cranks. For the
instruction of wise men and the amusement of fools." There were bitter
attacks on the "embalmed beef" sent to the troops in the field against
Spain and on imperialist expansion arising from the war.[6]

The third issue announced a grand banquet at the Mills in honour
of Train's seventieth birthday, to be given by the "13 Club". There were
certain rules for the diners to comply with: "No Politics, Religion,
Liquors, Table-Cloths, Napkins, Airs, Grace, Dirt, Doxology, Fads,
Freaks, Cranks, but Bon Vivants! And Cordial Welcome! Selah! Amen!"[7]
One of the Train-Donovan boxing exhibitions was promised to whet
appetites. The same issue contained a reprint of an article about him
entitled "The Most Eccentric Man in the World," highlighting his determination to be known by this magnificent nickname. In an interview for
the *Politeness Home Magazine*, Train spoke frankly and unrepentantly
about his life:

> *"I make frequent use of the words hell and damn. Why? Because I*
> *am the product of eight generations of Methodists. Back-slider be*
> *blanked. I was no more a Methodist than I am a Buddhist or an*
> *Anarchist. I don't believe in heaven or hell, God or devil, soul or*
> *immortality. My religion is my conscience, my belief is the brother-*
> *hood of man. After forty years of active life I have formulated this*
> *philosophy: Everything is worth having, nothing is worth worrying*
> *over; that philosophy is a sure cure for all diseases, such as greed*
> *and nervousness. All Americans ought to take it....*

You ask me if I am preparing now for my next great achievement? Sir, my next great achievement will be to live. Anybody can live a century and a half if he only knows how. Fountain of youth be blanked! That is not the way to do it. It is through the stomach. The American stomach is killing off all the best Americans...

I read newspapers constantly, blank them! They call me a crank; lunatic, and accuse me of eccentricity. All right. I accept the term eccentric. I define it as being without fixed orbit. Some newspapers defend me. Why defend? Am I a rogue, dishonest? Have I ever done wrong? Criminals, only, are defended. They insult me by defending me. If I am insane, as they say I am, then I am not to be defended, but pitied. Do you catch?...

Every morning at seven o'clock, ten newspapers are thrust into my room through the transom. I have finished them at nine. In the afternoon I have six more, and I distribute the sixteen among the policemen in Madison Square. I never attend theaters, lectures, operas, or concerts. I read current literature as long as I can swallow the mental food offered by latter-day literary cooks. They are nearly all bad cooks – philosophers, novelists, scientists – all fool cooks. When I am nauseated I turn to the great poet, a master mind, a real thinker, Ralph Waldo Emerson...

Have twice run for President of the United States. I ran on the Citizen Ticket against Grant and Greeley. I lost because people wanted the White House occupied by Democrats or Republicans and not by a citizen. Ever see this watch, presented me by the people when I lost? It meant 'Thanks. You did your best.' But there is only one Citizen in all the United States and I am he. There ought to be more."[8]

The *Penny Magazine* for April 1900 showed that Train still had supporters. A Stephen Maybell of San Francisco made the following declaration:

"Citizen George Francis Train for President of the United States!
    Platform: Repudiation!
    I nominate George Francis Train for President of the United States of America!
    I propose that he be elected on a platform containing but one plank, but one word; REPUDIATION – Repudiation of the bonds!

George Francis Train is the greatest statesman that America has produced!

The highest degree in the understanding thereof, and therein is the consummation of all knowledge.

I gladly crown him with the recognition of his wonderful genius, and I would do all in my power to have not only his country, but all the world recognize and appreciate, as he deserves, this great American.

I would vote for him for President; I would do more, I would vote for him for Dictator, without time or limit, constitution or restraint.

If there were enough people who knew him as I know him he would be the next President of the United States.

What we need is a Revolution — a Revolution that will wipe out the bonds and free the country forever!

What we need is a Revolution that will sweep forever away the whole present corrupt system of government, a Revolution that will usher in a reign of Justice to Labor!

George Francis Train is the man to elect to bring about this Revolution.

Come, Americans! If you love your country, if you would give your life for its glory, if you would give your vote for its Liberty, give your vote for George Francis Train for the next President of the United States!"[9]

The magazine apparently prospered, since it was turned into a weekly on July 20, 1900. Train was still editor and, ignoring Mabell's words, he supported William J. Bryan and Adlai E. Stevenson in the presidential election. Train had decided to pass on the opportunity to run for the most exalted position in the land.

Eventually the magazine floundered, although Train still had his supporters, as the following letters show:

"New York, Sept. 2. '01

Citizen George Francis Train,
New York

My Dear Citizen — The article in the Omaha Mercury does you but scant justice. Men and their lives are part of the history in the times in which they live, and you are no exception. Your work will not be fully recognized until you have stretched many years below the sod. It seems that all great things must be viewed at a distance, so it is with tall buildings, oil-paintings, history and man. It is too bad that this is so, for the encouragement that a man of genius requires, for he is but mortal, comes at an hour when his senses are stilled, and he does not hear the air filled with the glamour of his glory. Yours has been a life filled with the doings of one hundred lives, still unappreciated, except to the few that know, how many nitches you have cut in the mountain of progress.

You have climbed higher, and have reached loftier heights, than the millions that make up the mass, and they do not understand it, and in consequence think you queer. You were the first to open our land of liberty from sea to sea, and when the flag of progress will be fully unfolded, your name will be high upon its banner, as a man of keen perception, fine intuition, marvellous integrity of reasoning ability, and a man who was thirty years before the times in which he lived. But you are still young, and time has been kind to you, and who knows that within you lie greater deeds than those you have done, and which have made your name one known to the smallest thinking youngster, in this, our fair and glorious land.

With my best wishes always yours,
Carleton Simon." [10]

Replying to the foregoing, from the president of the Hundred-Year Club of New York and a leading medical specialist, Mr Train wrote as follows:

"Cher Citoyen [Dear Citizen] Dr Carleton Simon:

Thank you young and old friend for kind words. As you admit I am still alive (and kicking)! I intend to double my age! Your Hundred Year club an early corpse! I live on fruit and grains; have eaten no cadavers for quarter of century! Omaha Mercury is only paper that does me justice! (See article No. 4 mailed you today!) Editor of Mercury got me out of self! Hiding in clouds! He found me in Arctic Polar Regions! Have you had justice from newspapers? You will always get it from your old friend.

GEORGE FRANCIS TRAIN" [11]

Train particularly valued the following gushing tribute from his old friend D. O. Mills:

"New York, September 30, 1901.

Hon. GEORGE FRANCIS TRAIN,
Mills Hotel, Bleecker St., New York.

My Dear Citizen:

   The many appreciative notices that have come to my attention of your distinguished talents of early years lead me also to send you a line of appreciation, particularly as touching the part played by you in some of the great commercial enterprises that have so signally marked the nineteenth century, notably in the Merchant Marine, and in the building of the Union Pacific Railroad, in the conception and construction of which you bore so distinguished a part.

   The present generation, with its conveniences of travel and communication, can not realise what were the difficulties and experiences of the merchant and traveler of those early days when you were engaged in the China trade, and your Clipper Ships were often seen in the port of San Francisco.

   The long voyage around the Horn, the danger experienced from sudden attack by Indians while traversing the wild and uninhabited country lying between Omaha and the Pacific Coast, are experiences which even an old voyager like myself questions as he speeds across the continent, privileged to enjoy the comforts of a Pullman car, and a railroad service that has shortened the journey from New York to San Francisco from months to a few days. In recalling the many years of our pleasant acquaintance by sea and land, not the least is the remembrance of your kind and genial spirit, and I am glad to see that you have lost none of your sincere wish to do good.

                                   With kind regards.
                                   Very truly yours,
                                   D. O. MILLS."

Towards the middle of 1902 Train was approached by F. W. Halsey of D. Appleton and Co. with a proposal. Halsey was a former newspaperman who knew all about Train. He asked him to write an autobiography.

Train agreed and the next morning Halsey's assistant, an expert stenographer, arrived in the little room on the top floor of the Mills Hotel. He sat down in the room's only chair, the same one that America's wealthiest man, the financier J. Pierpont Morgan, had sat in not long before when he called on Train and talked with him for an hour about shipping, while Train and D.O. Mills sat on the bed opposite.[12]

Over several weeks in July and August Train dictated his life during one or two hours over two or three days a week. Altogether it took a total of thirty-five hours of dictation to accomplish the task. Train dictated his life off the top of his head, though he did make a brief outline so he would not wander too far from the tracks. Train's dedication was characteristic:

"TO THE CHILDREN
and to the children's children
in this and in all lands
who love and believe in me
because they know
I love and believe in them."

In his preface Train explained:

"I have been silent for thirty years. During that long period I have taken little part in the public life of the world, have written nothing beyond occasional letters and newspaper articles, and have conversed with few persons, except children in parks and streets. I have found children always sympathetic and appreciative. For this reason I have readily entered into their play and their more serious moods; and for this reason, also, have dedicated this book to them and to their children.

For many years I have been a silent recluse, remote from the world in my little corner in the Mills Hotel, thinking and waiting patiently. That I break this silence now, after so many years, is due to the suggestion of a friend who has told me that the world of to-day, as well as the world of to-morrow, will be interested in reading my story...

I beg my readers to remember that this book was spoken, not written, by me... It may not, in every part, agree with the recollections of others; but I am sure that it is as accurate in statement as it is blameless in purpose. If I should fail at any point, this will

*be due to some wavering of memory, and not to intention. Thanks
to my early Methodist training, I have never knowingly told a lie;
and I shall not begin at this time of life...*

*Although I am a hermit now, I was not always so. All who read
this book must see that. I spent many happy years in society — and
never an unhappy year anywhere, whether in jail or under social
persecution...*

*A last word as to myself. Readers of this book may think I have
sometimes taken myself too seriously. I can scarcely agree with
them. I try not to be too serious about anything — not even about
myself. When I was making a hopeless fight for the Presidency in
'72, I made the following statement in one of my speeches:*

*'Many persons attribute to me simply an impulsiveness, and an
impressibility, as if I were some erratic comet, rushing madly
through space, emitting coruscations of fancifully colored sparks,
without system, rule, or definite object. This is a popular error. I
claim to be a close analytical observer of passing events, applying
the crucible of Truth to every new matter or subject presented to my
mind or my senses.'*

*I think that estimate may be used to-day in this place. It does
not so much matter, however, what I may have thought of myself or
what I now think of myself. What does matter is what I may have
done. I stand on my achievement.*

*And with this, I commit my life-story to the kind considera-
tion of readers.*

Citizen GEORGE FRANCIS TRAIN.

The Mills Palace,

September 22, '02."

A reporter for the New York *World* asked Train whether he hoped for a
monetary return from the book. Citizen Train replied: "What do I want
with money? I have all I need. It only costs me $3 a week to live. If I had
more money I would only have to give it away. No, I didn't write it for
money."

"Did you write it to place yourself right before the public?" came
the next question.

*"My dear Sir, I am a legal lunatic. Why should I not talk out of
my head? Place myself right with the public? How can a peanut*

convention know about a cocoanut? The people who compose it have never seen a cocoanut. They don't know what it is. The peanut convention considers the cocoanut, deliberates wisely, and passes a resolution that the cocoanut is a large peanut. And how can the cocoanut find out what it is until it sees another cocoanut like itself? I am a cocoanut." [13]

The book sold well, proving that Train still had a certain magnetic hold on the public's imagination. One critic described it as "a spirited and interesting story, but contains many inaccuracies and some statements which can only be regarded as deliberate falsehoods. To the end he was the showman, and had to appear as the hero in every incident." The *Times* literary supplement declared: "This is the most frankly egotistical Book of Reminiscences we remember to have read." [15]

Sometime in 1903, during a visit to his daughter Sue at her home in Stamford, Connecticut, Train became ill with what was diagnosed as smallpox by the local authorities. They insisted that he be isolated in the local pest-house and they burned all his clothes, including a bundle of manuscripts which he had with him. Train retaliated by threatening them with a fifty-thousand-dollar damages suit. Though this was never pursued, the eccentric's stay in the lazaret cost the community two thousand dollars. [16] Eventually Train recovered completely from his illness and was released. Once again turning down his daughter's offer of a home with her, he returned to his little refuge at the "Mills Palace".

Among Train's admirers was James Clifton Robinson, managing director and engineer of the London United Tramways, who was known by the nickname "Tramway King". In his youth he had been an office boy to George Starbuck, junior, an associate of Train's in the British Tramway enterprise. On February 21, 1903 the following kind tribute from Robinson appeared in the New York *Press*.

"My Dear Mr. Train — It seems but yesterday that, as a very small boy I came under the magnetism of your eloquence in inaugurating the first European street tramway in my native place of Birkenhead, August, 1860. You will realize the effect it had upon me when I say that from that day to this I have steadfastly pursued the course you then dictated in the introduction and development of tramways. You will, I fear, hardly remember the minor part I played in the drama during your sojourn in England in the early sixties, or of my career under your auspices during the latter part

of that decade, but I have never ceased to think of and admire your splendid personality. This influence has remained with me through life, and any success which has attended my labors has, I am bound to say, been largely due to my early association with your, at that time, brilliant career. You will find your name prominent in all the records of my achievements, and I am glad, indeed, to have this opportunity of acknowledging the grand example you set me in pioneering tramways enterprise under conditions and difficulties which you alone can understand, and which you have so graphically described in the story of your eventful life. With every good wish for your welfare and happiness, believe me, my dear old chief, sincerely yours,

Feb. 3, 1903. J. CLIFTON ROBINSON."[17]

[1]   Don C. Seitz, *Uncommon Americans* (The Bobbs-Merrill Company, Indianapolis, 1925), p. 180.

[2]   Quoted in Willis Thornton, *The Nine Lives of Citizen Train* (Greenberg, New York, 1948), p. 283.

[3]   *Ibid.*, p. 286.

[4]   http://www.ibhof.com/mikedon.htm

[5]   Quoted in Willis Thornton, above, n. 2, pp. 292–293.

[6]   *Ibid.*, p. 293.

[7]   *Ibid.*

[8]   *Ibid.*, pp. 294–295.

[9]   *Ibid.*, pp. 296–297.

[10] From a newspaper clipping in the Carleton Simon Papers at Albany University, New York.

[11] *Ibid.*

[12] Willis Thornton, above, n. 2, p. 298; http://www.obits.com/morganjp.html

[13] *Ibid.*, p. 300.

[14] Charles E. Lee, "The English Tramways of George Francis Train" in *Journal of Transport History* (1953), Vol. I.

[15] *The Times*, January 25, 1905, p. 27.

[16] Don C. Seitz, above, n. I, p. 182.

[17] *New York Press*, February 21, 1903, reproduced in George Francis Train, *My Life in Many States and Foreign Lands* (republished by Adam Gordon, Buckingham, 1991), p. *iii*.

TWENTY-FOUR

Onward to Immortality

George Francis Train died on January 18, 1904. For some months it was obvious to observers that his legendary health was not what it once was and that he was not going to live, as he believed, to a fabled old age of 150 years or more. By mid-January he was confined to bed in his cluttered little room at the Mills Hotel. It must have been quite a shock to his system to be laid up and powerless to do anything about it. However, he had plenty of friends from inside the hotel, and beyond in the outside world, who called regularly on him. By Sunday, January 17, it was obvious that this was an illness from which Train would not recover. Sue was sent for. For the next two days she sat beside her father's bedside, caring for him. Though Train's body was failing him, his mind was as clear as ever. Despite his determination to recover and his will to live, Train weakened gradually. On Monday night Sue heard her father softly murmur: "all right soon again..." before falling into unconsciousness or a deep sleep.[1] After an hour it become clear that he would never wake. His doctor and close friend Carleton Simon, whom Train had met through their mutual interest in phrenology, pronounced that his death was due to heart failure as a result of the onset of nephritis (chronic Bright's disease) which the good doctor had been treating for some months. Doctor Simon did not hesitate to declare that the alleged smallpox from which Train suffered at Stamford was in reality merely fever and a skin eruption, which were symptoms of nephritis.

News of Citizen Train's passing made front page news in several of the following day's newspapers. His extraordinary life's adventures were detailed, as well as his eccentricities and accomplishments. The evening edition of the New York *World* carried the following story:

"'CITIZEN' TRAIN PASSES AWAY AT MILLS HOTEL NO. 1

Attack of Nephritis Proves Fatal, and One of the Most Interesting Americans Dies in His Little Room with No One to Comfort Last Moments but His Doctor.

HIS LIFE ONE FULL OF EXCITING INCIDENTS
AND ADVENTURES

Lost Family by Yellow Fever in New Orleans at Age of Four-Carved Out Own Fortune and Made Himself a Factor in the Affairs of the World.

George Francis Train is dead in his little room in the Mills Hotel in Bleecker street, where for years he has paid his twenty cents per night, the same as other lodgers. He died of nephritis. He was attended by Dr Carleton Simon who is also making arrangements for the funeral. Though Mr. Train had been ill some days no whisper of his condition reached the outside world. He died just before midnight.

Of the circumstances concerning the death of this remarkable man nothing is known. The servants and attendants at the hotel are reticent. They are so trained. Mr. Train was nearly seventy-eight years old. Mr. Train lived on the top storey of the Mills Hotel in a little room, possibly eight feet long and six feet wide. He had lived in that room ever since the hotel was first opened. In it is a single bed, a dresser, a tiny table and a chair. Many distinguished men have sat in that chair while 'Citizen' Train entertained them with a dignity and a graciousness that was almost kingly.

No matter whatever else his graciousness or kindness led him to do, Mr. Train did not up to the time of his death consent to shake the hand of man or woman. For fourteen years he would not speak to man or woman. Children he loved and adored. He believed that old people absorbed from children what he called psychic force, while adults subtracted that force especially the stronger ones from the weaker. Mr. Train's most recent illness, before the trouble which caused his death, was an attack of small-pox in May of last year, while he was at the home of his sister [sic] in Stamford, Mrs Susan M. T. Gulager. Mr. Train always contended he had only measles."

The newspaper report concluded with its own opinion of him: "Eccentric, lovable, brainy and courageous, George Francis Train was a remarkable man."

Another newspaper reprinted Train's last lecture announcement, which he had sent out to newspaper editors before his illness had taken hold. It was proof, if any was needed, that Train had every intention of living his life to the fullest up until the very last moment:

"George Francis Train. Immanuel Pfeiffer.
Cher Citizens! (Citoyens!) Managers! Lecture Bureaus! Clubs!
Odd-fellows! Masons! Theatres! Opera Houses! Lecture Halls!
(Politeness Postmasters.)

ADVANCE LECTURE PROGRAMME.
Citizens George Francis Train and Immanuel Pfeiffer – Lecture
Campaign!
Sea to Sea against Medicals! Legals! Clericals!
Two Victims to M.D's! (Loaded for Big Game!)
Septuagints versus Professions! (Open to Debate!)
Something New under Sun! (Truth! Manhood! Courage!)
Abolishing 'Jenner-ism!'
Impeaching Doctors!
Pest! Pox! Plague - Poisoners! (Stampeded!)
Pfeiffer's Lessons for Public Schools! (20,000,000 tots!)
Ego Mania, Run Mad!
Cheers and Hisses Defied! (Red-Hot Talk Exposing Graft-Ism!)
(R)Evolution Lunacy of Thirty-Million-Aire Omaha-El-Dorado!
Train Ligue will be published on which G.F.T. was jailed! (Bible
Quotations.)
Lecture Bureaus! Societies, – Forums!
(Crowded Houses Sighted!)
Publishers wanted for Score of G.F.T. Books!
Typewriter and Stenographer en Route!
(Appletons did not Exhaust this worldwide Personality in Alpha of
Alphabet!)
Syndicate High class Lawyers will soon move on Omaha Cathay
Ship! (Thirty Millions!)
Our Home Rights. Twenty-five cents a year! Five cents at News
Stands, Cheapest and Best Magazine of Cosmos! Million-
Circulation ahead! Address, Bedford, Mass.
Citizen Train's $50,000 suit (Stamford) and Immanuel Pfeiffer's
$30,000 (Boston) will soon be in active Eruption!
(Co. Editors (O.H.R.) will soon Round World in Thirty Days,
Cutting Citizen's Record One-Half." [2]

News of Train's death spread quickly. So many people came to Train's little room in the Mills to pay their last respects that it was decided to move the body to the Merritt and Campbell undertakers' parlour in West 23rd Street. Train lay in state there from six p.m. in the evening of the twentieth until the burial at 1.30 p.m. on the twenty-first. Around one hundred and fifty people were waiting to pay their respects when the funeral parlour opened its doors. A third of these were children, many of whom carried flowers.

Throughout the evening a continuous stream of visitors arrived, some merely curious, but the great majority evidently intent on paying a sincere tribute. Great heaps of flowers piled up around the quarter-oak casket. Moses King's flowers bore the inscription: "Genius, Philanthropist, Patriot." A tall cross woven of flowers came from George P. Bemis of Omaha, accompanied by a message saying that only illness had prevented him from being there. Hundreds of other messages of condolence arrived in a steady stream, most of which were personal and not given out publicly. Train's death was mourned around the world. A contemporary from his Australian days recalled: "With all his shortcomings... he was a man of many good parts. To those in want or distress he was profuse in his liberality, and many a man with whom things had gone ill had abundant cause to remember him with gratitude."[3] The Omaha Real Estate Exchange resolved that Omaha had lost "one of its earliest and most enthusiastic friends... a prophet of the West, living to see his most sanguine predictions realized."[4] The flag of the Train school in Omaha, named in his honour, was lowered to half-mast. Clifton Robinson, now a Member of Parliament, sent his condolences from faraway England.

Until almost midnight, reported the New York *American*, there was no break in the long line of people coming to pay a last tribute to the Citizen. Robert B. Roosevelt, uncle of President Theodore Roosevelt, came and looked silently on the dead. At his elbow was:

> "...a ragged man, clutching the collar of his coat against the sunken throat, his hands red from the cold he had endured in his walk from the Mills Hotel. And near this man were a little boy and girl, hand in hand, and in the free hand of each was a white rose with a bit of bright green fern. The children cast soft, shy glances at the dead man's face. They seemed to feel nothing of awe or fear. For the lips of the dead man were smiling quite the same as he used to smile when he sat with the little children in the park...".[5]

Throughout the bitterly cold January night, more than two thousand children came to pass the bier. Little floral tokens, mostly single flowers, were dropped on and all about the coffin. Many very small children were lifted up that they might look on the calm, kindly countenance. One woman brought a crippled girl and lifted her up beside the bier. "You must always remember him," she said, "remember him when you pray. He was very good to you when you were hurt."

"He came to see me when I was in the hospital," said the child. "He told me stories."[6]

Through tears, many others told what Train himself had never told – how he had helped them in their time of need. "You owe your life to a trained nurse he provided when you were ill," a mother told the child she led by the hand.[7] People who had never known or seen one another before found themselves suddenly bound by common ties of having received timely help from a man who lived on a few dollars a week, but who had found money, somehow, for others in need.

One well-dressed, handsome schoolboy placed a bunch of white carnations among the flowers, with a card on which was stiffly written, "Jack." The boy stood a little while, then suddenly sobbed outright. Several persons looked at the boy and, seeing this, he turned away and said with a sort of defiance in his voice: "He liked me!"[8]

Carleton Simon made the funeral arrangements. Among the pallbearers were: Dr W. Hanaford White of the Society for Psychic Research; Clark Bell, ex-president of the Medico-Legal Society, who had defended Train in the lunacy hearings thirty years before; Moses King, a life-long friend; J.L. Thomas of Mills Hotel No. 1; Charles A. Montgomery, president of the Vegetarian Society; and Dr Simon himself.

Only a few members of the family and a few friends attended the funeral services. The soprano soloist of St Paul's Church sang, "Lead, Kindly Light" and "Nearer, My God, to Thee", which had been Train's favourite hymns, notwithstanding his atheism. Two members of local theatrical companies also sang. The public was not admitted, for reasons explained by Dr White: "Mr Train had certain ideas regarding religion... and it was not thought fair to admit the public who might think Mr. Train's ideas of religion were queer."[9] The huge quantities of flowers, except for a few transported with the coffin to Greenwood Cemetery, Brooklyn, for the burial, were distributed to the Citizen's fellow residents at the Mills Hotel and to patients in various children's hospitals.

With the family's consent, Dr Simon and Dr Edward Spitzka examined Train's brain. It was found to weigh 53.8 ounces, which the examining physicians ranked twenty-sixth in a list of the brain weights of one hundred and six famous men, a full six ounces greater than the average.

No will was found among the clutter of papers in the boxes and trunks in the little room at the Mills Hotel. It did not matter, since Train no longer owned anything of much value. The Citizen had died with precisely what he had possessed when his father put him aboard the ship for New England as a child: the clothes on his back. He had completely balanced his accounts with life.

Train's occasional nemesis, Jules Verne, died the following year. The funeral was held on March 28. It was an elaborate affair, with parties of soldiers and schoolchildren, politicians and clergy. Among the great crowd that followed the bier to the cemetery was a strange Englishman. He had learned one phrase off by heart, which he repeated to the family as he shook each of them by the hand: "*Courage, courage, dans la dure epreuve qui vous atteint.*" [Be brave in the sore trial you face]. Was he, as some of them later wondered, the ghost of Phileas Fogg come to pay his last respects?[10]

Verne's son, Michel, erected a wonderfully apt memorial over his father's grave. It shows the bearded Verne, his hair tossed by the sea winds, breaking free of shroud and tomb, rising with a magnificent gesture from the dead. Above it are cut his name and the words: "ONWARD TO IMMORTALITY AND ETERNAL YOUTH."

No doubt Train and Verne would have agreed with the sentiments.

Now that Train had passed away, few looked past the last eccentric decades of his life to analyse his solid achievements. One of those who bothered to do this was the *World-Herald* of Omaha, Nebraska. It paid Train a sincere tribute, acknowledging a debt that Omaha could never repay:

> "*Omaha has lost the best of its earliest friends in the passing of George Francis Train in the 75th year of his age. None need shrink from making this announcement. In the early days Mr. Train gave his ardent friendship to a then unknown frontier town, and by his international reputation as an orator, a business man, and a champion of human kind, placed it on its upward march and helped it to become a flourishing city...*
>
> *He was often so flippantly called a madman. What madness has ever wrought so grandly? In his later years it is thought his unusual*

mental powers unbalanced his mind, this accounting for the many eccentricities of his later life. If it were so, it was a grievous ruin over which none but the expression of sorrow can hold place, and in that sorrow there can be no more sincere mourners than the people of this city, for whom he cherished a stalwart affection...

Poor Train! He was a 'man of sorrows.' He bore his burden without complaint, and at his bier there could be no brighter flowers than those contributed by the men of Omaha who knew and loved him at his best." [11]

Other periodicals also began to re-evaluate Train's life in depth, looking beyond his widely acknowledged eccentricity. On January 30, 1904, *The Outlook* published an eloquent analysis of his character:

"The line that separates insanity pure and simple from excessive eccentricity is a fine one, and it might be hard to decide upon which side to place the singular personality of George Francis Train, who was wont at one time to call himself the sanest man alive, at others the greatest 'crank' in the world. The mere fact that he did recognise his megalomania or exuberant egoism shows conclusively that his mind had its sane side...". [12]

The *Bookman* magazine also offered a penetrating analysis:

"Train was a sort of stormy petrel, appearing in the most unlikely places whenever there was any social or political disturbance, and always plunging into it with the zest of one who loved trouble for its own sake...

Train had a natural dislike for every form of constraint and for every form of convention. He loved to run contrary to the prejudices of conservative people... He was certainly ill-balanced to a degree, but it is also just as certain that he never was insane." [13]

It seemed that even the widely published eccentricity of his latter years could not negate the extraordinary achievements of his earlier days. The *Dictionary of American Biography* took the view that:

"in spite of his eccentricities and mad escapades – he styles himself 'Champion Crank' – Train was a man of no small ability nor unimportant achievements. That his influence on American shipping and British street railways was considerable is recognized. In

his sensational performances, moreover, there was an element of
practical joking that gave them a touch of humor and satire."[13]

As late as 1938 Train and his masses of writings were paid the kind of
offhanded tribute by the writers of *American Authors 1600–1900* that he
would have appreciated. Train was described as an:

> *"[e]ccentric reformer, multi-millionaire, and miscellaneous*
> *writer... At an early age he had already begun his twin careers of*
> *pioneer money making... and of wholesale espousal of numberless*
> *causes, the latter marked by innumerable pamphlets, lectures, and*
> *newspaper articles. These causes included woman suffrage, free*
> *thought (though later he believed himself possessed of psychic*
> *power), and many others... [He] probably was never really crazy,*
> *only an extreme eccentric who thought it amusing to shock peo-*
> *ple... His writing had no literary value, but is of interest histori-*
> *cally and psychologically. He was a gorgeous crank."*[14]

When Willis Thornton wrote the first biography of Train's life he
lamented that none of those who were close to Train in his heyday were
still alive. Even his children had passed away. His grandchildren only had
childhood memories of a fine, grey, laughing man whom they saw
sometimes at Christmas at his daughter's home. He would bring great
bags of Chinese lychee nuts, or come tumbling into the room dressed
in a huge polar bear skin, direct from Santa Claus at the North Pole! A
distant relative, Arthur Train, had a few words to say about "that eccentric old connection of mine":

> *"After he had gone somewhat 'ga-ga,' [he] used in Union Square to*
> *hold Sunday morning services of what he called 'The Church of the*
> *Laughing Jackass'. Whether George Francis intended to refer to*
> *himself by the term I know not, but, dotty as he undoubtedly was,*
> *I am inclined to suspect that there was method in his mad-*
> *ness...".*[16]

This was a view shared by others who had known Train as well. Don C.
Seitz, who while working as editor of the Brooklyn *Daily Eagle* had
known Train, wrote: "Eccentric, he was indeed, but much of it was
planned, not spontaneous. He had heaps of fun with himself and the
world at large."[17]

On April 5, the American Institute of Phrenology, of which Train was a member, met and paid tribute to him. Phrenology is the study of the structure of the skull to determine a person's character and mental capacity. This pseudo-science was based on the false assumption that mental faculties are located in brain "organs" on the surface of the brain and can be detected by visible inspection of the skull. Though it is now completely debunked and is recognised as having no scientific merit or basis in fact, it was not always so.[18]

Until the early 1900s it was a very popular science, especially in the United States. Train was one of its devotees, having been interested since being introduced to it by James McHenry in the 1850s while Train was in Liverpool. He accompanied McHenry on a visit to Bridges, the most famous phrenologist. Train was hooked on it after the phrenologist told him things about himself that Train had supposed no-one knew. Train was astonished: "Up to this time, I had not taken any stock in the science, which I set down as charlatanry...". At first Train accused McHenry of prepping Bridges, but he vehemently denied this, so Train had to accept his word.

Train's curiosity was awakened and he decided to conduct an investigation of the "science." He went to London to consult another famous phrenologist, who would have no idea who he was. Train still was not satisfied when the man declared: "You will be either a great reformer, or a great pirate. It merely depends upon the direction you take in Ethics!" He saw every phrenologist he could reach, even going as far as France and Germany to do so. Finally he saw one of the greatest phrenologists, Dr L.N. Fowler, so that he could get an absolutely impartial reading. The phrenologist placed his hands on Train's head and exclaimed: "Jehu, what a head!" Then he went on to give an impressive reading. Train was finally satisfied. He remarked that it was the most complete and accurate statement of his mental powers that he had ever received from anyone. Over the years he had kept an interest in phrenology.

As it turned out, it was Dr Fowler's daughter who kicked off the Institute's proceedings with a brief overview of Train's interest in phrenology and an account of an examination she had made of him herself.

> "[I]t will be interesting to our readers to know what phrenology has to say about him, for he was a man who has been much misunderstood and criticised...
>
> It sometimes takes a man who is considered to be eccentric to

bring about reforms; so it appeared in the case of Geo. Francis Train. As we have said, Mr Train was not understood...

I had the pleasure to examine Mr. Train on March 1, 1891, and said of him:

> 'Phrenology can account for, as no other science can, the peculiarities of such a character and head as the one before us.
>
> The head is unusually large and well developed. The basilar portions, giving energy, force and executive power, are exceptionally well defined. There is tremendous force here, reminding one of the force of Niagara as it passes down over the Horseshoe Falls, or like an avalanche that slips down some steep mountain peak, and hurls with it rocks, stones and trees. His head indicates that he will allow neither prejudice nor old-fogyism to deter him from the course that he has set himself to run, or the task that he has undertaken. His head is remarkably broad an inch above the base of the brain, or that section which surrounds the ears, which indicates that whatever he undertakes to do will be uncommon, massive and exceptionally large in conception and outline. He will give himself to extensive plans, rather than to microscopic detail work, and the organ of sublimity is excessively developed.
>
> His perceptive intellect, being remarkably full and active, shows unusual gifts in working out definite, useful and practical plans, inventions and schemes of work. He is not a man to imitate others, and will be more original in his style of thinking than one in a thousand. He will think of things that will arouse the interest of others.
>
> He is not calculated to live a smooth, easy life. If he had his choice to live his life over again, he would choose the rough, pioneer work of practical reform, rather than the life that is strewn with roses, soft-cushioned and smooth.
>
> Another conclusion that we draw from his remarkable head comes from the development of the crown. He is an exceptionally independent man. He hates to be beholden to

anyone. He will dare to say what other men would tremble over saying.

He is fond of children, and the helplessness and simplicity of their lives appeals to him in a remarkable way. He should be able to suit himself to the young as well as to animals and pets. His spirit of reform will show itself in his love for both children and the young, hence we judge that he will ever keep his spirit from growing old.

His sympathies form another very strong characteristic. He will not allow them to be wasted, but he will have quite a distinct regard for the wants of others, largely through his benevolence. He will support public reforms and philanthropic agencies.

His intuitions are very strong, and they come to him like a flash of lightning. He will read through a person's spoken words and actions what their hidden motives are, and although he may not always act on his first impressions, yet he is a man who will form strong opinions concerning his fellows.

That he has literary talent, is to be seen in his strikingly developed forehead. He is a fact collector, and his language being striking, and peculiarity strong and effective, and should arouse the interest of others in what he has to tell them. The organ of language works with his comparison and causality in giving him more than ordinary spontaneity of thought, and when he writes, he describes what he has seen as though he were speaking to a person.

His strong points of character, having been accentuated by a remarkable career, have thrown him into an atmosphere which can only be appreciated by being understood, and lived.

He has a strong sense of wit, and does not mind how much good-natured raillery he creates around him, even if the fun comes back upon himself.

To sum him up in a sentence, he should be known as a reformer, an agitator, an explorer, a brilliant public speaker, a successful business man of great force and ability, and a writer of exceptional originality.'

Many of Geo. Francis Train's eccentricities can be allowed to pass out of sight in the light of what he actually accomplished.

His strongest characteristic was his independence of mind, which he carried to an unusual extreme.

He showed a remarkably developed memory. His brain showed a superior degree of complexity in its morphological surface. There were no lesions of any kind and no deformity, atrophy or anomaly to be found.

The brain weighed 1,525.5 grains or 53.81 ounces.

The celebrated scientist who does not believe in phrenology, says that he possessed a brain of unquestioned vigor and superior mental capability, or one of the best ever recorded."[19]

Following a short speech by the chairman, Dr McGuire, Dr Carleton Simon addressed the meeting. After a moving tribute to Train, he gave an account of the autopsy on Train's brain in which he had assisted.

"It is with a feeling of pleasure that I am able to present to this Institute, in preference to all others, the death mask of my friend and patient, Geo. Francis Train. Of course, it was with a feeling of deep regret that such a mask was taken, but I felt that I was simply carrying out his own wishes, and desires of his family, for it was his special request that a mask be taken and presented to this Institute, — as he was well acquainted with its promoters and officers, and had often discussed their work with me.

In presenting this mask to you, I feel not alone honored that this task should have been allotted to me, but as well feel that were he here, he would be glad that he is able to contribute something for science. It will also give you, and others to come, an opportunity to study this noble man, for I am sure that the eccentricities he possessed should be better understood than they were when he was alive.

Mr Train was always willing to contribute his life to science, and this is exemplified in a little incident that occurred about eight years ago. I was making some experiments with the ultra-violet rays, at [the] time not understood, and was using tremendous currents of electricity in my work. I happened to remark to Mr. Train that I was looking for a subject upon whom to try my experiments, but felt it would be difficult to find someone, as the experiments were exceedingly dangerous. With that spontaneity which Mr. Train always showed, he said at once, 'You are at perfect liberty to experiment with me, as long as science be benefited, even though I die under the experiment.' This one incident shows the generousness, nobility and unselfishness of the man.

He was a man who loved the simple, the things close to nature, for he loved solitude, the flowers, the birds and little children. The eccentricities of the man hindered him from being properly understood, but he lived a life of purity and studiousness, as well as one of activity. In fact, few men live the life he did, and therefore his life can not be understood until his standard of thinking can be attained. His language was always definite and exceedingly brief. A word of his was so concrete and so masterfully chosen, as to be equivalent in meaning to a volume of some men... He was a philanthropist of the highest order and fullest sense, appreciating sympathy, kind-hearted to a fault, although he did not court praise or admiration for whatever good he did. The world has seen few great men who had no enemies, but Geo. Francis Train had none, for he was beloved by everyone he came in contact with. He died a beautiful death; his limbs crossed, his hands serenely clasped together, his eyes closed, and with a smile of deep mysterious understanding, he passed away." [20]

Dr Simon read a poem by Train on the "Life and Death of Robert Ingersoll". *The Phrenological Journal* explained that this poem explained Train's "views regarding life and death. He did not believe in wearing crape or mourning, but he considered that life and death should be surrounded with flowers." [21]

At the close of the meeting Miss Fowler "tastefully" accepted Train's death mask from Dr Carleton and thanked him for his "interesting and very valuable speech". She concluded that she hoped the members would allow their brains to be preserved and should indicate their willingness to the Institute to do so at their convenience.

Dr Carleton Simon was right when he said that Train's genius would only be recognised years after his death. He had, after all, achieved a great deal in life. Though his achievements were overshadowed by his eccentricities in life, many of the causes which he chose to support, resulting in him being labelled an eccentric, now seem progressive and are widely accepted. In his time they were the sure sign of a madman. Everyone had their opinion about Train, ranging from "a genius" to "a madman", but it is his own words that best illuminate his extraordinary life:

> *"I have lived fast. I have ever been an advocate of speed. I was born into a slow world, and I wished to oil the wheels and gear, so that the machine would spin faster and, withal, to better purposes. I suggested larger and fleeter ships, to shorten travel on the ocean. I built street-railways, so that the workers of the world might save a few minutes from their days of pitiless toil, and so might have a little leisure for enjoyment and self-improvement. I built great railway lines — the Atlantic and Great Western, and the Union Pacific — that the continent might be traversed by men and commerce more rapidly, and its waste places made to blossom like the rose. I wished to add a stimulus, a spur, a goad — if necessary — that the slow, old world might go on more swiftly, 'and fetch the age of gold,' with more leisure, more culture, more happiness. And so I put faster ships on the oceans, and faster means of travel on land."*

[1] Quoted in Willis Thornton, *The Nine Lives of Citizen Train* (Greenberg, New York, 1948), p. 303.

[2] Newspaper clippping from an unknown source in the Carleton Simon Papers at Albany University, New York.

[3] W. Craig, *My Adventures on the Australian Goldfields* (London, 1903), pp. 197–198.

[4] Quoted in Willis Thornton, above, n. I, p. 304.

[5] New York *American*, January 21, 1904.

[6] Quoted in Willis Thornton, above, n. I, p. 305.

[7] *Ibid.*

8   *Ibid.*

9   *Ibid.*, p. 306.

10 Peter Costello, *Jules Verne, Inventor of Science Fiction* (Hodder & Stoughton, London, 1978), p. 220.

11 Quoted in Willis Thornton, above, n. I, pp. 309–310.

12 *Ibid.*, p. 310.

13 *Ibid.*

14 *Dictionary of American Biography* (Scribner, New York, 1936), Vol. 9, pp. 626–627.

15 Stanley Kunitz and Howard Heycroft, *American Authors 1600–1900* (6th edition, H.W. Wilson, New York, 1964), p. 757.

16 Arthur Train, *Puritan's Progress* (Scribner, New York, 1931), cited in Willis Thornton, above, n. I, p. 311.

17 Don C. Seitz, *Uncommon Americans* (The Bobbs-Merrill Company, Indianapolis, 1925), p. 182.

18 *Encylopedia Britannica* (15th edition, Chicago, 1994), Vol. 9, pp. 407–408.

19 Edw. Anthony Spitzka, ed., "Proceedings of The Amercian Institute of Phrenology" in *The Phrenological Journal* (May 1904), pp. 158–160.

20 *Ibid.*, pp. 161–164.

21 *Ibid.*, p. 162.